Church History

Church History

Simonetta Carr

Reformation Heritage Books
Grand Rapids, Michigan

Church History
© 2022 by Simonetta Carr

All rights reserved. No part of this book may be used or reproduced in any manner whatsoever without written permission except in the case of brief quotations embodied in critical articles and reviews. Direct your requests to the publisher at the following addresses:

Reformation Heritage Books
3070 29th St. SE
Grand Rapids, MI 49512
616-977-0889
orders@heritagebooks.org
www.heritagebooks.org

Scripture taken from the New King James Version®. Copyright © 1982 by Thomas Nelson. Used by permission. All rights reserved.

Printed in the United States of America
22 23 24 25 26 27/10 9 8 7 6 5 4 3 2 1

Library of Congress Cataloging-in-Publication Data

Names: Carr, Simonetta, author.
Title: Church history / Simonetta Carr.
Description: Grand Rapids : Reformation Heritage Books, 2022. | Includes index. | Audience: Ages 9 and up | Summary: "An overview of 2000 years of church history, filled with color images to draw in the attention of young readers and illustrate important people, places, and events" — Provided by publisher.
Identifiers: LCCN 2022000034 | ISBN 9781601788566 (hardcover)
Subjects: LCSH: Church history—Juvenile literature. | BISAC: JUVENILE NONFICTION / History / General
Classification: LCC BR150 .C37 2022 | DDC 270—dc23/eng/20220131
LC record available at https://lccn.loc.gov/2022000034

For additional Reformed literature, request a free book list from Reformation Heritage Books at the above regular or email address.

Contents

NOTE TO THE READER vi

INTRODUCTION 1

PART 1
THE EARLY CHURCH (30–312) 2

PART 2
THE CHURCH IN LATE ANTIQUITY (312–622) 14

PART 3
THE EARLY MIDDLE AGES (622–1000) 40

PART 4
THE HIGH MIDDLE AGES (1000–1517) 54

PART 5
THE PROTESTANT REFORMATION (1517–1600) 80

PART 6
A TROUBLED CENTURY (1600–1700) 100

PART 7
A TIME OF REVIVALS (1700–1789) 122

PART 8
A CHANGING WORLD (1789–1914) 142

PART 9
THE MODERN WORLD (1914–2000) 198

GLOSSARY 249

INDEX 257

ACKNOWLEDGMENTS 266

Note to the Reader

This book may include some words that are unfamiliar to you. The first time they appear, they will be in bold type (**like this**), which will show that you can find their meaning in the glossary at the back of the book.

If you find an unfamiliar word that is not in bold type, you can check the glossary to see if a variation of that word is included. For example, the word *liberalism* is in the glossary, but not the word *liberal*. When you find the definition of *liberalism*, though, you can figure out that a *liberal* is someone who believes in *liberalism*—and you will know what all of that means. Because there may be words in this book unfamiliar to you that aren't in the glossary, it's a good idea to read this book (and any book) with a dictionary close by so that you can understand what you are reading and improve your vocabulary by learning new words.

Also, you will notice that the first time people are mentioned in this book, their names are followed by the dates of their birth and death. If these dates are not there, it could be that the person was mentioned earlier in the book or that the dates of his or her birth or death are unknown.

The abbreviation *ca.* before a date stands for the word *circa*, meaning "about." It shows that we are not sure about the date of a person's birth or death. The abbreviation *b.* before a date stands for *born*; we give only people's year of birth when they are still alive or when we don't know the year that they died. The abbreviation *d.* stands for *died*. We give only the year of a person's death when we don't know the year he or she was born. Even if we have only approximate years of a person's birth or death or only the year of their birth or death, it helps us to know the era when they lived.

Another important tool at the back of this book (and many other books) is the index. An *index* is an alphabetical list of topics, names of people, and names of places included in this book with the page numbers where they are mentioned. It can help you quickly find where, for example, the city Constantinople is mentioned, a person like C. S. Lewis is discussed, or a topic like the French Revolution is covered. In an index, people are listed by their last names first, so if you want to find out more about Lewis, you would look under *L* for Lewis, C. S. If people have a title (like king, queen, or pope) with no last name, look them up under their given name—for example, look under *H* for Henry VIII, King of England; or *G* for Gregory I, Pope.

Like with anything you read, if you have questions about what you find in these pages, talk with trusted people who can help you understand: your parents, a teacher, or a minister, for example. Asking questions—and discovering good answers to them—is one of the best ways to grow.

Introduction

From eternity past, before the creation of this world, God intended to have a people whom He would love forever, enjoying their company as they enjoyed His. His plan has always been the same: "I will be their God, and they shall be My people" (Ezekiel 37:27).

Adam and Eve's rebellion in the garden of Eden, when they sided with Satan against God, didn't catch God by surprise. In His wisdom, He had already decided to bring about the only remedy that would allow Him to show His perfect justice and His perfect love. He would come to earth in the person of His Son, fully God and fully man, to live the perfect life Adam would fail to live and take on Himself all the sins of His people.

In the Old Testament, the people of God lived by faith in this Savior to come. They called Him Messiah (corresponding to the word Christ in the Greek New Testament), or Son of David. Since Jesus's birth, God's people have been living by faith in the Savior who has come as promised.

Jesus told His disciples that He would build His church, and nothing could destroy it (Matthew 16:18). He was not talking about a church building. He was talking about His people. In fact, He promised that He would always be with His people in spirit, even after His return to His Father in heaven (Matthew 28:20).

He has kept His promise. For over two thousand years, Christ has continued to preserve His church even when it seemed like it was going to be destroyed.

You can read about the first years of the church in the Bible in the book of Acts. There, we see how it became organized and how it brought the message of salvation through Christ first to Israel, where Jesus and His disciples lived, and then to other nations around the Mediterranean Sea.

This book starts after the resurrection of Jesus and His commission of the twelve **apostles** and ends at the beginning of the twenty-first century. History is much more complicated than a simple overview, but this will give you a general idea of how God preserved His church and His **gospel**, His message of good news, throughout the centuries and what challenges the church had to face. Hopefully, it will make you want to know more about this fascinating story and especially about the God who has planned it and keeps it going toward an even more exciting future.

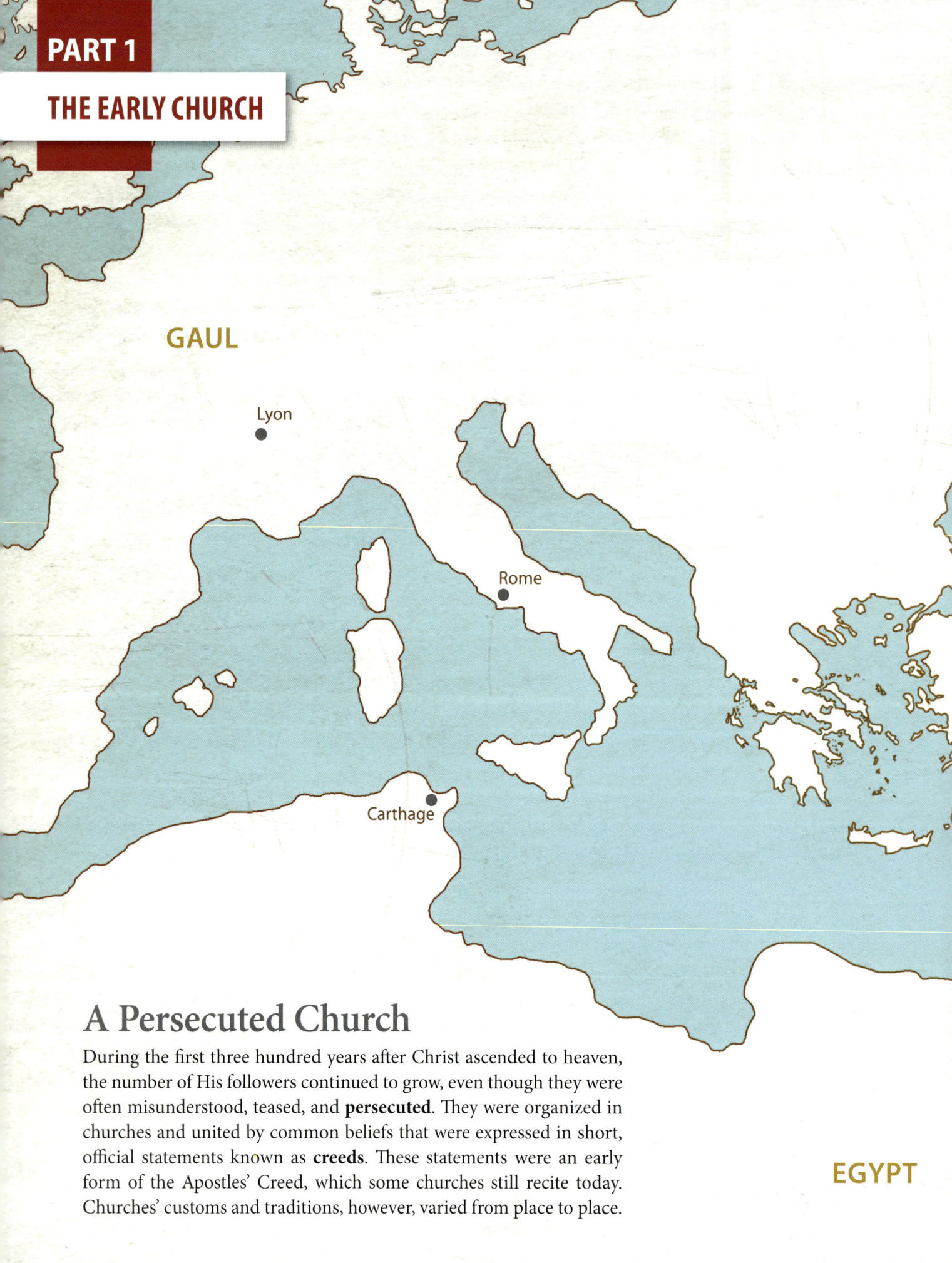

PART 1
THE EARLY CHURCH

GAUL

Lyon

Rome

Carthage

EGYPT

A Persecuted Church

During the first three hundred years after Christ ascended to heaven, the number of His followers continued to grow, even though they were often misunderstood, teased, and **persecuted**. They were organized in churches and united by common beliefs that were expressed in short, official statements known as **creeds**. These statements were an early form of the Apostles' Creed, which some churches still recite today. Churches' customs and traditions, however, varied from place to place.

30–312

ca. 30 — The Roman authorities crucify Jesus. His friends bury Him, and after three days He rises again. He then commissions His disciples to preach the gospel and establish churches. These specially commissioned disciples are called apostles.

ca. 33 — A blinding light stops the Jewish religious leader Saul of Tarsus on his way to Damascus, where he was going to arrest Christians. Jesus commissions him to take the gospel to other nations outside Israel. Saul changes his name to Paul.

49 — The apostles hold a church council in Jerusalem. They discuss how God has fulfilled His promises of creating for Himself a people of all nations, not just Jews.

64 — Nero blames the Christians for a fire that burned much of Rome. He cruelly persecutes Christians in Rome.

177 — Pressed by the people of Lyon, in today's France, the Roman government imprisons, tortures, and kills many Christians.

249 — The first general persecution of Christians in the Roman Empire under Emperor Decius occurs.

301 — King Tiridates III of Armenia proclaims Christianity as the state religion, making Armenia the first official Christian country.

303 — The worst persecution against Christians starts during the reign of Diocletian.

THE EARLY CHURCH

WHY PERSECUTION?

"If they persecuted Me, they will also persecute you," Jesus told His disciples (John 15:20). His words proved true soon after He returned to heaven at the end of His earthly mission, as we read in the book of Acts. The early Christians were persecuted by Jewish leaders who didn't recognize Jesus as the Messiah (Savior) their scriptures (what Christians know as the Old Testament) had predicted.

Many Jews thought Jesus was lying about being the Son of God. They also thought the idea of the God who had made the heaven and the earth dying on a Roman cross, the most humiliating and cruel punishment at that time, was outrageous and offensive. That was not the Messiah they had been expecting. They wanted a strong man who could deliver them from the Romans, who had taken over their land.

The Greeks and Romans were used to stories of men like Hercules becoming gods through acts of courage and strength. But the story of the God who became man and died a shameful death like a common criminal seemed so foolish that they made it the subject of cartoons.

Most of the time, however, Greeks and Romans allowed people to practice other religions. They had many different gods and adopted gods from other nations. They even respected the Jews for their ancient religion. Christianity, instead, looked like a new religion, with strange teachings and ceremonies that were easily misunderstood. For example, when in the Last Supper Christians repeated Jesus's words that the bread is His body and the wine His blood, the Romans called them **cannibals**.

The Romans became particularly concerned when the Christians refused to worship other gods. Often, if a disaster struck, the Romans blamed the Christians for angering the gods. And when the Romans required people to worship the spirit of the emperor's household as a god, the Christians' refusal to do so was seen as a rebellion against the government.

The earliest-known wide persecution of Christians in Rome was started in the year 64 by Emperor Nero, who blamed them for a fire that destroyed much of the city. Most of the time, however, it was the common people who complained about Christians to the

The Amphithéâtre des Trois-Gaules in Lyon, France, where many Christians were killed by wild beasts—a common form of punishment in the second half of the second century

GUILHEM VELLUT, FLICKR

authorities. This is what happened in 177 in Lyon, in today's France, where the locals, plagued by wars and disease, blamed the Christians for angering the gods and dragged them to the authorities for punishment. Most Christians were imprisoned. Some were tortured, and about forty-eight were killed.

Other times persecution came directly from the emperors. Even the worst persecutions, however, failed to stop the Christians, who believed that dying for their faith was an honor. Those who died because of their faith were called **martyrs**, from a Greek word meaning "**witnesses**." The Christians' courage and devotion were a witness of their faith and drew others to the gospel.

The first general persecution of Christians in the Roman Empire happened in 249 under Emperor Decius, who demanded everyone's participation in sacrifices to the gods, even if it was just by eating the meat of sacrificial animals. Those who obeyed received a certificate called a *libellus*. Those who were found without a *libellus* were imprisoned, tortured, and sometimes killed.

An even worse persecution was launched in 303 during the reign of Diocletian. Churches were burned, Bibles were destroyed, and thousands of Christians were killed. By this time, however, Christians had become so numerous and well liked in their communities that many Romans defended them.

Did You Know?

Death by crucifixion (being nailed to a cross) was such a horrible form of punishment that it was usually done outside the city. The sight of people hanging on crosses served as a warning for people coming into a city. Crucifixions were really a form of torture because it could take hours or even days of terrible suffering for a person to die. The Romans, who had probably learned this method from the Persians or Carthaginians, didn't use it to punish Roman citizens. Because the apostle Paul was a Roman citizen, he was probably beheaded.

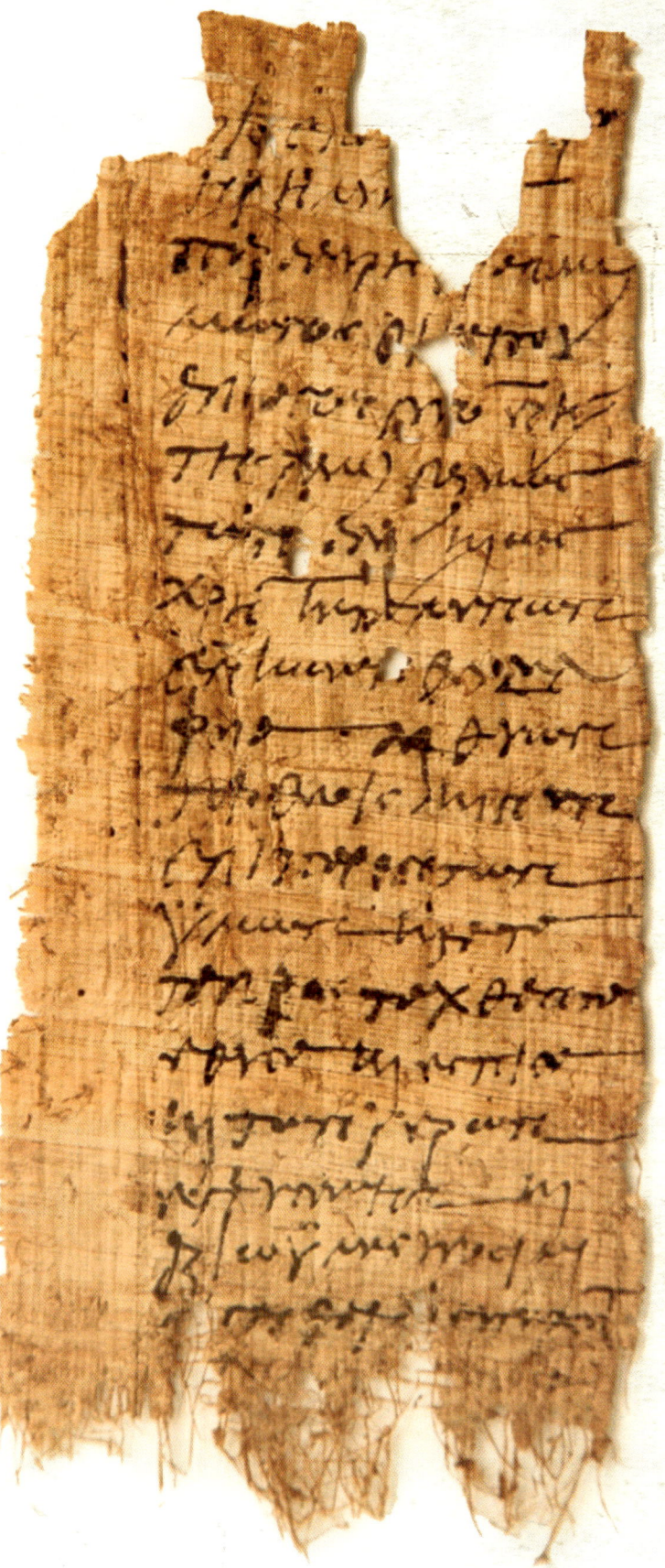

In order to avoid persecution, Christians had to show a certificate (*libellus*) declaring that they had performed a sacrifice to the Roman gods. This *libellus* was required during the persecution under Emperor Decius. The signature line reads, "We, the Aurelii Serenus and Hermas, saw you sacrificing."

LUTHER COLLEGE ARCHIVES, DECORAH, IOWA

THE SPREAD OF CHRISTIANITY

Before leaving this earth, Jesus told His disciples,

> All authority has been given to Me in heaven and on earth. Go therefore and make disciples of all the nations, baptizing them in the name of the Father and of the Son and of the Holy Spirit, teaching them to observe all things that I have commanded you; and lo, I am with you always, even to the end of the age. (Matthew 28:18–20)

His disciples took this commandment seriously and spread the good news of Jesus's life, death, and resurrection both in Israel and in other nations. It was really good news because it told people that because of Jesus's obedience, sacrifice, and victory over death, there was a bright future in store for all those who trusted in Him.

He was really the Christ (a Greek word for Messiah) the Jews had been expecting, but He was not just their Savior. He had come to save people from all nationalities. And He had not come to give the Jews political freedom from the Romans, who were there just for a time. He had come to free them from the bondage of sin—something no human being could do.

Accustomed to the idea that there were many gods who kept fighting each other and had to be kept pacified with constant sacrifices, people found the Christian message of a God of never-ending love to be wonderful news. This good news is known as the gospel. Those who received the gospel spread it to others, sometimes traveling long distances to do so.

This sounded strange to ancient people, who usually believed in the gods of their region and didn't care what people living in other places believed. In fact, they were glad if the foreigners' gods were weak. But Christians believed that Christ died to save the whole world and that everyone should hear this good news.

We don't have a record of all the early missionary travels. According to some sources, the apostles

The monastery of Khor Virap in Artašat, Armenia, was built in the seventh century on the site where Gregory the Illuminator was imprisoned for thirteen years. The prison cell is still under the monastery, which was remodeled several times. The mountain in the background is Mount Ararat.

DIEGO DELSO, DELSO.PHOTO

Thaddeus and Bartholomew brought the gospel to Armenia, while the early **evangelization** of India is attributed by some to the apostle Thomas and by others to Bartholomew. In any case, according to the historian Eusebius of Caesarea (ca. 260–339), in the late second century there was already a community of Christians in India who had a copy of the Gospel of Matthew.

Most of the time, the gospel was spread by Christians who spoke to their neighbors or to people they met while traveling for work or pleasure or because of persecution. As new Christian communities grew, they often asked a larger community to send a **bishop** to assist them.

Some ancient historians were surprised that a religion whose followers were so persecuted and despised continued to spread—first slowly, then faster and faster. At the end of the first century, of the sixty million people in the Roman Empire, less than ten thousand were Christians. By the year 300, at the time of the Diocletian persecution, at least six million people called themselves Christians in spite of the dangers and hatred against them.

THE FIRST CHRISTIAN NATION

According to the ancient historian Agathangelos, Armenia was the first nation to adopt Christianity as its official religion. This happened in 301, during the reign of King Tiridates III (ca. 250–330).

As the story goes, Tiridates, charmed by the beauty of a Christian **nun**, Hripsime, called her to his palace, where he asked her to marry him. When she refused, he tried to take her by force, but she fought him off and won. Disappointed and embarrassed, he tried to convince the **abbess** of the **convent** to order Hripsime to obey him. When she also refused, he killed the thirty-three nuns in the convent.

After this, he was struck by a condition similar to that of King Nebuchadnezzar in the Bible (see Daniel 4). It was then that Tiridates's sister Khosrovidukht urged him to call a Christian man out of his prison to pray for him. The man's name was Gregory (ca. 240–332), later known as "the Illuminator," which means "giver of light." Gregory had been in prison for thirteen years for refusing to worship one of Armenia's **pagan** gods.

Healed through Gregory's prayer, Tiridates professed faith in Christ. Wanting his people to do the same, he officially declared Armenia a Christian nation.

THE EARLY CHURCH • 7

Some Men and Women of the Early Church

MARTYRS—GIVING THEIR LIVES FOR CHRIST

IGNATIUS (ca. 35–ca. 107) was bishop of Antioch, in today's Turkey. He was arrested because of his faith and sent to Rome under guard. The news spread quickly even without TV and internet, and Christians rushed to meet him at every stop he made along the way. They were encouraged by his brave and cheerful attitude. He was killed in Rome, probably in the Circus Maximus.

> *My only wish is to attain Jesus Christ.*
> —IGNATIUS OF ANTIOCH

POLYCARP (ca. 69–155) was bishop of Smyrna, in today's Turkey. To the Roman authorities who encouraged him to save his life by cursing Christ he replied, "Eighty-six years I have served Christ, and he never did me any wrong. How can I blaspheme my King who saved me?" He was burned at the stake.

CYPRIAN (ca. 200–258) was bishop of Carthage. When Emperor Decius began to persecute Christians, Cyprian went into hiding so he could keep the church encouraged and united. He encouraged the church to forgive those who out of fear gave up their faith—as long as they repented. Years later, he boldly faced a new wave of persecution and was killed.

BLANDINA (ca. 162–177) was a young slave. She was arrested during the persecution at Lyon, in today's France, and tortured day and night. Throughout this time she encouraged other young people to stay strong. She was killed by a raging bull in a Roman **arena**.

A mosaic depicting Perpetua and Felicitas, as a fifth-century artist imagined them

PHOTO BY NICK THOMPSON, PUBLISHED WITH KIND PERMISSION OF OPERA DI RELIGIONE DELLA DIOCESI DI RAVENNA

PERPETUA AND FELICITAS (both d. 203) were a noblewoman and a slave from Carthage, in today's Tunisia. They were both young mothers. (Felicitas gave birth to a baby a couple days before she was killed.) They were killed for refusing to deny their faith. Perpetua is remembered for the diary she kept during her imprisonment, helping us to understand how Christians were persecuted.

Blandina was killed by a raging bull in a Roman arena.

FROM THE MARTYR'S MIRROR, 1660, BETHEL COLLEGE LIBRARY AND ARCHIVES

> *I cannot be called anything other than what I am, a Christian.*
> —PERPETUA OF CARTHAGE

APOLOGISTS—INTRODUCING CHRIST TO THE WORLD

Initially, Christians wrote to instruct, reassure, and comfort other Christians. For example, local bishops would write letters to their churches. By the middle of the second century, some began to address their writings to outsiders in order to explain the Christian faith. We call these writers **apologists**.

It was a challenging task because few people at that time had ever heard of Jesus, and few, apart from the Jews, knew much about the Old Testament and the Messiah it announces. The apologists had to start from scratch. Often, they had to defend Christians against the accusations of those who had heard only strange and negative things about Christianity.

JUSTIN (ca. 100–165), called Martyr, was a **philosopher** from the region of Samaria, near Israel, who discovered that Christianity was the only "safe and reasonable" **philosophy**. His writings were addressed to both the Jews (to help them understand that Christianity is the fulfillment of their scriptures) and to the pagans. He also wrote letters to emperors to explain that Christians were of great value to Rome. Despite this, he was arrested and killed, together with some of his students.

A Roman mosaic in Ostia Antica, Italy, showing a philosopher talking. The clothes this man is wearing are probably similar to what Justin Martyr wore as a sign of his profession. Beards were also common among philosophers.

FR. LAWRENCE LEW, O.P.

CLEMENT (ca. 150–ca. 215) became the head of a school for new believers in Alexandria, Egypt. He wrote many important works, including *Exhortation to the Greeks*, in which he encouraged educated Greeks and Romans to hear the gospel of Jesus. While fragments of hymns from the early church exist, his "Hymn of the Savior" is the earliest known complete hymn of the church.

ORIGEN (ca. 185–ca. 253) was a teacher and writer from Alexandria, Egypt. He wrote a convincing reply to Celsus, a Roman who believed that Christianity was a new and dangerous religion. Celsus thought Christians were absurd because they followed a dead carpenter. He also thought that God would never come down to earth—it's man who needs to raise his mind to God. Origen replied that it's precisely the opposite. God reached down to man because man is not able to reach up to God. His clear and logical replies confirmed that Christians were not as absurd and unintelligent as Celsus accused them of being.

Origen was also the first person who tried to write an organized explanation of Christian beliefs. Ultimately, not all of his thinking was considered biblical by the church, but his writings raised important questions Christians needed to face.

> *We understand that God, the Creator of all things, is superior to the things that are to be changed. If, therefore, on some points we teach the same things as the poets and philosophers whom you honor, and on other points are fuller and more divine in our teaching, and if we alone afford proof of what we assert, why are we unjustly hated more than all others?*
> —JUSTIN MARTYR

Great Questions of the Church

DO WE NEED HIGHER KNOWLEDGE?

Since Jesus's message was still new, some people interpreted it in different ways. Soon the church realized the danger of straying from the teachings of the apostles, who had been with Jesus and knew what He taught. In fact, the apostles had to deal with some false teachings in their churches and had described them in their letters and in the book of Revelation.

There were different reasons why some people strayed from the apostles' message. Some thought that it was too simple and there was a higher knowledge still to be discovered. Today, these people are called **Gnostics**, from the Greek word *gnosis*, meaning "knowledge."

The Gnostics were not one united group. The word is used for different groups who had similar beliefs. Some Gnostics claimed to have received special revelations directly from Jesus that were superior to the message of the apostles. Most of them believed that everything we can see and touch is inferior to what is spiritual. Some explained the evil in the world by saying that there are two gods—one good and one bad, or one inferior to the other.

One person who held this second view was Marcion (d. ca. 160). He is not included with the Gnostics because he didn't believe that knowledge is the key to salvation. He still believed we are saved by faith in Christ, but he thought that Christ was the son of the good god of the New Testament, who was different from the harsh god of the Old Testament. The New Testament frequently quotes the Old Testament, so Marcion removed the Old Testament references. Both the Gnostics and Marcion had many followers, although the Christian community was united in rejecting their teachings.

Irenaeus (ca. 130–ca. 202), a pastor from Asia Minor who served in Lyon, France, studied the gnostic teachings and wrote a book to explain why they were different from what Jesus had taught, even though they used similar words, and how they were illogical and based on suppositions. He also explained that both the Old and the New Testaments talk about one God who created everything good, for a good purpose, and who is bringing this purpose to a glorious end in Christ.

We call his book *Against Heresies*. Originally, the Greek word for **heresy** meant "a choice." By Irenaeus's day it meant a "wrong choice." His purpose was to encourage Christians to keep to the scriptural teachings of the apostles. He included a prayer for the Gnostics, saying that he loved them "better than they seem to love themselves."

Another important apologist who wrote against the Gnostics was the North African Tertullian (ca. 155–ca. 240), who was also the first apologist to produce a great number of Christian works in Latin, the language of the Western Roman Empire; before this, most Christian works had been written in Greek, which was the language of the East. Some of his works were also addressed to the Jews and to pagan philosophers.

> **Think about It**
> - What's wrong with wanting to discover more about God than what the Bible has revealed?
> - Was it safer for Christians to trust the teachings of the apostles or the teachings of the Gnostics? Why?
> - Did the Gnostics' interpretations help them to understand the Bible, or did they take them further away from it? Why?
> - Explain how the Bible is one unified story, with just one God from beginning to end. What's the theme of the story?

We don't have any images of Irenaeus from the time when he was alive. This is how nineteenth-century sculptor Carl Rohl Smith imagined him to be.

ORF3US, WIKIMEDIA COMMONS

Daily Life of Early Christians

Sometime in the second century, a Christian wrote a letter to a man named Diognetus, who was curious to know how Christians worshiped and what they believed.

He explained that Christians didn't look any different from the people around them. They lived in the same communities as the others, dressed like them, ate the same types of food, and spoke the same languages. A Christian in Greece looked like any other Greek, and a Christian in Africa looked like any other African.

But they were different in other ways. They lived in their own countries as though they were only passing through. They performed their duties as citizens of their countries, but they remembered they were first of all citizens of heaven. They loved everyone, even those who persecuted them. When people insulted them, they answered with a blessing.

Their faith affected their attitudes and decisions. For example, Christian parents didn't abandon their babies like Greek or Roman parents often did, and husbands and wives valued their faithfulness to each other.

The objects left from that time show some of the Christians' preferences. For example, they chose carefully the symbols and pictures used in jewelry designs. They avoided not only pictures of gods or **idols** but also images of swords or bows (Christians tried to live at peace) or wine cups (Christians drank wine or beer in moderation). They liked images of doves, fish, anchors, and ships. The fish became a Christian symbol because the letters of the Greek word (*ixthus*) were the first letters of the words in the Greek phrase "Jesus Christ Son of God Savior."

In the center of this terracotta oil lamp from the fourth century, you can see a Christian symbol: the Greek letters *chi* (X) and *rho* (P), placed one over the other. These were the first two letters in the Greek word *Kristos* (Christ). People used oil lamps to light their homes. These letters reminded Christians that Christ is the light of the world.

THE WALTERS ART MUSEUM, BALTIMORE

Sometimes, the first and last letters of the Greek alphabet, *alpha* (A) and *omega* (Ω), were placed next to the *chi-rho* symbol as a reminder of what Jesus said in Revelation 1:8; 21:6; and 22:13: "I am the Alpha and the Omega, the Beginning and the End."

MONIEK SPAANS, ISTOCK

THE BISHOPS—OVERSEEING THE CHURCHES

Initially, the word *bishop* (*episkopos* in Greek) simply described an overseer of a church and probably had the same meaning as **elder**. After a while, each church started to have one bishop in charge.

By the fourth century, larger cities such as Antioch, in today's Turkey; Alexandria, in Egypt; Rome, in today's Italy; and Carthage, in today's Tunisia, had one bishop over all the churches in the city. But the authority of bishops varied from city to city.

The clothes worn by most bishops and **archbishops**, today known as **vestments**, were not a Christian invention. They were similar to the clothes worn by noblemen or government authorities.

A SAMPLE OF WORSHIP IN THE EARLY CHURCH

This picture of a Christian family was painted on a wall of the **catacombs** of Saint Gennaro, Naples, Italy. The family's hands are raised in prayer because that's how most people prayed in those days instead of bowing their heads and closing their eyes, as most Christians do now.

GIANNI CIUNFRINI
(WITH PERMISSION FROM CATACOMBE DI NAPOLI)

In a letter to Emperor Antoninus Pius (86–161), Justin Martyr explained how Christians worshiped in Rome. The worship service included reading the Bible, instructions (preaching), prayers, and the **sacrament** of the **Eucharist** (now also called the Lord's Supper). This followed the example given by the apostles in Acts 2:42: "And they continued steadfastly in the apostles' **doctrine** and fellowship, in the breaking of bread, and in prayers."

Justin explained that on Sunday, Christians traveled from different places to get together for worship. Then they would read some writings from the Bible, either Old or New Testament, and the person leading worship would explain them to the others.

After that, they had prayer and the Lord's Supper, with bread and wine that was diluted with water, as the ancient Romans and Greeks did. If people were not able to leave their homes, the **deacons** would bring the Lord's Supper to them.

At the end of the service, people gave an offering for the poor.

Justin explained that Christians worshiped on Sunday instead of the Jewish Saturday because Sunday represents the first day of creation and especially because "Jesus Christ our Savior on the same day rose from the dead."

The Lord's Supper is also described in the Didache, an important document from the early church that gives one example of how Christians celebrated it every Sunday.

Did You Know?

- Today, the Roman Catholic Church still mixes the Eucharist's wine with water.

- In the early church, when the Bible was read and explained, the preacher would sit and the **congregation** would stand. Over time, each bishop began to sit on a special chair called in both Latin and Greek the *cathedra*. Later, the word *cathedral* was the name of a church where a bishop regularly preached.

DID THE EARLY CHRISTIANS READ THE BIBLE?

Until the invention of the printing press in the fifteenth century, the main way to duplicate a document or book was to copy it by hand—on scrolls or on sheets of parchment made from animal skins. Books were expensive, and only a few people owned them. Most people heard the Bible read in church on Sundays.

The first Christians used the same books the Jews considered inspired by God. Today we call them the Old Testament. Since there was no New Testament yet, the first Christians just called them "the books." At the same time, the churches started to pass around some letters written by the apostles. In the course of time, they recognized that some of these letters were as inspired by God as the Old Testament books. These, together with the Gospels, the book of Acts, and the book of Revelation, made up the New Testament, a title given in the beginning of the third century.

Paul died around AD 65, so all his letters were written before then. Three of the Gospels—Mark, Luke, and Matthew—were also written by AD 70. The Gospel of John was written in the 80s AD.

Irenaeus, who wrote around the end of the second century, included many New Testament references in his works, showing that these books were well known and their authority was recognized. In 367 Bishop Athanasius (ca. 296–373) of Alexandria produced the first existing list of the New Testament books, which were almost the same as those we have today. Then, in 397 the **Council** of Carthage officially recognized as the inspired Word of God the books of the Old and New Testaments, which the church has been using ever since.

A UNITED CHURCH

Irenaeus pointed out that while the Gnostics had many different theories, the Christian churches, no matter where they were, were united through the Bible. This unity was very important to Christians. This is why Cyprian refused to recognize baptisms performed by heretics or by people who had separated from the church. He is remembered for saying, "Outside of the church there is no salvation," and "He cannot have God for his Father who does not have the church as his mother." He meant that people couldn't call themselves Christians if they didn't belong to what was recognized as the church—a community of believers present in many nations and united in their faithfulness to the recorded teachings of the apostles. Those who didn't consider themselves part of this community and taught things that were not in the Bible were inventing a different religion.

At the same time, Irenaeus explained that churches can have some minor differences. For example, at a time when Christians were questioning the best time to celebrate Easter, he thought it was acceptable for the churches in Rome to celebrate it at one time while the churches in the East chose a different date.

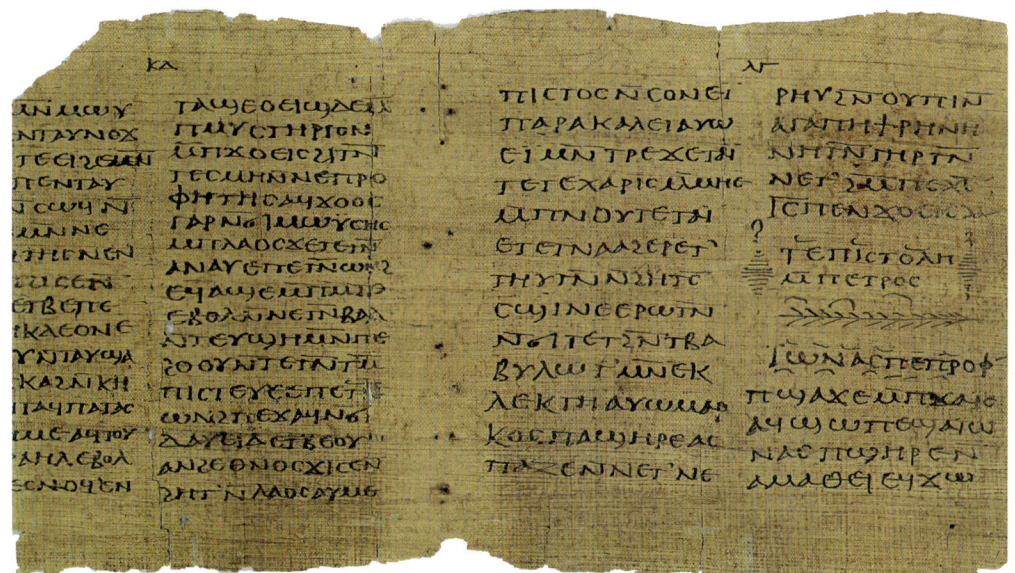

MS 193. The Crosby-Schøyen Codex, Egypt, third century. These two pages show the end of the first letter of Peter and the beginning of the book of Jonah. This is the earliest existing manuscript of the book of 1 Peter in any language and the earliest complete manuscript of the book of Jonah in any language, as well as the oldest book in private ownership.

SCHØYEN COLLECTION, OSLO AND LONDON

PART 2

THE CHURCH IN LATE ANTIQUITY

Most **scholars** today call the period between the fourth and eighth centuries Late Antiquity—a period of gradual change from the ancient world to the Middle Ages.

A Recognized Church

Things changed drastically for Christians in 313, when Emperor Constantine I (ca. 272–337), who had declared himself a Christian, proclaimed that Christianity was a legal religion. For the first time, Christians found favor with the Roman government and were able to worship freely. In fact, Constantine commissioned the building of large churches. This declaration was a turning point in church history. It became known as the Edict of Milan because it was issued in Milan, Italy, which was the capital of the Western Roman Empire from 286 to 402.

312–622

312 — Following a military victory, the Roman emperor Constantine I declares himself a Christian.

313 — Constantine puts a legal end to the persecution of Christians.

325 — Constantine calls the first Council of Nicaea to discuss, among other things, whether Jesus is fully God. This is the first ecumenical council, with representatives from the whole church.

337 — King Mirian III makes Christianity the official religion of Georgia, a region of Eastern Europe.

361–363 — The Roman emperor Julian tries to return the empire to its original religion.

367 — The Christian bishop Athanasius makes a first complete list of the books of the New Testament.

380 — Emperor Theodosius I makes Christianity the official religion of the Roman Empire.

381 — The first Council of Constantinople (second ecumenical council) agrees that the Holy Spirit is fully God and refines the Nicene Creed.

382 — The Council of Rome officially recognizes as the inspired Word of God the books of the Old and New Testaments, which the church has been using for some centuries.

405 — Jerome finishes the official translation of the Bible into Latin.

410 — The Visigoths' raid on Rome signals the collapse of the Western Roman Empire.

412 — Augustine of Hippo begins to oppose the teachings of Pelagius.

418 — The Council of Carthage officially condemns Pelagius's teachings.

451 — The Council of Chalcedon (third ecumenical council) affirms that Jesus is fully human and fully divine, one person with two natures.

476 — The Germanic general Odoacer ends the Western Roman Empire by deposing its last emperor.

THE CHURCH IN LATE ANTIQUITY

One of the ancient gates of Iznik, where Nicaea was located
CAROLE RADDATO, WIKIMEDIA COMMONS

Great Questions of the Church

IS JESUS REALLY GOD?

The Bible teaches that there is only one God. It also teaches that Jesus is both God *and* the Son of God. How can this be? This question puzzled the early Christians. Arius (ca. 260–336), an elder in Alexandria, Egypt, tried to solve this puzzle by saying that Jesus is not God in the same way the Creator is. He said, for example, that God the Father is eternal, while Jesus had a beginning, which means He was created. Arius even invented a jingle to explain his idea—"There was when He was not"—meaning that there was a time when Jesus didn't exist. (The jingle was catchier in the original Greek.) Today, the **Jehovah's Witnesses** believe the same thing. Also, the **Mormons** believe that Jesus was the first created spirit, not the Son of God.

Throughout the Roman Empire, bishops, elders, and common people began to take sides for and against this elder so much that there were arguments in the markets and fights in the streets. In 325, Emperor Constantine tried to bring peace by calling a meeting of bishops in the city of Nicaea (today's Iznik, Turkey). It was the first church meeting ever called and presided over by an emperor. It was also the first **ecumenical** council, a meeting of representatives of the whole church, from both the East and the West.

About two hundred bishops came. They discussed the main teachings people had been circulating about Jesus. The vast majority believed that the Father and the Son were one God but distinguished one from the other. That explained why Jesus could say, "I and My Father are one" (John 10:30) *and* could also pray to the Father.

In the end, the bishops wrote a statement declaring that Jesus was of one substance with the Father, and Constantine approved this wording. Constantine gave Arius the choice of signing the statement or going into exile. Arius chose exile.

The Council of Nicaea didn't put an end to the arguments. A few cities ended up having two bishops, one in favor of Nicaea and one in favor of Arius.

There were also people who believed the Father and the Son were two different gods altogether and others who thought the Father and the Son were just one god appearing in two different forms—sometimes as father and sometimes as son. The confusion continued throughout the century.

Politics also had a lot to do with this matter because some emperors defended Arius's views while others opposed them. Bishop Athanasius of Alexandria, one of the greatest defenders of the decisions made at Nicaea, was exiled five times by different emperors for his firm belief that Jesus Christ is fully God.

This golden medallion, showing the head of Emperor Constantine I, was created to celebrate the thirtieth year of his rule, which lasted from 306 to 337.

THE WALTERS ART MUSEUM, BALTIMORE

Think about It

- Some people say Jesus never declared specifically that He was God's only Son. Even though He didn't, He certainly approved of those who did say it. For example, when Peter said, "You are the Christ, the Son of the living God," Jesus replied, "Blessed are you, Simon Bar-Jonah, for flesh and blood has not revealed this to you, but My Father who is in heaven" (Matthew 16:16–17). He told Peter that his answer was exactly right. Find more verses showing that Jesus agreed with those who said He was God.

- Created or uncreated, same substance or similar substance…does it really matter? Can't we just love Jesus without understanding who He really is? Why not?

- If Jesus had not been God, was His death on the cross enough to save us? Can a man die for someone else's sins? Explain your answer.

- If Jesus was not really God and could not save us, then how should we view Him? We would be forced to see Him as just a good example to follow, which is how many people want to see Him today. But would you want to follow someone who says he is something he is not?

- Read John 1:1, 3, 14; 17:5; and 20:8. How do they prove that Jesus is God?

THE CHURCH IN LATE ANTIQUITY • 17

THE THREE CAPPADOCIANS

Three men were particularly instrumental in helping the church to understand the Trinity, along with the importance of seeing each person (God the Father, God the Son, and God the Holy Spirit) as equally **divine**.

Two of these men—Basil (ca. 330–379) and Gregory (ca. 335–395)—were brothers. The third was a close friend also named Gregory (ca. 329–ca. 390). We distinguish the two Gregories by the place where they were born or lived: Basil's brother was called Gregory of Nyssa, and their friend, Gregory of Nazianzus. They are often known as the Cappadocian Fathers because they served in the area of Asia Minor known as Cappadocia.

> *I cannot think of the One without being quickly surrounded by the splendor of the Three; nor can I think of the Three without being immediately carried back to the One.*
> —GREGORY OF NAZIANZUS

Think about It

- Why are some truths about God impossible to explain with human words?

- How can human explanations end up creating a different God from the one who has revealed Himself in the Bible?

- Read Matthew 3:16–17 and John 14:26. What do they tell you about the Trinity?

HOW CAN GOD BE ONE IN THREE PERSONS?

The churches had been obeying Jesus's last commission: "Go therefore and make disciples of all the nations, baptizing them in the name of the Father and of the Son and of the Holy Spirit" (Matthew 28:19). People wondered who exactly the Holy Spirit was.

Those who believed that the Father and the Son were two different forms of the same god taught that the Holy Spirit was a third form. In other words, they thought that God manifested Himself sometimes as the Father, sometimes as the Son, and sometimes as the Holy Spirit. This doesn't agree with the Bible, in which Father, Son, and Holy Spirit are often manifested at the same time in their different roles. For example, at Jesus's baptism in Mark 1:9–11, Jesus is in the water, the Holy Spirit descends like a dove, and the Father speaks from heaven.

Ultimately, the church realized that any attempt to explain the **Trinity** with human illustrations is flawed. It's best just to say that Father, Son, and Holy Spirit are one God in three persons. This a mystery that only God can understand. That doesn't mean we should not try to learn more about it. As long as we stay faithful to the Bible, learning about the Trinity can help us to know God better and to be filled with wonder at His greatness.

In 380 Emperor Theodosius I (ca. 347–395) defended the teaching of the Trinity when he made Christianity the official religion of the Roman Empire. He said, "According to the apostolic teaching and the doctrine of the gospel, we believe the one **deity** of the Father, the Son, and the Holy Spirit, in equal majesty and in a holy Trinity."

The Cappadocian Mountains provided a place of quiet for Christians who wanted to spend time in meditation and were a refuge for those who were persecuted. Some Christians carved their homes inside the mountains. Later, whole monasteries and churches were carved in these rocks, and images were painted on the inside walls.

#1923#, FLICKR

Daily Life of Early Monks

Before the **conversion** of Constantine, the church regularly expected persecution. Martyrs and confessors (those who stayed faithful to their beliefs under threats) were held in great honor as spiritual heroes.

Constantine's decision to legalize Christianity brought much relief but also laziness and insincerity. Since Constantine and nearly all of his **successors** professed to be Christians, many people converted to Christianity out of convenience. They went to church but spent most of their time living for money and entertainment like the pagans did.

A few believers—especially young people—wanted to get away from all that. They left their money and possessions and moved to isolated places where they could spend their time in meditation and prayer. They became known by the Greek word *monachoi*, which means "solitary." In English, we call them **monks**. Some monks lived together in communities, and some lived completely by themselves.

In one of his writings, John Chrysostom (ca. 354–407), a bishop of Constantinople who spent some years as a monk, explained that the monks who lived together usually slept on straw mats in separate rooms and followed a common rule. They wore simple tunics under rough clothes made of camel's or goat's hair. Their diet was simple: bread and water, unless they were sick and needed a little more nourishment.

Every day, they rose before dawn and gathered to sing psalms and hymns and to pray. Then they performed their daily tasks. Chrysostom thought it was important for monks to spend time working, especially to help the poor.

> *Incomprehensible! How could the son of respectable middle-class parents with a good education and excellent prospects for a steady comfortable life leave his home to go off and join a company of dirty vagrants [wanderers]!*
>
> —THE REACTION OF AN UPSTANDING CITIZEN OF ANTIOCH TO THE MONKS' LIFESTYLE AS RECORDED BY CHRYSOSTOM

JOHN CHRYSOSTOM

John was later called Chrysostom, a Greek word meaning "golden mouth," because he was an excellent preacher. His prestigious position provoked the jealousy of other bishops and the anger of Empress Eudoxia (d. 404), who resented his sermons against her extravagant lifestyle. In the end, Eudoxia had Chrysostom exiled. He died in 407 when, already weak, he was forced to walk many miles in bad weather.

THE CHURCH IN LATE ANTIQUITY • 19

EXTREME MONKS

One of the most famous fourth-century monks was an Egyptian named Antony (ca. 251–356). Initially, he lived with other like-minded men in the desert near his village. Later, he decided to move deeper into the desert and live there by himself, eating bread and water provided by visiting friends. He lived 105 years.

Antony's life was not peaceful. His doubts and temptations grew even stronger when he was alone with his thoughts. But many Christians admired him for fighting them, and his example inspired others to do the same. Monks became the new Christian heroes. They were often called "God's athletes."

One man, Symeon (ca. 389–459), took this challenge even further. After living in a **monastery** for ten years, he moved out on his own, sat on a small platform on top of a pillar, and stayed there for almost forty years, until he died. Over time, he had more pieces added to the pillar until it became over twenty feet tall. People came from all over the region to see this man who lived suspended between heaven and earth. Some brought him bread and water or milk to help him survive.

CHURCH BUILDINGS

Initially, Christians met in someone's home. But when Christianity became Rome's preferred religion, there was a need for larger places of worship. The Jewish temples were not a good model because they were meant for priests to offer their sacrifices and not for large crowds. Christians found a good model in the **basilica**, a building where Romans held official meetings, court cases, and even military drills. Basilicas featured a wide space in the middle with two rows of columns on either side. In most cases, a separate building, called a baptistery, was built next to the basilica as a place where Christians could get baptized.

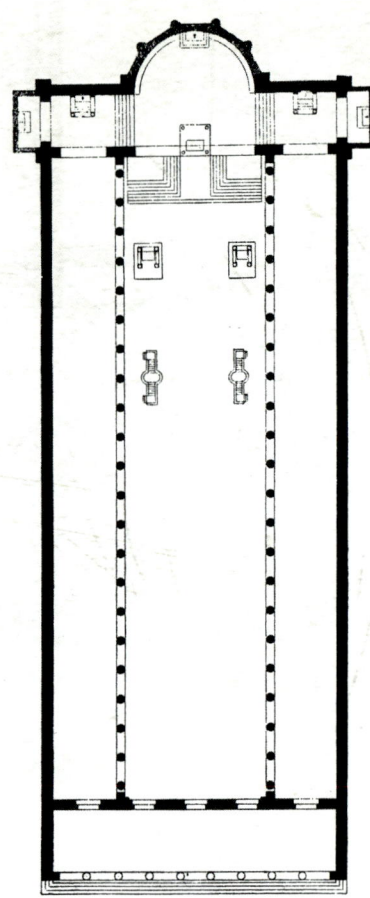

This floor plan of the Basilica of Santa Maria Maggiore in Rome is typical of Christian basilicas.

GEORG DEHIO/GUSTAV VON BEZOLD, WIKIMEDIA COMMONS

Symeon's Pillar used to be quite high, but after he died, visitors chipped away at it in order to take home some pieces. Now it looks more like an egg. The church around the pillar, built after his death, is the oldest surviving **Byzantine** church.

ARIAN ZWEGERS, FLICKR

The Revolutionary Nature of Christian Love

THE FIRST HOSPITAL

Basil of Caesarea, one of the three Cappadocian Fathers, was also attracted to the life of monks. He was about to join a monastery when his sister Macrina (ca. 327–379) gave him a different idea.

Macrina was a young woman whose fiancé had died just before their wedding. Instead of finding another husband, she decided to devote her life to the care of the poor and convinced her widowed mother, Emmelia (d. 375), to use the family home to create a religious community. There, the family and some like-minded people lived together, devoting their time to prayer, service to others, and singing hymns.

When Basil returned home from his studies, the house was quite different from the wealthy Roman *domus* of his youth. He realized that Macrina's life of service was much closer to Christ's example than a life of isolation would be.

With this new vision, he founded or reformed several monasteries. He is famous for building a large compound that included a hospital and a home for the orphans and elderly, all staffed by physicians and nurses. Special care was given to lepers, who were usually abandoned by society. It was the first hospital of this kind and was completely free of charge because Basil and his friends and family encouraged others to give money.

Basil's work was revolutionary in his day, so much so that Emperor Julian (331–363), in his effort to bring back the empire to the worship of the Roman gods, tried to teach the priests of his Roman religion to do good works similar to those of Christians. Julian's plan never materialized, and the emperors who reigned after him continued to support Christianity.

AGAINST SLAVERY

Macrina's brother Gregory of Nyssa was the first-known preacher to speak out against slavery. His condemnation came in the course of a sermon on Ecclesiastes 2:7, a passage where the author of the book listed his servants as part of his riches: "I acquired male and female servants, and had servants born in my house. Yes, I had greater possessions of herds and flocks than all who were in Jerusalem before me."

The word *servants* in the original Greek text that Gregory read really meant slaves. Many of Gregory's hearers had slaves. Some were or had been slaves. They probably thought Gregory would talk about the emptiness of riches. They might even have expected an exhortation to masters to be kind to their slaves.

But Gregory did more. He reminded slave owners that God made all human beings in His image (Genesis 1:26). "He who knew the nature of mankind rightly said that the whole world was not worth giving in exchange for a human soul," Gregory said, referencing Jesus's words in Matthew 16:26 and Mark 8:36.

Some people believe that Gregory might have been inspired by the example of his sister Macrina, who had persuaded their mother, Emmelia, to free all their slaves, treating as equals those who chose to stay.

Gregory's words didn't have much effect because slavery had been around for centuries, and most people accepted it as normal. The famous Greek philosopher Aristotle (384–322 BC) thought the world was naturally divided into slaves and owners. Many more centuries had to pass until people realized that Gregory's words were true.

Great Questions of the Church

IS JESUS REALLY A MAN?

While the church was trying to find clear language to explain that Jesus was truly God, some Christians began to wonder if He was truly a man. In the Greek mythological tales, some heroes could become gods, but who had ever heard of a god becoming a man? To many people, this seemed beneath the dignity of a god.

To make this sound better, some people said that Jesus only looked like a man. Today, we call these people Docetists, from a Greek word meaning "to appear." An early form of Docetism was around even at the time of the apostles. The apostle John strongly condemned this type of teaching in his letters.

But even those who believed the biblical teachings couldn't understand how one person, Jesus, could be both God and man. A bishop named Apollinaris (ca. 310–ca. 390) tried to explain this by saying that Jesus was a true man, but the second person of the Godhead (God the Son) took the place of his soul. In other words, Jesus didn't have a human soul. It sounded reasonable, but it's not what the Bible teaches. Instead, the Bible tells us that Jesus was fully man and fully God. And since humans are composed of body and soul, to be fully man, Jesus had to have both a human body and a human soul.

Apollinaris's teaching was condemned in 381 at the first Council of Constantinople (today's Istanbul, Turkey). It was there that the Nicene Creed was worded in almost the same way we have it today. In 451 the same creed was confirmed in the Council of Chalcedon (a town near Constantinople), where they clarified that Jesus was "like us in all respects except for sin; begotten before the ages from the Father as regards his **divinity**." Both of these were ecumenical councils that included representatives of the churches from both the East and the West.

Like the Trinity, the two natures of Christ are a mystery that human minds can't fully understand.

Think about It

- The Bible teaches that "since by man came death, by Man also came the resurrection of the dead" (1 Corinthians 15:21). Would God be just if He punished an angel or another being for sins committed by a human? Explain your answer.

- The reason why the church fought strongly against any teaching that Jesus is not fully God and fully man is that these teachings deny the gospel, which tells us that Jesus, being God, became one of us in order to rescue us from sin and death. Can teachers who deny the gospel call themselves Christians? Explain your answer.

- Read 1 John 1:1–2; 4:3; and 2 John 7. Explain how they tell us that Jesus was really a man.

JESUS IN THE NICENE CREED
(as published at the Council of Constantinople)

We believe…in one Lord Jesus Christ, the only-begotten Son of God, begotten of the Father before all worlds; God of God, Light of Light, very God of very God; begotten, not made, being of one substance with the Father, by whom all things were made. Who, for us men and for our salvation, came down from heaven, and was **incarnate** by the Holy Spirit of the virgin Mary, and was made man; and was crucified also for us under Pontius Pilate; He suffered and was buried; and the third day He rose again, according to the Scriptures; and ascended into heaven, and sitteth on the right hand of the Father; and He shall come again, with glory, to judge the living and the dead; whose kingdom shall have no end.

Some images produced in the fifth century to illustrate scenes from the Council of Chalcedon

Some Men and Women of the Church in Late Antiquity

POETS AND WRITERS

An image of the three Cappadocian Fathers—Basil of Caesarea, Gregory of Nazianzus, and Gregory of Nyssa—on the walls of the Church of the Holy Savior in Chora in Istanbul, Turkey. No one knows what these men looked like, but this is how an artist imagined them to be. The robes with geometric patterns are typically Cappadocian.

DAVID EDWARDS

GREGORY OF NAZIANZUS, one of the Three Cappadocians, was also a poet who considered his poetry a work done for God's glory. He thought his poems could be helpful both to himself and to others who might be having similar experiences.

In you, the One,
all things abide,
and all things endlessly run to you
who are the end of all.
Father, Son, and Holy Spirit.
Amen.

—GREGORY OF NAZIANZUS

EUSEBIUS OF CAESAREA (ca. 260–339) wrote many books on history and one on the geography of biblical places. His most famous work is *Church History*, an account of the main events of the early church from the period of the apostles to his own time. Even though the book is not as complete and precise as we would like, it is still a valuable resource because Eusebius had access to documents that are now lost.

ATHANASIUS, bishop of Alexandria, wrote a book about Antony's life that portrayed the monk as a hero, fighting both demons and wild beasts. The book became a best seller.

A piece of stone with a portion of a sermon by Athanasius. In antiquity, people used pieces of stone or broken pottery when they didn't have paper, which was expensive. A piece of stone or pottery with writings is known as an **ostracon**. The writing on this particular ostracon is in Coptic and was made in Thebes, Egypt, in the seventh century.

THE MET

The Church of Saint Jacob of Nisibis, built between 313 and 320, where Ephrem served as deacon. Among the oldest churches in Turkey, it was built by Jacob of Nisibis, who was Ephrem's teacher.

GARETH HUGHES, WIKIMEDIA

EPHREM OF SYRIA (ca. 306–373) used his hymns to explain correct teachings about the Bible. He had a great ability to describe both God's splendor and common human feelings. Some of his hymns included portions to be sung specifically by women, who in many ancient cultures were excluded from religious practices. He believed Christian women should be as armed against false teachings as men.

AMBROSE OF MILAN (ca. 340–397) is considered the father of Christian hymns in the West because he introduced the custom of singing hymns to Western Europe. His hymns were composed of four lines with eight syllables per line and were based on Bible passages. Later hymns in the same style were called Ambrosian hymns.

EGERIA was a Christian woman who took a long trip around 381–384 to visit some of the places mentioned in the Bible, such as Mount Sinai and Jerusalem. Her account of her travels, written for her friends at home, helps us learn about some Christian traditions and ways of worship in Late Antiquity. For example, she wrote about how the church prepared new believers for baptism, how many hours of preaching and worship there were on the Lord's Day, and how Christians celebrated special days like Easter, Jesus's ascension, and the wise men's visit to Jesus (Epiphany).

AUGUSTINE (354–430), bishop of Hippo (today's Annaba, Algeria), wrote a book about his life from the time he was a baby until his decision to serve God. The book, called *Confessions*, is a long prayer to God written with an honesty which was rare at that time. Some people consider it to be the first autobiography of the Western world. He also wrote many other books, sermons, and letters. One of his most famous books is *The City of God*, which he wrote to comfort the Christians in Rome after the Visigoths' **sack** of the city in 410. He explained that God does not live in any city on earth and Christians belong to a heavenly city.

You have made us for Yourself, and our hearts are restless until they rest in You.
—AUGUSTINE OF HIPPO

PRUDENTIUS OF SPAIN (ca. 348–after 405) worked for a time as governor, then served at the imperial court in Milan. Around 392 he retired to devote his time to writing poetry. His poems follow the style of the classical Roman poets. To fight the teachings of Arius, he stressed the divine nature of the three persons of the Trinity. In contrast to the Gnostics, he emphasized the beauty of God's creation. Some of his poems have been turned into hymns. One of the most famous is "Of the Father's Love Begotten."

*Of the Father's love begotten
Ere the worlds began to be,
He is Alpha and Omega,
He the Source, the Ending He,
Of the things that are, that have been,
And that future years shall see,
Evermore and evermore!*
—PRUDENTIUS OF SPAIN, translated by H. W. Baker

THE CHURCH IN LATE ANTIQUITY

Great Questions of the Church

WHO NEEDS GRACE?

When Augustine of Hippo wrote a prayer asking God to give him the grace to obey, he didn't know those words would spark one of the most important debates in the history of the church.

It all started when a British monk named Pelagius (ca. 360–ca. 420) wondered why Augustine would ask God for grace to obey. After all, he thought, if God asked human beings to obey Him, He must know they could do it. Adam and Eve had just left a bad example, but no one has to follow it.

Augustine and his mother, Monica, as shown by a modern artist

EZIO POLLAI

From reading the writings of the apostle Paul, Augustine understood instead that when God told Adam that by eating the forbidden fruit he would "surely die," He meant a spiritual death. Since Adam's sin, every human being is born spiritually dead and unable to remedy the situation. Only God's grace can bring human beings to life in Jesus Christ and give them the ability to believe and obey. Without God's grace, they can only continue to sin (see Philippians 2:13).

Soon, other Christians joined this controversy—some in favor of Augustine, some supporting Pelagius. In 418 the church council of Carthage (in today's Tunisia) agreed with Augustine and officially condemned Pelagius's teachings. Augustine called this the Council of Africa because Carthage was the main Christian center in that continent and the council gathered bishops from every African province.

The same judgment was repeated at the third ecumenical council held in Ephesus (in today's Turkey) in 431 and at the Council of Orange (in today's France) in 529.

Augustine is considered the greatest **theologian** of the early Western church. His influence has continued throughout the centuries.

Think about It

- Would people who say, like Pelagius, that they can earn their own salvation really need a savior?

- If we don't need a savior, why did Christ have to die?

- Do you think it's possible for human beings to obey all God's laws perfectly? Explain your answer.

- What comes first—our faith or God's grace? According to Augustine, do we believe so we can receive God's grace, or does God give us grace so we can believe?

- Is it comforting to know that God does everything that's needed for our salvation? Why or why not?

- Read Matthew 19:25–26; John 6:44; Romans 11:6; Ephesians 2:1, 8–9. How would you use these Bible passages to explain to someone that human beings can't save themselves?

HOW AUGUSTINE EXPLAINED IT

Augustine used an interesting formula to explain how the human nature has changed because of Adam and will change again in Christ.

1. Before Adam's sin in the garden of Eden, he and Eve *had the ability not to sin*. Sadly, by rebelling against God, they chose sin and death.

2. Since Adam's fall, the human nature has become so corrupted that human beings, in themselves and without God's intervention, *are not able to keep themselves from sinning*.

3. Because of Christ's sacrifice, however, those who are in Him will eventually be in a condition that's even better than that of Adam and Eve in the garden. They will *not be able to sin*.

Bible Translations

By the time the church met for the Council of Carthage, both the Old Testament, originally written in Hebrew, and the New Testament, originally written in Greek, had already been translated in several languages.

Both Greek and Latin were essential languages in the Mediterranean region and were largely understood by educated people, although Greek was mostly spoken in the eastern portion of the Roman Empire and Latin in the western portion. The most important Latin translation of the Bible was done by Jerome. It became the official version in the Western church for centuries after the knowledge of Greek and Hebrew became largely lost to it.

The Bible was also translated into Syriac (spoken in Edessa in today's Turkey) and different forms of Coptic (spoken in Egypt). During the fourth century, it was translated into Gothic (spoken in parts of today's Germany), Armenian, Ethiopic, and Georgian.

JEROME

Born in Stridon, in today's Slovenia, Jerome (ca. 341–420) received an excellent education. After spending some time in the desert as a hermit, he became first a priest and then a secretary for the **pope** in Rome. He also became an advisor to a group of women who wanted to study the Bible more seriously. Later, when he moved to Israel and Palestine, some of these women followed him. Together, they built a monastery and three convents.

Sixth-century ostracon with an ink inscription in Coptic of portions of the Bible (Job 29:1–30:7 and Isaiah 38:1–20), recording the prayers of Job and Hezekiah.

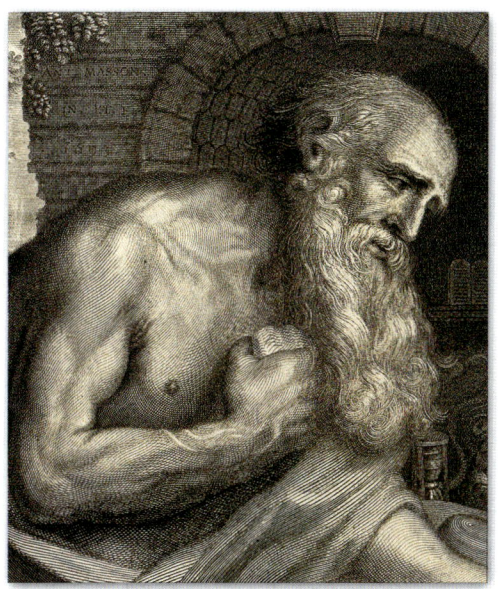

Jerome, as the French artist Antoine Masson portrayed him in a 1693 line engraving

WELLCOME LIBRARY, LONDON

THE CHURCH IN LATE ANTIQUITY • 27

More Men and Women of the Church in Late Antiquity

EARLY MISSIONARIES

Not all religions emphasize the importance of sharing their faith with others, but Christianity is based on a great historical event, Christ's resurrection, which has to be announced along with its meaning: salvation from God's punishment of the world because of sin. No one could know about this event if no one announced it, and the Bible teaches that no one can be saved without believing and trusting in the Christ who rose from the dead.

That's why from the dawn of Christianity many Christians have gone throughout their country and abroad to announce this message. Some missionaries preached first to the rulers of each land because if the rulers were converted, the whole kingdom would follow.

The inscription on this large stone records Ezana's conversion to Christianity and his military victories.
TVEDE, SHUTTERSTOCK

FRUMENTIUS (ca. 300–after 380) was traveling on the Red Sea with his brother Edesius and their uncle when some raiders attacked their ship. The brothers were sold as slaves to King Ousanas of Aksum, an area including today's Ethiopia, who employed them as tutors for his son Ezana (ca. 323–ca. 365/370). The brothers taught the king and his family about Christ and promoted building a local church. After they gained their freedom, Edesius returned to his hometown, Tyre, in today's Lebanon, where he became an elder. Frumentius accompanied him part of the way but stopped in Egypt to ask Bishop Athanasius to send a missionary to Aksum. Athanasius thought Frumentius would be the best man for the task, so he **ordained** him bishop and sent him back.

Frumentius continued to spread Christianity throughout Ethiopia. Around 356 the Roman Emperor Constantius II (ca. 317–361) asked Ezana, who had become king, to send Frumentius back to Alexandria to be ordained again by the new bishop, George. Knowing that both Constantius and George were followers of Arius, who didn't believe that Jesus was fully and eternally God, Frumentius refused, with the approval of the king.

Later, some monks came to Aksum to take the gospel to the countryside and to translate the Bible into the local language, Ge'ez. In the early sixth century, the kingdom of Aksum was still an important center of Christianity.

MARTIN OF TOURS (ca. 316–397) was one of the most active missionaries in spreading the gospel throughout Gaul, today's France. Born in what is now Hungary, he was forced by his military father to become a soldier at age fifteen. At age twenty-three, he convinced his commander to let him go to serve Christ. After spending ten years as a monk, he was ordained bishop. He founded many monasteries, which he saw as bases for bringing the gospel to the countryside. While he fought hard against false doctrines, he interceded with the emperor against the practice of killing people of different beliefs.

Aksum was apparently the first kingdom to print a cross on the back of their coins as a symbol of their state religion. The golden gild on this cross was added by a user who wanted to emphasize the value of the cross of Christ. Other Aksum coins show Christian inscriptions, such as "Joy and peace to the people" and "He conquers through Christ."

WITH PERMISSION OF WILDWINDS.COM, EX ROMA NUMISMATICS, E-SALE 67, LOT 523

NINO (d. 335)—According to tradition, Nino was an enslaved Christian woman who taught the gospel to King Mirian III (d. 361) and Queen Nana of Georgia, a nation in Eastern Europe. Apparently, the king was impressed by Nino's example, but the turning point was a hunting trip when the king was blinded so that he could see nothing but darkness. When his pagan gods proved of no avail, he prayed to the God of Nino and regained his sight. This episode awoke the king's interest in Nino's teachings. He converted and ordered the construction of a church building, the Svetitskhoveli Cathedral in Mtskheta. He also asked the church in Constantinople to send more missionaries and a bishop to oversee them. Nino continued to announce the gospel until her death in 335. She was buried in the Bodbe Monastery in Kakheti, Georgia. Two years after her death, around 337, King Mirian made Christianity the official religion of his kingdom.

A carving on the tomb of King Mirian III at Samtavro Monastery in Mtskheta, Georgia. His wife, Nana, is buried in the same monastery, which apparently the king ordered to be built.

GURO GABASHVILI, WIKIMEDIA COMMONS

PATRICK (ca. 385–461) is probably the most famous fourth-century missionary. Born in Roman Britain (which corresponds to today's England and Wales), he was captured at age sixteen by a band of Irish raiders and taken to Ireland as a slave. Six years later, he was able to escape. He eventually felt compelled to return to Ireland as a missionary. In a long letter, he explained how he was opposed by some Irish chiefs and even by some Christians who didn't understand his mission. Still, he persisted and took the gospel to parts of Ireland where it had never been taken before and baptized thousands of people. He was not the first Christian to arrive in Ireland, but he was the first to go outside the boundaries of the Roman Empire (Rome had never conquered Ireland) with the specific purpose of preaching the gospel to as many people as possible. In this, he left an example to many others.

If I be worthy, I am ready even to give up my life most willingly here and now for his name.

—PATRICK OF IRELAND

THE CHURCH IN LATE ANTIQUITY

HOW BISHOPS BECAME POPES

As the Christian population kept growing and became more recognized, the church had to become more organized, and bishops took on more authority. Problems started when some men wanted to become bishops in order to gain influence, riches, and power.

For the first two centuries, no bishop had greater influence than any other. It was common for a bishop or a group of bishops to correct one another. In time, the bishops of the largest cities started to claim greater authority.

As far as we know, the first bishop to openly claim supreme power over the others was Stephen I (d. 257) of Rome. To support his claim, he said that his authority had come from the apostle Peter, following a long line of bishops. He took Jesus's words "You are Peter, and on this rock I will build My church" (Matthew 16:18) to mean that Peter was going to be the church's supreme leader, even though the early church was led by a council of apostles and Paul had to correct Peter quite strongly for his attitude toward Christians who were not born Jews (Galatians 2:11–14).

In the fifth century, Leo I (ca. 400–461) took this claim one step further. He said that when the bishop of Rome speaks, it is actually Peter speaking directly through him.

Many opposed this claim. To make things worse, sometimes different men said they were Peter's successors. For example, in 366 two rivals—Ursinus (d. ca. 385) and Damasus (ca. 304–384)—were each elected bishop of Rome at the same time. The competition produced a wave of violence, until most of the supporters of Ursinus were killed.

Initially, the word *pope*, which simply means "father," was used as another way of saying bishop, particularly in the largest cities. After a while, the title was used for the most important bishop of the area. It was not until the eleventh century that *pope* started to be used exclusively for the bishop of Rome. Today, the same title is given to the Coptic **patriarch** of Alexandria and to all priests in the Greek Orthodox Church.

Today's popes still say they are direct successors of the apostle Peter. There is no historical proof that Peter was ever a bishop of Rome (this is not mentioned in the book of Acts, in the letters of Paul, or in Peter's own letters) or that a line of popes came down from him, but the idea is part of Roman Catholic beliefs and traditions.

The artist who created this statue in the fourteenth century dressed St. Peter as a pope to encourage people to see him as the first pope. Since Peter is often represented holding the keys of heaven, some people believe that he actually stands at the heavenly gates to let people in.

THE WALTERS ART MUSEUM, BALTIMORE

Did You Know?

Initially, popes kept the names they were given at birth. The first pope to change his name was John II (d. 535), who thought his birth name, Mercurius (a messenger of the Roman gods), was not suitable for a pope. In contrast, a pope named Formosus (ca. 816–896) had no objections to his birth name, which means "handsome."

BISHOPS AND EMPERORS

While emperors had many ways of enforcing their power through laws, taxes, and military force, bishops had some advantages: they normally lived longer (most emperors were killed by their enemies), knew their local areas, and could help their people more effectively. Many bishops ran programs to feed the poor and gave quick assistance in emergencies. For example, in 378, Bishop Ambrose of Milan rescued the prisoners of the disastrous battle of Adrianople with money collected from his churches. In 452, Leo I, bishop of Rome, convinced Attila the Hun (ca. 406–453) not to invade his city. These acts made them popular with the people, unlike emperors, who enlisted young men and collected taxes.

Also, emperors were often busy with emergencies, so a persistent bishop could often win an argument. For example, in 385 Emperor Valentinian II (371–392) and his mother, Justina (d. 388), both followers of Arius, demanded the use of two churches in Milan (still the capital of the Western Roman Empire) to worship in a way that didn't recognize that Jesus was fully and eternally God. When Bishop Ambrose refused, the emperor asked him to surrender at least one church. Ambrose didn't budge. When the emperor sent his troops to take the church by force, Ambrose and all the members of his church barricaded themselves inside the building, singing loudly until the soldiers had to leave.

MARY AND OTHER SAINTS

The word *saint* comes from the Latin *sanctus*, which means "set apart." The New Testament writers called all Christians saints because they are set apart for Christ. Over time, the church began to use this word more specifically for Christians who showed extraordinary devotion to Christ—for example, those who died for their faith. In time, some Christians started to pray to these saints, asking for special favors.

For some people, the saints were like the gods of the pagans. Just as the pagans had a god for every specific need (for example, a goddess named Juno for mothers and a god named Neptune for those at sea), some people assigned specific needs to individual saints. Mary, being the mother of Jesus, had a high place in this system. People argued that Jesus would always be willing to listen to His mother.

Around the fourth century, possessing some bones or objects that belonged to famous saints began to be considered a sign of prestige.

Places where the saints lived also became increasingly popular. Jerusalem became known as the Holy Land. Rome attracted many visitors by pointing out some places where the apostle Peter supposedly lived for some time and where the apostle Paul was supposedly imprisoned.

An artist's view of the meeting between Leo I and Attila

HERITAGE HISTORY

477–621

ca. 508 — Clovis, king of the Franks, is one of the first kings of Northern Europe to declare himself a Christian.

529 — The Council of Orange confirms and clarifies Augustine's teachings that faith is a gift of God that no one can have just by trying or wishing to have it.

596 — Pope Gregory I sends a group of monks to take Christianity to England.

After Rome

Although the western portion of the Roman Empire fell to Germanic tribes in the fifth century, much of its culture persisted. In fact, the groups who attacked it adopted many of its customs.

In the meantime, the eastern portion of the empire continued to exist until 1453, when it was conquered by the Ottomans. During that long period, it was considered the natural continuation of the Roman Empire. Today, it is commonly known as the Byzantine Empire, from the ancient name of its capital, Byzantium.

Over time, East and West became increasingly different in many aspects of their culture, such as language, art, and architecture. For example, people in the West continued to speak Latin, but people in the East spoke Greek.

Eventually, their churches became completely independent from each other. The Eastern church, known as the Orthodox Church, called their main leaders patriarchs, while the Western church, known as the Roman Catholic Church, called their main leader pope. The word *orthodox* means "correct," and the word *catholic* means "universal" (even though the Roman Church was still limited in space). The two churches started out similarly but became different over time.

THE CHURCH IN LATE ANTIQUITY • 33

More Men and Women of the Church in Late Antiquity

PREACHING CHRIST NORTH OF ROME

The missionary activity of the church increased in Late Antiquity, particularly under the supervision of Gregory I (ca. 540–604), the first pope to officially support foreign missions. In 595 he sent a group of missionaries to Britain, where he had planned to go himself before becoming pope.

The first missionaries were mostly monks sent by the church who had no earthly possessions and could move around from place to place. Many monasteries became bases where new missionaries were trained and where the local people could attend worship and receive further instruction.

Kings had an important role in spreading Christianity because they could decide on the official religion of their kingdom. In many cases, their wives became Christian first.

CLOTILDE (ca. 475–545), wife of Clovis (ca. 466–511), a powerful king of the Franks (a group of tribes in northern Gaul), tried hard to convince her husband to become a Christian. When their first son died soon after being baptized, Clovis thought it was a punishment from their pagan gods, who were angry about the baptism. Finally, after a victory in battle, Clovis agreed to be baptized, and his people readily agreed to do the same.

COLUMBA (ca. 521–597) was an Irish **abbot** who was based in Iona, a small island off the west coast of Scotland, and brought the Christian message to that region. Lots of legends were built around his life, including a story that he encountered the Loch Ness Monster.

AUGUSTINE OF CANTERBURY (d. 604) was the man in charge of Gregory I's mission to Britain. He received permission from Ethelbert (d. ca. 616), king of the province of Kent, England, to preach the gospel. Ethelbert knew something about Christianity because his wife, Bertha (d. ca. 603), was a Christian. Ethelbert allowed the missionaries to stay in Canterbury, the main city in Kent, but he wasn't interested in their religion. We know he eventually professed faith in Christ because in 601 Pope Gregory referred to him as a Christian king.

This cross on the island of Iona, Scotland, is carved in a typical style of the Celts, which was an ancient European population.
RANDALL FRIESEN

Did You Know?

The tradition of counting the years from the birth of Christ as anni Domini (AD, meaning "years of the Lord") started around the year 525 with a monk from Scythia (in Eastern Europe) named Dionysius Exiguus ("Denys the Short," ca. 470–ca. 544). In his research on the date of Easter, he used what he believed was the year of Christ's birth as the starting point. This system was widely adopted two hundred years later, when the English monk Bede (ca. 673–735) used it in his history of Christianity. Today, scholars believe that Jesus was born four to seven years before the date chosen by Dionysius.

This abbey in Bobbio, Italy, was founded by Colombanus. It became a center of learning. The monks living there were strong defenders of the Council of Nicaea's decisions about Jesus being fully God at a time when the Lombards, who ruled over much of Italy, believed the opposite.

MONGOLO1984, WIKIMEDIA COMMONS

COLUMBANUS (543–615), also an Irish abbot, became a missionary to France and other parts of Europe, bringing with him the strict rules he had learned in Irish monasteries. The community of monks in the **abbey** he founded in Luxeuil, France, became so large that they had to take turns participating in the customary singing of praise. Because of this, the abbey became famous for its non-stop singing. Columbanus was also a poet, writer, and scholar. He reminded Christians that all believers, whether they travel or not, are "sojourners and **pilgrims**" on this earth (1 Peter 2:11).

PAULINUS (d. 644) was a bishop assigned to help Ethelbert's daughter Ethelburga (d. 647) when she was given in marriage to the pagan King Edwin (ca. 585–633) of Northumbria, an English region. Paulinus and Ethelburga worked hard to convince Edwin to convert to Christianity. He finally agreed, but before asking his people to do the same, as kings normally did, he asked for his counselors' advice. A nobleman at Edwin's court compared life on earth to the flight of a sparrow that enters the castle from one door and quickly goes out another. "So this life of man appears but for a moment," he said. "What follows or indeed what went before we know not at all. If the new doctrine brings us more certain information it seems right that we should accept it." Edwin was baptized in 627.

MANUALS ON REPENTANCE

The Bible teaches us to repent of our sins, ask for forgiveness from both God and those we have wronged. In the case of a serious sin like murder or a sin that had hurt many people, the early church asked sinners to show their repentance publicly. Sometimes the church assigned a harsh punishment.

In the sixth century, some Irish monks came up with a new system, encouraging people to confess their sins privately to a priest and assigning them special acts to show their repentance. To make things easier, the monks compiled some books called penitentials, which prescribed a particular act, or **penance**, for each type of sin. In the early penitentials, the penalties for sin could be tough.

When the Irish monk Columbanus went to Gaul, he brought this custom with him and wrote his own penitential.

The Church of St. Mary and St. Ethelburga in Lyminge, Kent, England, where Ethelburga was buried. Founded by Ethelburga, this church was rebuilt a few centuries later, but some parts of the original structure are still there.

GNANGARRA, WIKIMEDIA COMMONS

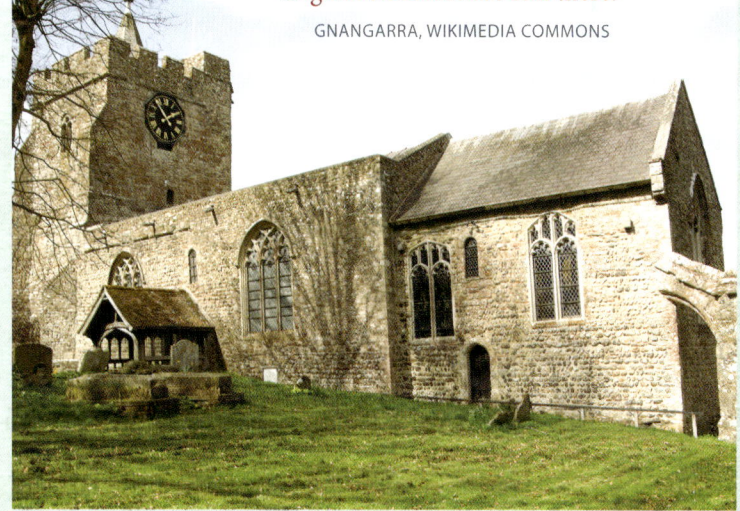

Preaching Christ in Asia

By the sixth century, travelers to the East could already find churches in faraway places such as India, Sri Lanka, and the Arabian Peninsula. These churches were founded by missionary monks sent by the so-called Church of the East, which grew beyond the eastern borders of the Roman Empire. Often, the gospel message was spread by merchants or travelers. Both missionaries and merchants traveled on the Silk Road, a vast network of connected caravan routes used to transport Asian goods like silk, jade, perfumes, and spices, as well as Western goods, especially horses. The Silk Road is marked in red on the map on these pages. The Church of the East also sent missionaries to distant lands in both Asia and Arabia.

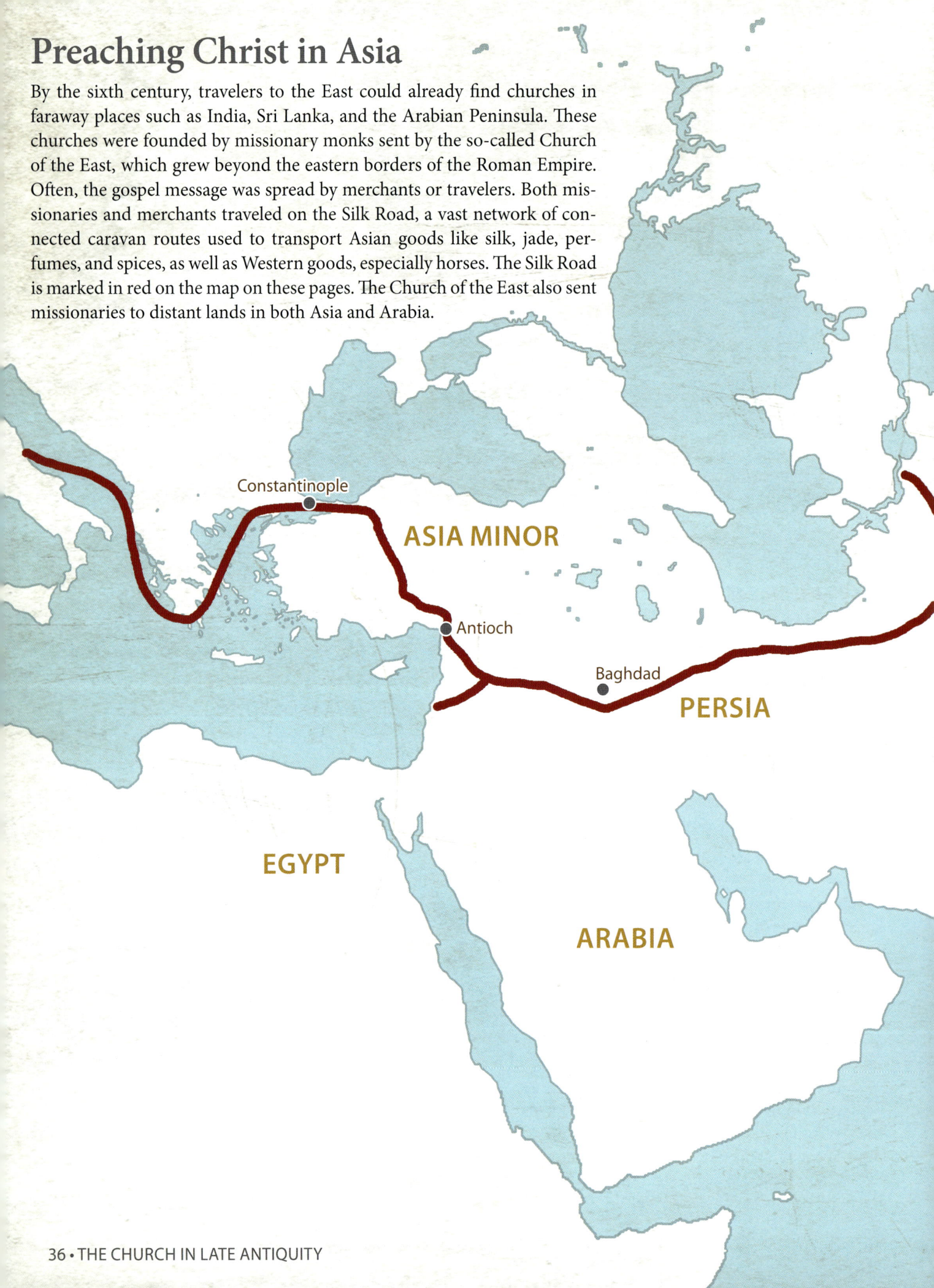

THE CHURCH OF THE EAST

The Church of the East took shape in what is now eastern Turkey and Iraq (in what was then the Persian Empire) and spread over much of Asia and Arabia – going much further than missionaries in the West did at that time.

After Constantine I made Christianity legal, the Persian kings began to resent Christians because they had some connections with Persia's bitter enemy Rome. The actual persecution, which lasted from about 341 to 367, was often carried out by the priests of the Zoroastrian religion, which was based on a supposed conflict between equal spiritual forces of good and evil. As it often happens, Christians came out of the persecution with greater strength.

In reality the Church of the East didn't have strong ties with Rome and declared its official independence in 424. It was headed by a patriarch and spoke Syriac, a form of Aramaic, the language spoken by Jesus. The Syriac translation of the Bible was one of the first ever completed.

The patriarchs of the Church of the East encouraged the building of monasteries where monks preached, cared for the people in their communities, and trained more missionaries. Most monasteries included schools and hospitals. The churches established by these monks were led by a bishop. Timothy I of Baghdad (727–823), one of the most influential patriarchs of the Church of the East, sent over eighty missionaries to many regions of Asia and Arabia and kept in regular contact with them. He believed that preaching the gospel was an urgent task.

CHINA

According to Chinese sources, the first official group of Christian missionaries arrived in the capital of China (today's Xi'an) during the reign of Emperor Taizong (598–649), who carefully examined their Chinese translation of portions of the Bible. An official imperial decree mentions a Persian monk by his Chinese name, Alopen, and describes his teachings: "The meaning of the teaching has been carefully examined; it is mysterious, wonderful, calm; it fixes the essentials of life and perfection; it is the salvation of living beings; it is the wealth of man. It is right that it should spread through the empire."

Taizong ordered the building of a monastery for twenty-one monks and the translation of the writings Alopen had carried with him.

Overall, Christianity enjoyed about a century of peace in China, interrupted by a time of persecution under the Buddhist Empress Wu Zetian (624–705), one of China's most powerful rulers. Although **Buddhism** was still fairly new in China, she made it the official religion and stirred up mobs against the Christians. She also destroyed many monasteries and churches.

A greater blow to Christianity was given in 845, when Emperor Wuzong (814–846) banned all foreign religions (including Christianity and Buddhism). Foreign Christians were forced to leave the country, and Chinese men and women who had become monks and nuns had to find other occupations. Some small Christian communities, however, survived.

Ancient merchants traveled in caravans of camels and horses to carry goods to other lands along the so-called Silk Road.

FDECOMITE, WIKIMEDIA COMMONS

INDIA

A sixth-century merchant named Cosmas reported that he saw churches in India and Sri Lanka during his travels. One of these was in Malabar, in south-western India. According to tradition, the church there was planted when an Armenian merchant named Thomas of Kana arrived there with a group of seventy-two families, a bishop, and some deacons. According to Syrian documents, they were sent by the patriarch of Babylon. The group was well received by the king of the region, Coquarangon, who gave them land and privileges.

Other kings gave the same warm welcome to other groups of Christians. Some of these Christians arrived in India when the Arabs took over their lands.

This upright, ten-foot-tall slab of stone, also known as a stele, was built in 781 to commemorate the introduction of Christianity in China. It includes the history of the Christian mission to China with the names of the missionaries, starting with Alopen. Initially erected in the Daqin Temple of Chang-an, it was discovered in Xi'an in 1623.

THIERRY OLLIVIER, ART RESOURCE

Did You Know?

The monks from the Church of the East lived simply with few possessions. When one bishop wanted to retire in comfort in Baghdad, Timothy I reminded him that monks traveled long distances by foot with only a walking stick in their hand and a small bag on their shoulder. When monks planted a monastery, the people in the community were glad to help build it because they understood the benefits they were going to receive.

The patriarchs in Baghdad kept in touch with the missionaries in distant lands through messages that were sent along the Silk Road. The monasteries built along those roads provided lines of communication.

Indians wrote their official contracts on sheets of copper. This image shows the copper plates given in 849 by King Sthanu Ravi to the Syrian Christian leader Maruvan Sapir Iso. It grants land for the construction of a church near Kerala, India. The script is Vatteluttu.

CHALLIYAN AT MALAYALAM, WIKIPEDIA

Daqin Pagoda is the earliest existing church building in China. It was built in the style of the pagoda (a Chinese memorial or temple). Unlike non-Christian Chinese temples, it faces east.

J. COSTER, WIKIMEDIA COMMONS

Did You Know?

If you attended a school in the Syriac-speaking world, you would be required to memorize and recite all the psalms in the Bible. A few lines from Psalms 1 and 2, written in Syriac, were found on a piece of pottery in Panjikent (in today's Tajikistan). Pieces of broken pottery, known as ostraca, were often used by students to practice their lessons. This ostracon ends with some words that were probably used in Syriac churches: "Your glory, God of Hosts, which fills heaven and earth."

PART 3
THE EARLY MIDDLE AGES

A Church Facing New Challenges

As was the case with Late Antiquity, historians differ on fixed dates for the beginning and ending of the Middle Ages. This book uses the first year of the **Islamic** era (622) as its start and Martin Luther's nailing of his Ninety-Five Theses to the church door (1517) as its end. It also divides the period into Early Middle Ages (622–1000) and High Middle Ages (1000–1517). (If you have never heard of the Islamic era or Luther's theses, keep reading this book.)

Some people have referred to the Early Middle Ages as the Dark Ages. In time, however, most people have come to understand that these centuries were not darker than other times in history. Like every age, the Early Middle Ages had its own challenges, and the church had to find ways to respond. Being made up—as always—of sinful people depending on God's grace, the church responded well in some cases and not as well in others. But it continued to strive to bring the gospel to others, to provide a place of security and protection in a violent society, and to promote knowledge and science as means to know the God who created all things.

622–1000

- **622** — Muhammad flees to Medina from Mecca; this is considered the first year of the Islamic era.
- **636** — Jerusalem falls to the Arabs.
- **732** — Charles Martel stops Islamic invaders at the Battle of Tours.
- **800** — Pope Leo III crowns Charlemagne as *Imperator Romanorum* (emperor of the Romans)—the first emperor in the West since the fall of Rome.
- **843** — The Carolingian Empire is divided between the three surviving sons of Louis the Pious.
- **863** — Byzantine missionaries Cyril and Methodius bring the gospel to the Slavs.
- **960** — Denmark becomes the first Viking kingdom to adopt Christianity.
- **962** — Pope John XII crowns Otto I, king of Germany, as emperor. Otto declares that his authority surpasses that of the pope.
- **988** — Prince Vladimir of Kyiv adopts the Greek Orthodox faith as the official religion of Russia.

THE EARLY MIDDLE AGES • 41

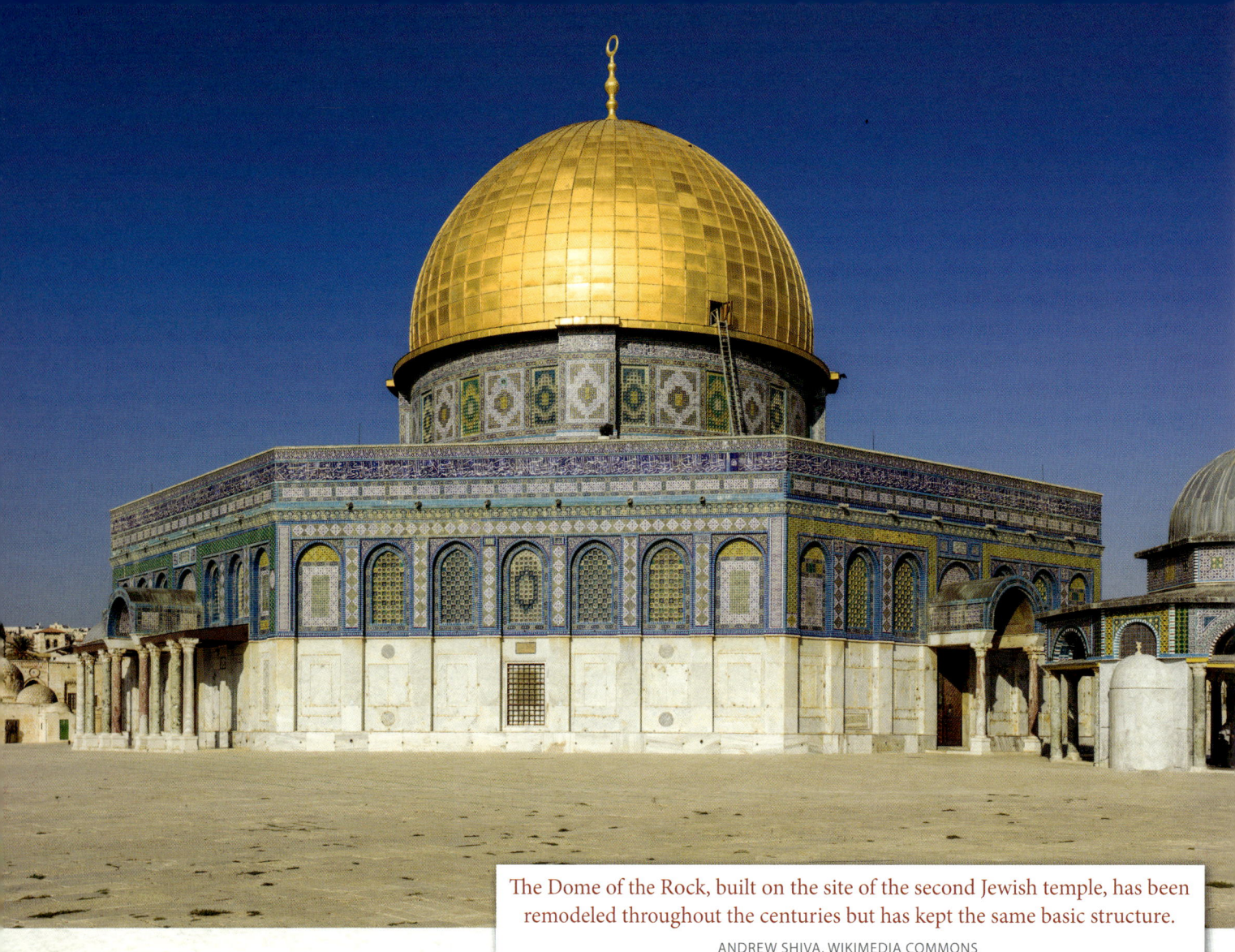

The Dome of the Rock, built on the site of the second Jewish temple, has been remodeled throughout the centuries but has kept the same basic structure.
ANDREW SHIVA, WIKIMEDIA COMMONS

The Rise of Islam

In 622 the people of Mecca, in today's Saudi Arabia, expelled from their town a man named Muhammad (ca. 571–632), who believed he had received a message from Allah, meaning "the God." Muhammad didn't know how to write but passed on the message to his followers, who wrote it down in a book called the Qur'an, meaning "recitation." The Qur'an told people to stop worshiping idols and to live and worship according to specific rules.

Muhammad and some of his followers moved to a town now known as Medina, about two hundred miles north, where they built a new community. It was the start of a new religion, **Islam**, meaning "submission." The followers of Islam, called **Muslims**, used military force to establish their influence in the area and to claim an ancient building in Mecca called Ka'ba, meaning "cube," which became their sacred location.

When Muhammad died in 632, his followers included only a small group of Arab tribes. But they continued to conquer lands in the name of their religion not only in Arabia but also in Africa, in the Byzantine Empire, in Persia, and in many Asian regions, taking over major Christian cities like Damascus, Antioch, Jerusalem, and Alexandria, with their surrounding regions. In Jerusalem, to the astonishment of both Jews and Christians, they built a **mosque** in the place of the ancient Jewish temple.

In 711 some Muslim forces began a conquest of the Iberian Peninsula, which includes Spain and Portugal.

Fearing they might move farther north, the Frankish armies of Charles Martel (ca. 688–741) stopped them in 732 at the Battle of Tours. Martel was also able to free other territories from Islamic rule. By that time, however, the Muslims were already controlling much of the area from southern Iran to Spain. Their presence and ideas had a great influence in the region.

Islam claims that Allah is the same as the God of Abraham. In reality, the Qur'an interprets the accounts in the Torah (the historical books of the Old Testament) quite differently than the Jews do. Islam is also very different from Christianity because it teaches that Jesus was only a prophet who was inferior to Muhammad, that He didn't really die on the cross, and that God is wrongly described as the Trinity.

A thirteenth-century illustration depicting the Battle of Tours, from the *Great Chronicles of France*
LEVAN RAMISHVILI, FLICKR

CHRISTIANS UNDER ISLAMIC RULE

The treatment of Christians under Islamic rule varied from place to place and from time to time. Some Christians converted to Islam to find acceptance in their community. Most of the time, those who stayed faithful to their Christian faith were allowed to practice it as long as they didn't attack Islam in public. For example, the Byzantine patriarch Timothy I (d. 823) had a long and peaceful private discussion with the Muslim **caliph** al-Mahdi (ca. 745–785), and the Christian theologian John of Damascus (ca. 675–ca. 750) was free to oppose Muslim teachings in his writings.

Around 851, when the Byzantine emperor Michael III (ca. 839–867) planned a diplomatic journey to convince Caliph al-Mutawakkil (822–861) not to attack his territories, the caliph asked him to send someone who could explain to him the meaning of the Christian Trinity. The emperor chose twenty-four-year-old Cyril of Thessalonica (ca. 826–869), who replied, "I will gladly go forth for our Christian creed. For is there anything in the world sweeter to me than to live and die for the Holy Trinity?" Cyril prepared himself by studying the Qur'an and quoted both that book and the Old Testament, which Muslims respected.

While private discussions were allowed, speaking in public in a Muslim country against Islam or renouncing the Islamic faith were considered crimes punishable by death. Between 850 and 851, forty-eight Christians were executed in Cordoba, Spain, for one of these reasons. To avoid these confrontations, many Spanish Christians left their country.

Great Questions of the Church

MAY WE MAKE PICTURES OF JESUS?

The second of God's Ten Commandments says,

> You shall not make for yourself a carved image—any likeness of anything that is in heaven above, or that is in the earth beneath, or that is in the water under the earth; you shall not bow down to them nor serve them. For I, the LORD your God, am a jealous God, visiting the iniquity of the fathers upon the children to the third and fourth generations of those who hate Me. (Exodus 20:4–5)

Traditionally, the Jews and early Christians understood that we should not make any image for the purpose of worship.

When it comes to pictures of Jesus, there is another problem. Since no one knows how He looked, any picture of Him is bound to be a false image. Those who defended images of Jesus thought they would just be a reminder to Christians that He became a man for their sakes. Those who opposed images thought that pictures could represent Him only as a man and not as God since the only way to know and worship Him as both God and man is through the Bible.

The situation became alarming when people started to light candles in front of images of Jesus and saints or to kiss them. The Muslims, who allowed no images of anything in their mosques and no images of Allah or Muhammad anywhere, thought Christians were idol worshipers.

Some Byzantine emperors tried to put a stop to this practice. In 726 Leo III (ca. 680–741) banned all religious art in the empire. The ban continued with his successors until 786, when Empress Irene (ca. 752–803), ruling in place of her underage son, resumed the old custom. In 787 she called a council of bishops at Nicaea (the seventh ecumenical council). Under her supervision, the bishops decided that images could be made as long as they were not worshiped. They could be venerated, meaning "respected," because of the persons they represented. In reality, this change of words didn't make much difference because people used the images as they had before.

Less than thirty years later, history repeated itself with a ban on images instituted in 814 by Byzantine Emperor Leo V (d. 820) and lifted in 842 by Theodora (d. after 867), his grandson's wife, who, like Irene, ruled for her underage son.

Through all these changes, there were periods of great violence, with protesters and strong persecution by the emperors of those who opposed them.

The Church of Hagia Irene, Istanbul, was built in the fourth century and was reconstructed a few times. This simple cross without an image of Jesus was ordered by Emperor Constantine V (718–775), who was against the use of images in churches.

NINA ALDIN THUNE, WIKIMEDIA COMMONS

In 794 King Charles of the Franks (742–814; later called Charlemagne, meaning "Charles the Great") called a council of bishops in Frankfurt, in today's Germany, to discuss, among other things, the Byzantines' decision about images. One of these bishops, Theodulf of Orleans (ca. 750–821), had written a long document to explain why images should not be used in worship. One reason he gave is that God has always communicated to His people through words, not images. The objects God used in the Old Testament as symbols were only supposed to teach people about Christ. Now that Christ has come, the symbols are useless. Christians don't need to go back "from the truth to an image, from the body to the shadow," Theodulf said. In the end, the bishops determined that images could be used for educational purposes but not to venerate or worship.

Many of the bishops and popes in the West didn't see any problem in making images. A strong exception was Claudius (d. after 827), bishop of Turin, Italy. Shocked by the number of images he found in the Italian churches, he personally destroyed them, provoking a chorus of angry complaints. He also spoke against prayers to the saints, which he considered **idolatry**, and against religious trips to Rome if they were done to earn merit with or forgiveness from God.

Today, Roman Catholic and Orthodox churches still have images of Jesus and saints, each following their different style. Many **Protestant** churches avoid all images. In those churches that have pictures or images, people don't usually kneel, light candles, or place flowers before them. **Reformed** churches believe there shouldn't be any image of God or Jesus at all, in or outside the church, because it will always be a false image and lead to false worship.

Think about It

Do you have images in your church? Whether you do or not, ask your pastor or parents to explain the reasons behind that decision.

A nineteenth-century statue of Charlemagne in Paris, France

LUC VAN BRACKEL, FLICKR

The Popes Look North

On Christmas Day, 800, in the Basilica of St. Peter's in Rome, Pope Leo III (750–816) surprised the world by crowning Charlemagne *Imperator Romanorum* (emperor of the Romans).

This act was especially shocking because after the fall of Rome, the Byzantine emperors had considered their reign a rightful continuation of the Roman Empire. After all, they reasoned, only the western part of the empire had fallen. And if the Roman Empire was continuing, what gave the pope the right to crown someone else as Roman emperor?

Leo claimed this right through an ancient document signed by Constantine I giving the popes control over a large part of the Roman Empire, including Constantinople.

In reality, the document was an eighth-century fake. This was proven in 1439 by the Italian scholar Lorenzo Valla (1407–1457). What gave the deception away were the writing style and some obvious contradictions. For example, the document included Constantinople as a **patriarchate**, a title used two hundred years after Constantine's death. But most people in the year 800 didn't know this, so they believed what the church told them.

Leo proclaimed Charlemagne emperor because Charlemagne, unlike the Byzantine rulers, had come to his help when the Lombards were threatening Rome. Declaring someone emperor was a powerful way for a pope to show his authority over rulers.

BYZANTINE ICONS

Called icons, religious images in the Byzantine Empire were different from those in the West and continue to be different in the Orthodox Church. First, they are flat and two-dimensional with few details. They also look distorted to avoid showing the characters' true features and emotions. These rules are meant to help the viewer understand that the images are not true representations. For some people, it was a way to keep the Second Commandment since these were flat images, and not "carved," or engraved.

The subjects are made to look spiritual by the use of light and gold. Many times the light seems to come from inside the subject.

An Orthodox icon depicting the biblical prophet Elijah

TED, FLICKR

The index page of a Gospel Book from the ninth century. Charlemagne and his court valued the type of orderly handwriting found in this index, known as Carolingian minuscule. Colorful decorations, known as illuminations, were also treasured.

THE MET MUSEUM

THE CAROLINGIAN RENAISSANCE

As emperor, Charlemagne extended his empire from the Atlantic Ocean to today's Austria and from northern Germany to Rome. His reign marked a period of cultural **revival** that is often called the Carolingian Renaissance. One of his first moves was to call to his court some of the best scholars in Europe in order to educate his court and organize other schools throughout the empire.

These scholars were led by the English Alcuin of York (ca. 735–804), who wrote textbooks and created a standardized curriculum for all schools, following the classical *trivium* and *quadrivium*. The *trivium* included grammar, logic, and rhetoric (the art of speaking well); and the *quadrivium* included arithmetic, geometry, astronomy, and music, which was considered a science. Alcuin's program became the standard for all schools in the Middle Ages.

Did You Know?

- Alcuin was an important influence on Charlemagne and spoke to him honestly. In 796 he openly opposed the king's use of force to convert pagan tribes to Christianity. "How can one force a man to believe what he does not believe?" he said. "You may force him into being baptized, not into believing." Instead, he insisted on the importance of preaching and teaching and spoke to the bishops to convince them to promote peace. Apparently, his persistence bore good fruit because there are no more recorded forced baptisms after 796 during Charlemagne's reign.

- Alcuin's scholastic method of teaching in questions and answers is evident in a book titled *Discussions between Pippin and Professor Albinus*. Pippin was a son of Charlemagne, and Albinus was one of Alcuin's nicknames. Some answers are poetic. For example, the answer to the question, "What is the sea?" is "The path of daring, the boundary of the earth, the separator of territories, the resting-place of rivers, the source of showers, a refuge in dangers, a grace among delights."

  The most familiar of Alcuin's riddles is "Three there have been: one never born and once dead; another once born, never dead; the third once born and twice dead." The answer is Adam, Elijah, and Lazarus.

Many **medieval** monasteries were far from cities. They were places where monks tried to spend their time in prayer and other occupations without distractions. Some, such as Saint Michael's Abbey in northern Italy, were convenient stops for pilgrims who traveled on foot from northern Europe to Rome.

LUCA XINO, FLICKR

Daily Life in Medieval Monasteries, Convents, and Abbeys

Monasteries, convents, and abbeys were important in the Middle Ages. Along with preaching, monks provided services for the people around them, including health care, charity, education, and support. Men who joined these communities were usually attracted by the well-regulated lifestyle, which they thought could bring them closer to God. Some women joined convents or abbeys to find protection in a dangerous world, especially if they were widows.

These religious communities were busy places where monks could study and practice a trade, such as writing, copying and illustrating texts; teaching; growing fruit and vegetables; cooking; and making products like cheese, wine, and natural remedies.

Usually, people who joined these communities had to make a **vow** to spend the rest of their lives there and obey their rules. Some people, known as **secular** canons or secular canonesses, were allowed to take only some of the required vows. In some cases, young men could go to a monastery to study without becoming a monk.

At times, people who couldn't or didn't want to live in a religious community could ask those who did to pray and even to do penance for them. For example, if people couldn't pray and fast for the amount of time a priest prescribed when they confessed their sins, they could ask a monk or nun to do it for them. This was particularly true of noblemen, who were often engaged in wars. In return, the noblemen would give the monasteries money and properties.

Often, parents sent one or more of their children to become a monk or nun. Some rich parents even built abbeys for their daughters to ensure they would have a safe place to live.

Not every child accepted their parents' decision. Some ran away. Others stayed in a monastery for the wrong reasons, enjoying the benefits without caring about the rules. One young man, Gottschalk of Orbais (ca. 804–ca. 870), protested in front of a religious court that he had been forced against his will and was released from his vows, but this was rare.

> *To Him a song I gladly sing,*
> *While waiting for Him, child sweet.*
> *A psalm in mouth, and in my mind,*
> *A psalm by day, a psalm by night,*
> *A song for You, most holy King,*
> *A sweet refrain, I gladly sing.*
>
> —GOTTSCHALK OF ORBAIS, in answer to a student who asked him to write a song. "How can I sing while I am in exile?" he asked at first. But then he realized God would still give him the joy and strength to sing to Him. A musical rendition of the whole song in Latin, with a medieval tune, is found here: https://www.youtube.com/watch?v=6A1iwCatTXA.

DAILY SCHEDULE OF MEDIEVAL MONKS

Benedict of Nursia (ca. 480–ca. 545) is considered the father of Western **monasticism** because he organized his monasteries according to strict rules that other communities copied.

The schedule of Benedictine monks was well structured. In winter, they woke up at two o'clock in the morning and met together to sing psalms. They went back to bed for an hour and woke up again at four o'clock for more singing. They rested until the rooster crowed, then went to their respective occupations, stopping twice in the morning to pray.

Lunch was at one o'clock in the afternoon—usually bread, two hot dishes, and fruits and vegetables when in season. The monks took turns serving. The servers on duty were allowed some bread and wine beforehand so they wouldn't be hungry while they served the others. Lunch was eaten in silence while a monk read some books by ancient Christian writers.

After lunch the monks could rest or walk around the courtyard. Then they worked again until evening prayer, followed by a small dinner before sunset, another prayer, and early bedtime. Their sleep was interrupted at ten o'clock for another hour of prayer, then they went back to bed until two o'clock, and the cycle started again. The shorter summer nights forced them to sleep less in order to fit in the same number of prayer times.

In spite of their busy schedule, medieval monks found time to play. This illustrated page of a prayer book in Latin (probably created by a monk) shows a group of monks playing blindman's buff, a form of tag. With a hood covering his eyes, the seated monk has to tag another player by following his voice and make him "it." Prayer books like this were very popular in the Middle Ages.

THE WALTERS ART MUSEUM, BALTIMORE

Some Men and Women of the Early Medieval Church

AUTHORS AND PATRONS

HILDA OF WHITBY (ca. 614–680) was an English abbess and one of the most influential women in the establishment of the church in England. She was an important organizer of the first official meeting of bishops in her area. Her abbey included both men and women. Some of the most important bishops, missionaries, and writers of her time came from there, including the famous Caedmon (d. ca. 680), the earliest-known English poet.

BEDE (ca. 673–735) was an English monk who wrote a history of Christianity in England. The book was an instant best seller and has been in copy or print ever since as the best source of information about English life in the Middle Ages. Bede wrote many other books, including instructional materials for children, and revised a translation of some books of the Bible into Old English. He was translating the Gospel of John into Old English when he died. The translation has been lost.

DHUODA (d. after 843) wrote one of the best compositions by a medieval woman. It was a handbook for her son William, who was living at the Frankish court. The manual included poetry, prayers, Bible lessons, word games, and some medieval interpretations of numbers. She especially encouraged William to pray, read the Bible, and keep trusting in God.

GOTTSCHALK OF ORBAIS (ca. 804–ca. 870) was a monk, missionary, and poet who wrote beautiful prayers to Christ as his Lord and protector. He also wrote a story of his life in the same style as Augustine's *Confessions*. At a council, a bishop and former teacher had him **flogged**, **excommunicated**, and imprisoned for teaching that God chooses those who will be saved and those who will not be. This was not a new teaching and could be supported by many Bible passages, but the bishop disagreed. Gottschalk appealed to the pope for justice, but by the time the pope called him to a meeting, he was too sick to go. He was buried as an unbeliever. Some of his writings were rediscovered and appreciated later.

KASSIA (ca. 810–ca. 867) was a Byzantine abbess and one of the greatest hymn writers of the Eastern church.

ALFRED THE GREAT (ca. 848–899) was king of Wessex from 871 to 886 and king of the Anglo-Saxons from 886 to 899. He promoted the translation of the Bible into Old English and personally translated some portions.

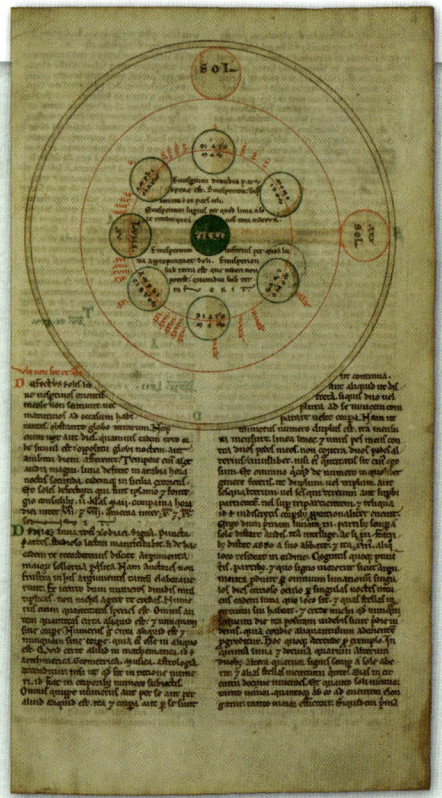

A page from a book of Bede's studies of the sky. This shows the phases of the moon. (The earth is in the center and the sun at the very top.)

WALTERS ART MUSEUM, BALTIMORE

Statue of Alfred the Great in Winchester, England

ELLIOTT BROWN, FLICKR

MISSIONARIES TO NORTHERN EUROPE

BONIFACE (ca. 675–754) was the most famous missionary to the Germans. As a young boy in England, he wanted to become a "pilgrim for Christ." When he was forty, he went on a missionary trip to Frisia, in today's Friesland, Netherlands. He was later sent to take the gospel to the Germans. During one last mission to Frisia, he and his team were attacked and killed by some local people. He is mostly famous for cutting down an oak tree the local people considered sacred and had devoted to their god Thor. This oak was creating a big problem because even some people who said they were Christian kept placing offerings in front of the tree "just in case." Before cutting the tree, Boniface challenged Thor to strike him down. Since nothing happened to Boniface, most of the people understood that Thor was unable to protect himself or others. Later, Boniface used the wood from the tree to build a church. Because of his emphasis on learning, he is also considered one of the fathers of the Carolingian Renaissance.

A statue of Boniface near the cathedral of the small German town Fritzlar
BJÖRN BIRKHAHN | DREAMSTIME.COM

ANSKAR (ca. 801–865), a Frank, was one of the rare Christians who was willing to go to Scandinavia at the time of the fearsome Vikings. He accepted calls first to Denmark and then to Sweden. After many attacks by both local people and Vikings, he was forced to leave. He built missionary bases in northern Germany with a vision of reaching the people further north. He also built schools for children and a hospital for people who could not afford a doctor. He often paid the ransom to free slaves and spoke to Christian slave traders to convince them to abandon their occupation. Christianity became accepted in Scandinavia in the tenth century when some kings converted.

LEOBA (ca. 710–782) was an English nun who arrived in Germany in 748, after Boniface invited her to help him in his missionary work. She oversaw a community of about thirty nuns and was very respected by the local people and by the rulers. Charlemagne's wife, Hildegard (ca. 754–783), often called her to the royal court to ask for her advice. Leoba was also known for her outstanding knowledge of the Bible. Boniface considered her an important part of the German mission and asked that after her death her grave be placed next to his. He is considered the first church leader to officially employ women as missionaries.

THEODULF OF ORLEANS (ca. 750–821), bishop, theologian, and poet, had a great influence on Charlemagne and his court. Along with the document used at the Council of Frankfurt to oppose the use of images in worship, he wrote other important papers. He also promoted a system of free elementary education for all taught by priests, monks, and nuns as part of their service to others. He is the author of the hymn translated as "All Glory, Laud, and Honor."

This statue commemorating Anskar, missionary to Scandinavia, was created in the twentieth century by Carl Eldth.
DEPENDABILITY, WIKIMEDIA COMMONS

MISSIONARIES TO EASTERN EUROPE

While Rome sent missionaries to northwestern Europe, the Byzantine church focused its missionary work in Eastern Europe. Much of this region embraced Christianity by the year 1100.

Cyril of Thessalonica and his brother Methodius (815–885) were the most famous missionaries to the Slavs, who had settled in today's southern Russia, Hungary, Czech Republic, and the Balkan Peninsula. They were both skilled with languages. The problem was, the Slavs didn't have a written language. The missionaries could speak to them but couldn't give them anything written. Since some Slavic sounds couldn't be reproduced with Greek characters, Cyril created some new, original characters. A version of those characters still bears his name, Cyrillic.

> *Does the rain not fall equally upon all people? Does the sun not shine for all, and do we not all breathe the air in equal measure? Why then are you not ashamed to recognize only three languages and command the other nations and races to be blind and deaf?*
> —CYRIL OF THESSALONICA

Cyril and Methodius received much opposition from German bishops who thought the Bible should be in only three languages: Hebrew, Greek, and Latin (the first two because the Bible was originally written in those languages, and Latin because they trusted Jerome's translation). Eventually, Pope Hadrian II (792–872) gave full approval to Cyril and Methodius's translating work. But after Cyril died, the German bishops found an excuse to imprison Methodius for two and a half years until Hadrian's successor, John VIII (d. 882), demanded his release. In spite of this, Methodius and his team managed to translate the Bible and other Christian writings into Slavic.

Some disciples of Methodius left Moravia, one of the historic Czech lands, during the persecution and found refuge in Bulgaria, whose king, **Czar** Boris I (d. 907), had converted to Christianity in 864. Boris encouraged the missionaries to develop a Bulgarian alphabet and to open a school where the Bible could be taught in the local language.

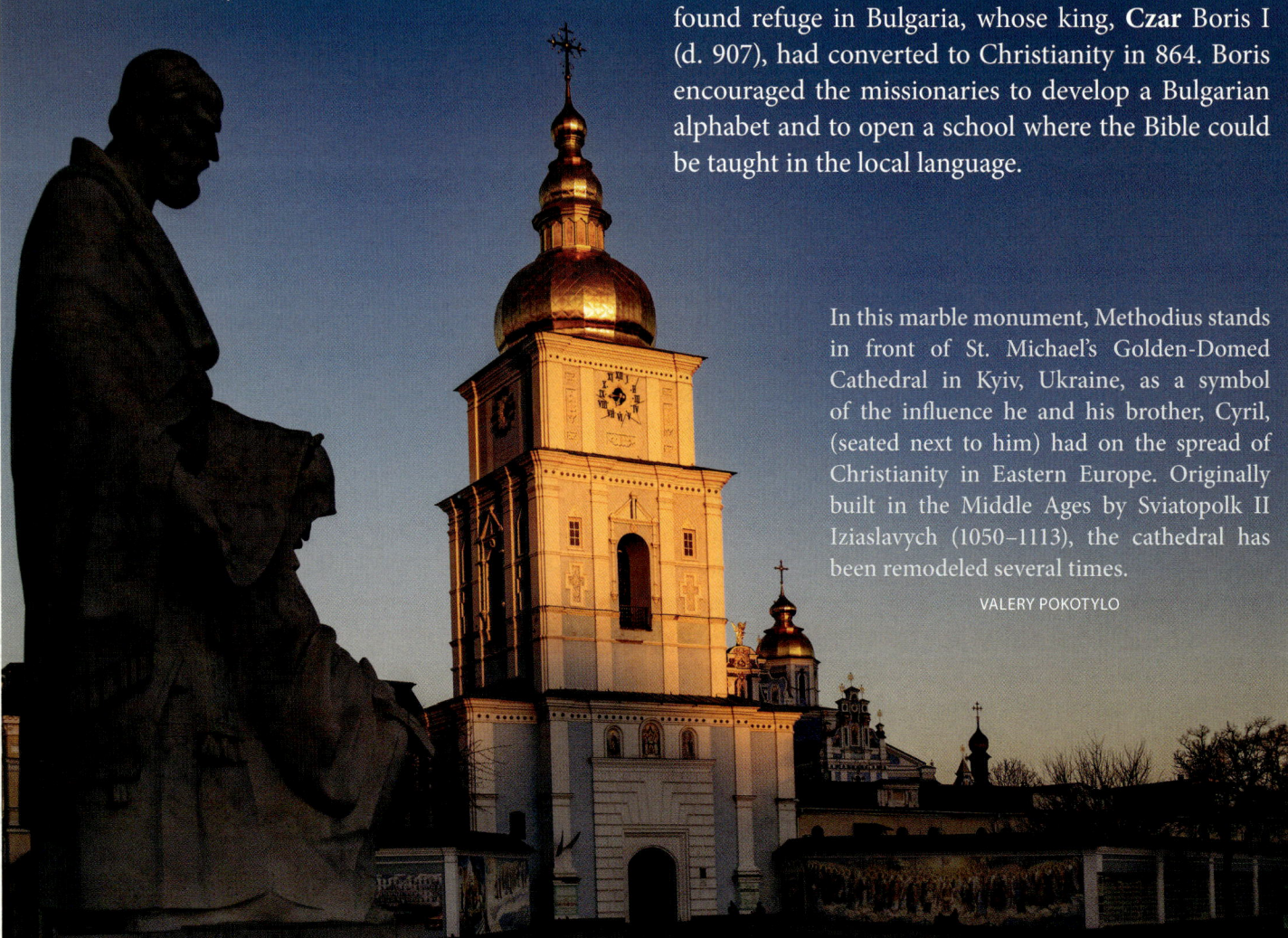

In this marble monument, Methodius stands in front of St. Michael's Golden-Domed Cathedral in Kyiv, Ukraine, as a symbol of the influence he and his brother, Cyril, (seated next to him) had on the spread of Christianity in Eastern Europe. Originally built in the Middle Ages by Sviatopolk II Iziaslavych (1050–1113), the cathedral has been remodeled several times.

VALERY POKOTYLO

The same marble statue of Cyril and Methodius, showing them writing the alphabet. To their right is a monument to Queen Olga and, to her right, a monument to St. Andrew, one of Jesus's disciples. According to a legend, he preached in the lands of Rus and planted a cross at the point where the city of Kyiv was built about four centuries later.

© THE REV'D GERRY LYNCH

Think about It

The German bishops were afraid that new Bible translations could have some mistakes, which is certainly possible. Not even Jerome's translation was perfect.

- What do you think? What's best—giving the people a Bible they can read, even if it might have a few imperfections, or keeping it from them for fear of mistakes? Explain your answer.

- Do you think the same Christ who has commanded His disciples to take the gospel to every nation will make sure that the same gospel is delivered correctly in other languages? Will mistakes be eventually discovered and corrected?

Christianity in Russia

According to tradition, the first person to spread Christianity in Russia was Queen Olga (d. 969), who ruled the region of Kyiv from 945 until 960 on behalf of her underage son Svyatoslav (943–972). The cruel death of her husband turned her into a fierce warrior who ruthlessly defeated her country's enemies, the Drevlians.

She apparently came into contact with Christianity in 954 in Constantinople when she visited Emperor Constantine VII (905–959). Even though Svyatoslav didn't follow his mother's faith, he allowed her to plant churches in Russia. Forty years later, her grandson Vladimir Sviatoslavich (ca. 958–1015), called Vladimir the Great, became a professing Christian too. According to traditional accounts, he chose the Orthodox Church over the Roman Catholic because he was impressed by the magnificent buildings and ceremonies of the Byzantine churches. His baptism marked an alliance with the Byzantine emperor Basil II (ca. 958–1025) and a marriage to the emperor's sister Anna (963–ca. 1011).

This seventeenth-century image of Vladimir shows him holding a staff mounted by a cross.

WIKIMEDIA COMMONS

THE EARLY MIDDLE AGES • 53

PART 4
THE HIGH MIDDLE AGES

- Under the patriarchate of Constantinople
- Under the patriarchate of Rome

Divisions and Crusades

For centuries the Church of Rome (also known as Catholic) and the church of the Byzantine Empire (known as Orthodox) were able to work side by side in spite of their differences, mostly related to worship and organization. Politically and culturally, however, they kept growing apart, and the gap became wider when the popes allied with the Frankish kings in the eighth century. One major problem was the pope's claim that he had authority over all Christian churches, including that of Constantinople. The division between East and West became definite in 1204, when Western **crusaders** invaded and captured Constantinople.

1000–1517

- **1077** — Emperor Henry IV is forced to ask for Pope Gregory VII's forgiveness at Canossa, Italy, one of the most important moments in the relations between church and state.
- **1095** — Pope Urban II calls for the First Crusade in the Holy Land.
- **1096–1099** — The First Crusade attempts to recover the Holy Land and establishes the Kingdom of Jerusalem.
- **1139** — The Second Lateran Council focuses on the proper behavior of priests, monks, and nuns and decides that priests should not marry.
- **1147–1148** — The Second Crusade ends with the failure to capture Damascus.
- **1187–1192** — The Third Crusade regains some lands (but not Jerusalem) from Saladin.
- **1201** — Pope Innocent III claims the right to appoint rulers, including the emperor.
- **1202–1204** — The Fourth Crusade ends with the raid of Constantinople, which marked a definite break between the Western and Eastern churches.
- **1208** — Pope Innocent III calls a crusade against a heretical group called the Cathars.
- **1215** — The Fourth Lateran Council announces important changes to the church and gives definite answers to questions until then unresolved, such as the view of transubstantiation.
- **1217–1221** — The Fifth Crusade fails to conquer Jerusalem.
- **1229** — Emperor Frederick II regains Jerusalem by negotiating a treaty with Sultan Al-Malik al-Kāmil.
- **1244** — The Muslims take back Jerusalem by force.

THE HIGH MIDDLE AGES • 55

THE CRUSADES

By 1095 Muslim troops had taken over much of the Near East and North Africa, once again coming dangerously close to destroying the Byzantine Empire. Emperor Alexius I Comnenus (ca. 1048–1118) asked several Christian rulers for help. While many were concerned, it was in 1095 that Pope Urban II (d. 1099) responded with a call to arms.

Urban appealed to the Christians' love for Jerusalem, the biblical holy city, which was now in the hands of Muslims. He encouraged those who had military skills to protect the Christians who had lost their lands.

Thousands of Christians responded with zeal, starting their march in 1096. They called themselves pilgrims and saw their expeditions as a way to do penance for their sins. Since many of them attached cloth crosses on their clothes, they later became known as crusaders (from the Latin *crux*, meaning "cross") and their expeditions, **crusades**.

These first crusaders took back Jerusalem in 1099, but a second crusade, meant to bring relief to the invaded city of Edessa, never reached its goal.

In 1187 the Muslims, led by Saladin (1138–1193), **sultan** of Egypt and Syria, recaptured Jerusalem and

Recapturing the Church of the Holy Sepulchre in Jerusalem became a major focus of the Crusades, as Christians believed that the church was built in the place where Jesus was buried.
JORGE LÁSCAR, FLICKR

other surrounding cities. This provoked a third crusade led by Emperor Frederick I (1122–1190) of Germany (nicknamed "Barbarossa," or "Redbeard"), King Philip II Augustus of France (1165–1223), and King Richard I of England (1157–1199) (nicknamed "the Lionheart").

This crusade suffered a major setback when Barbarossa drowned while crossing a stream. Philip returned home, while most crusaders continued to fight under Richard. They finally took back several cities (though not Jerusalem) and made a deal with Saladin.

Beginning in 1198, Pope Innocent III (1161–1216) promoted a fourth crusade to take back Jerusalem. This time, the crusaders planned to attack Egypt from the sea. They asked the ruler of Venice, Enrico Dandolo (ca. 1107–1205), to build enough ships for all the crusaders who had promised to go. They would pay once the ships were finished, they said.

By saying yes, Dandolo took a great risk because shipmakers had to stop working on other ships for an entire year, leaving the city without one of its main sources of income. In the end, only two-thirds of the promised crusaders turned up, and Venice received only two-thirds of the promised money.

Knowing that the crusaders were not able to pay him, Dandolo asked them to take back the city of Zara (in today's Croatia), which belonged to Venice. In spite of the pope's disagreement with this new venture, the crusaders accepted to make up for Venice's losses.

A statue erected in Châtillon-sur-Marne, France, in memory of Pope Urban II, who called people to fight in the First Crusade
FAB5669, WIKIMEDIA COMMONS

Another offer of money came from the Byzantine prince Alexius (ca. 1182–1204), who promised the crusaders money and assistance if they helped to restore him and his father, Isaac II (1156–1204), to the throne. They agreed, once again with the pope's disapproval, but, once crowned as Alexius IV, the prince could not keep his word. When a new contender, Alexius V (1195–1204), took the crown and commanded the crusaders to leave, the crusaders reacted by attacking Constantinople in 1204 and robbing it of many of its goods.

From 1217 to 1221, a fifth crusade tried to capture Jerusalem, this time by first conquering the Muslim sultanate of Egypt. They almost succeeded. Finally, in 1229 Emperor Frederick II (1194–1250) was able to gain control of the city by negotiating an agreement with the Egyptian sultan al-Malik al-Kāmil (1179–1238), nephew of Saladin. Frederick's mission is often known as the Sixth Crusade, even though these numbers were assigned later by historians, who have counted at least eight major crusades.

Frederick's victory was only temporary because in 1244 the Muslims took back Jerusalem. In 1453 they took over Constantinople, bringing to an end the Byzantine Empire.

An artist's view of the meeting between Francis of Assisi and Sultan al-Malik al-Kāmil

SEDMAK, ISTOCK

A statue of Saladin in front of the Citadel of Damascus

DOMINIC DAVEY, FLICKR

THE BIBLE AND THE SWORD

While most Christians in Europe and along the Mediterranean Sea were concerned about the fast advance of Islam and supported the crusades, some also wished for the Muslims to accept the gospel. In 1219 the Italian **friar** Francis of Assisi (ca. 1182–1226) visited Sultan al-Malik al-Kāmil. While there are no records of their conversations, it was a peaceful meeting. Decades later a Franciscan, Raymond Llull (ca. 1235–1315), insisted that some Christians should learn Arabic and the Qur'an in order to take the gospel to Muslims. While Muslims have some idea of God's love, he said, they know Him only as a Creator and not as a Savior who became man, lived, and died for sinners. He finally managed to set up a school to prepare missionaries to go to the Muslims. But when he went to preach the gospel in Béjaïa, in today's Algeria, he was stoned to death by a crowd of angry Muslims.

THE HIGH MIDDLE AGES • 57

POPES, BISHOPS, AND RULERS

Unlike the Christians in the East, who kept the Roman tradition of considering the emperor the head of the church, Western popes claimed this title for themselves, together with the right to appoint or **depose** bishops. But since the bishops owned a lot of property and held great authority over the people, Western rulers treated them as they would treat other leaders in their countries. They didn't see much difference between vassals (subjects who received lands or privileges in exchange for their loyalty) and bishops. Just as they gave vassals a symbol of their alliance (usually a sword or spear), they gave their bishops symbolic objects (normally a staff and a ring).

Some kings and emperors even claimed the right to appoint popes. To avoid this problem, in 1059 Pope Nicholas II (d. 1061) declared that only a chosen group of church leaders called **cardinals** could elect a pope.

Henry IV of Germany and Pope Gregory VII

One of the sharpest conflicts between a ruler and a pope happened in 1076, when the king of Germany, Henry IV (1050–1106), annoyed by the demands of Pope Gregory VII (ca. 1025–1085), claimed the pope had not been properly elected and demanded that he resign. In answer, Gregory excommunicated Henry and declared him unfit to rule. Excommunication meant that the church did not regard the king as a true Christian. In those days, it was a big punishment. It caused Henry to lose many supporters and gave his enemies hope of prevailing against him.

In the winter of 1077, one of the coldest anyone could remember, Henry crossed the Alps to face Gregory. Apparently, at first he wanted to fight back, but some advisers convinced him to ask for forgiveness. The pope was staying at Canossa, in northern Italy, in the castle of one of his supporters, Countess Matilda (1046–1115). A cousin of Henry and a powerful European ruler, she played an important role in the reconciliation.

Dressed in a rough sackcloth tunic, Henry stood barefoot outside the castle in the snow for three days. Gregory knew that once reinstated, Henry had no obligation to keep his word. But as a pope, he was supposed to forgive those who showed repentance.

Gregory announced that Henry was no longer excommunicated but didn't say he considered him fit to rule. Because of that, Henry's enemies in Germany tried to replace Henry with a new king.

In the end, Henry defeated his enemies, deposed Gregory, and appointed a different pope, Clement III (ca. 1025–1100), who crowned Henry emperor of the Holy Roman Empire, confirming his authority.

The broken tower on top of this hill is part of what remains of the Castle of Canossa. This is where Henry IV had to walk in the winter of 1077 to beg the pope for forgiveness.

ROBERTO PANCALDI

Henry II of England and Thomas Becket

About a century after Henry IV's walk to Canossa, the conflict between church and state also came to a head in England, this time between a king and an archbishop.

When the archbishop of Canterbury, the main religious authority in England, died in 1162, King Henry II (1133–1189) saw his chance to appoint someone who would be on his side. He chose his friend Thomas Becket (1118–1170).

Contrary to Henry's expectations, Becket didn't always agree with him. When Henry wrote a new code of laws giving the English kings the power to elect bishops; collect money from churches and monasteries; and punish priests, bishops, monks, and nuns who had committed crimes instead of leaving it up to the church, Becket refused to place on the official papers his seal, which would show his agreement.

An artist's view of Henry IV outside the Castle of Canossa waiting to reconcile with Pope Gregory VII
NSA DIGITAL ARCHIVE, ISTOCK

Henry felt betrayed. He became so angry that Becket fled to France for some time. Eventually, Becket returned but continued to oppose the king in many ways. Finally, Henry blurted out, "Who will rid me of this turbulent priest?" He probably meant this to be a careless remark, but four knights interpreted it as a command and stormed into the cathedral in Canterbury, where they murdered Becket.

The people of England were outraged to see an archbishop murdered inside a church. Henry had to ask for forgiveness and retract some of his new laws. He was also publicly flogged. As for Becket, the church declared him an official saint and built a shrine for him in the cathedral, which attracted many people. The shrine was destroyed in 1538, when King Henry VIII (1491–1547) declared that Becket had been a traitor to his king and ordered Becket's bones to be burned.

After Thomas Becket was murdered in 1170, he became the symbol of the conflict between church and state. Visitors at his shrine could buy badges like this one, which spread Becket's fame.
THE WALTERS ART MUSEUM, BALTIMORE

A **miniature** from an English psalter painted around the year 1250 depicts the murder of Thomas Becket. After Henry VIII condemned Becket in 1538, this image was hidden by gluing a piece of paper over it. It was discovered much later.
THE WALTERS ART MUSEUM, BALTIMORE

THE HIGH MIDDLE AGES • 59

Great Questions of the Church

WHY THE GOD-MAN?

Sometimes other people's questions help us better understand what we believe. In the eleventh century, an archbishop named Anselm (1033–1109) was puzzled by a question raised by Jews: Why was it necessary for God to become man?

Some Christians taught that after Adam's first sin, the devil had become the owner of every human soul, and Jesus had to die to take back these souls from him. That didn't really answer the Jews' questions. Couldn't God, being omnipotent, have saved His people another way? The Jews believed that God would send a savior, a messiah, but for God to actually take on a human body was seen as an unnecessary dishonor, disgracing God's majesty and glory.

Until then, most Christians had answered that yes, God could have done things differently, but He simply chose this way. Anselm, however, didn't believe the devil owned anyone's soul or that God owed anything to the devil. In reality, Anselm said, sin creates a problem for both humans and God. God cannot forgive humans without some payment because evil must always be punished, and humans don't have the ability to pay for their sins. Even if a payment were possible, as soon as people paid for one sin, they would commit another.

Besides, even the sins we consider small are a terrible rebellion against God and an offense to God's honor. It was something that people at that time of kings could easily understand because a rebellion against a king was always an affront to his honor.

Only one person could save humans from this terrible problem—someone who was fully God so that He could live a perfect life and take the terrible punishment that would crush any human being, and fully man because man sinned and man must repay.

This image of Anselm giving his book of meditations and prayers to Matilda of Canossa was originally painted during his lifetime. This doesn't mean it's accurate because it's possible that the artist never met the countess or Anselm.

BENEDIKTINERSTIFT ADMONT

Anselm wrote this reply as a conversation between him and a monk named Boso. He titled it *Cur Deus Homo*, which literally means "Why God-Man?" In time, the Western church adopted Anselm's explanation as its official answer to the question of why God had to become man. Later creeds added that God has to punish sin not only because it offends His honor but also because if He didn't punish evil, He would not be just.

Not everyone agreed with Anselm. Some Christians preferred the story of souls being the devil's property. A French scholar named Peter Abelard (1079–1142) made a different suggestion: Jesus died to show us God's love and give us an example to follow. This view created new problems. A French monk named Bernard of Clairvaux (1090–1153) explained that it would not be loving for God to crucify His Son in order to give us only an example of love.

> *If only God can make this satisfaction [for sin] and only a man ought to make it, it is necessary that a God-man make it.*
> —ANSELM OF CANTERBURY

ANSELM ON THE CRUSADES

"I advise you, I counsel you, I pray and beseech you, as one who is dear to me, to abandon that Jerusalem which is now not a vision of peace but of tribulation, to leave aside the treasures of Constantinople and Babylon, which are to be seized on with hands soaked in blood, and to set out on the road to the heavenly Jerusalem which is a vision of peace, where you will find treasures which only those who despise these [earthly] ones can receive."

—Anselm of Canterbury to a young man who was wondering if he should fight in the war to defend the Byzantine Empire

Bernard of Clairvaux, depicted by a fifteenth-century artist, in the white robe typical of the Cistercian monks

THE MET

Think about It

- Even though Jesus certainly gave us an example of sacrificial love, why would it be bad news if He came *only* for this reason? Do you think we could really match His example? Explain your answers.

- Was Bernard of Clairvaux right or wrong? Why? Would God be loving if He had willed His Son to be crucified only to give us an example of love? Why or why not?

- God's solution to the problem of humankind's rebellion against Him is so surprising that some people have become Christians just because they couldn't see how this solution could have been invented by a human being. What do you think? Can you see any other way for God to be perfectly just and loving in this matter? See Romans 3:23; Romans 5:12; 1 Corinthians 15:21–22; Hebrews 2:9.

Some Men of the Church of the High Middle Ages

REVIVERS OF MONASTIC LIFE

Some Christians tried to remedy the obvious problems in the church by founding new religious **orders**, hoping their members could be the examples of Christianity that popes and bishops failed to be. There were two types of religious orders, monks and friars: monks normally retreated to the country, and friars traveled around the cities to talk to people.

This painting of Bruno of Cologne was made in the fifteenth century. The artist, Girolamo Marchesi (ca. 1471–1550), didn't know what Bruno looked like but represented a typical Carthusian monk with a white robe and **cowl**.

THE WALTERS MUSEUM, BALTIMORE

This painting shows Anthony of Padua (ca. 1198–1231) taking his vows as a Franciscan friar. After taking their vows, those who wanted to join a community of friars, monks, or nuns would kneel and receive the distinctive clothes, or **habit**, of that particular community, or order. According to legend, Anthony was a Dominican before adopting the Franciscan rule. That's why two Dominican friars stand behind him holding the Dominican white habit with a black cowl while a Franciscan superior gives him the Franciscan brown habit.

THE WALTERS MUSEUM, BALTIMORE

In Germany **BRUNO OF COLOGNE** (ca. 1030–1101) adopted more drastic measures. He created an order where monks didn't just retreat to the country. They lived in individual cells with no contact with others except for daily worship meetings. This order was called Carthusian from the name of their first monastery, the Grande Chartreuse (*carthusium* in Latin).

In France **BERNARD OF CLAIRVAUX** (1090–1153) encouraged a disciplined Christian life in his order of monks, called Cistercian from the name of the place where it was founded. Most Cistercian monasteries were built far from cities in order to stay away from the riches that had corrupted other monks. The words of some famous Christian hymns, such as "O Sacred Head Now Wounded" and "Jesus, Thou Joy of Loving Hearts," were originally written in Latin by Bernard of Clairvaux.

In Italy **FRANCIS OF ASSISI** (ca. 1182–1226) shocked his family by abandoning everything and embracing a life of poverty and service to God and others. Soon he had many followers who did the same thing. While he never meant to create an organization, his followers did: after his death, they formed an order of friars called the Order of Friars Minor (or Franciscans). A woman from his hometown, **CLARE OF ASSISI** (1194–1253), founded a similar order for women called the Order of the Poor Clares (or Clarissas).

WALDO (1140–1218), also known as Valdes of Lyon, France, is considered the founder of a group called the **Waldensians**. Like Francis, Waldo preached simplicity and poverty. He commissioned the translation of the Bible in French, apparently the first translation in a modern language in Western Europe, and sent his men out to read the Bible to the people. He was excommunicated for preaching without the church's authorization. Most of his followers found refuge in the Italian Alps.

DOMINIC OF OSMA (ca. 1170–1221), from Spain, started an order of friars that could be trained to be preachers—a great need in the church at that time. Because of this, he placed a great emphasis on education. His order became known as the Order of Preachers, or Dominican Order. In England the Dominicans were called Black Friars because of their black capes.

The Grand Chartreuse, in the French Alps, was the first monastery built by Carthusian monks. In spite of frequent renovations, it still has the original design with individual cells for the monks, a common place of worship, and a common eating hall. The Carthusians supported themselves by raising sheep and growing grains, beans, and vegetables. Later, they took advantage of nearby iron mines to produce useful objects for sale.

FLORIEL, WIKIMEDIA COMMONS

THE CATHARS

A group called the Cathars, or Albigensians, reacted even more radically against the church's corruption. In trying to establish a purer church, they ended up rejecting many Christian doctrines and created a new religion. Like the early Gnostics, they believed there are a good god and an evil god and that everything material is bad, including the human body. Because of this, they thought Jesus's body looked real but was not, which means He never died or rose again. When they refused to change their views, the pope sent armies against them until there were almost no Cathars left. It was the first crusade launched against people who claimed to be Christian. The church officially condemned the teachings of the Cathars in 1215 at the Fourth Lateran Council, so called because it was held in the Lateran Palace, where Roman Catholic popes lived.

THE BOGOMILS

The Bogomils were a religious group that caused concerns in the Orthodox Church. They were similar to the Cathars because they believed that everything material is bad, so that Jesus could not have become man. They encouraged Christians to avoid most pleasures of life and to resist the religious authorities. This appealed to many Christians at a time when the Orthodox Church had become rich and powerful and many of its leaders seemed only interested in material things.

Inquisitions

As well as condemning the Cathars, the Fourth Lateran Council confirmed the institution of religious trials called **inquisitions**. Inquisitions were supposed to try every type of crime in the church. At that time, heresy was considered a crime to be punished, like stealing or murder.

In 1231 Pope Gregory IX (1145–1241) appointed the first official inquisitors of heresies—mostly Dominican and Franciscan friars. These inquisitors could arrest suspects on the testimony of two witnesses who could remain secret and had to answer only to the pope. In 1252 Pope Innocent IV (1195–1254) decreed that heretics who refused to give information could be tortured. Unrepentant heretics were given to the governing authorities to be executed, usually by being burned alive, which was regarded as a picture of the fires of hell.

Popular Religion

In the course of history, the great power given to inquisitors and the use of force against unbiblical teachings have caused many problems. But there were times when inquisitors were able to discover some issues that truly needed to be addressed.

One of these issues was the people's tendency to attribute special power to certain places, people, objects, or—in at least one rare case—animals. That's what happened in a region north of Lyon, France, where an inquisitor, Etienne de Bourbon (1190–1261), heard from many women about their prayers to Saint Guinefort Martyr. When Bourbon asked them more about it, he found out that Guinefort was a greyhound dog. According to the inquisitor, it all started when Guinefort's owners, finding some blood by their baby's empty crib, thought the dog had eaten the baby. After killing the dog, they heard a cry and found the baby safe under the crib, together with the body of a snake that Guinefort had killed. When the people in that area heard what had happened, they thought the dog had saved the baby and was in heaven. They began to pray to it, asking it to do miracles for their children. This story is unique and extreme, but it shows that people needed instruction to learn what the Bible really teaches about prayer, saints, and miracles.

More common was the people's faith in the power of **relics**. This belief grew during the Crusades, when crusaders brought back many relics from Israel and made them available to people. But many of these relics were fake, sold by people who simply wanted to make money from others who were easily fooled.

On important holy days, priests would carry reliquaries at the front of **processions**.

THE MET MUSEUM

Relics were often kept in richly decorated containers called reliquaries. This reliquary is said to hold a splinter from the cross on which Jesus died.

OPUSDEI28, WIKIMEDIA COMMONS

The image on this reliquary shows that the relic inside is a piece of bone from a saint's arm.

THE MET MUSEUM

Think about It

- For Roman Catholics, relics of saints are a connection between heaven and earth. In other words, they help believers to think about the person who is in heaven. During the **Reformation**, Protestants taught people that the only links God has given us between heaven and earth are God's Word (the Bible) and the two sacraments of baptism and the Lord's Supper. Which of these views seems more biblical to you? Explain why.

- While most Roman Catholics deny that relics have any power in themselves, many people still find it comforting to place their trust in those objects. Do you see why people might have this response to an object? Think of some examples when a common object (not necessarily a relic) made someone feel more secure. How can this tendency to trust an object become dangerous for a Christian?

> *Imagine, Reverend Master, what great blame is laid on **prelates** of the Church and others who, by reason of their office or their profession, are responsible for preaching to such persons, but instead take their ease, enjoying themselves in their pretty rooms in the large towns and villages. In the meantime, souls, for whose salvation Christ died, are perishing from lack of spiritual nourishment.*
> —VINCENT FERRER (1350–1419), Dominican preacher, on the lack of good preaching in the medieval church

READING AND HEARING THE SCRIPTURES IN THE HIGH MIDDLE AGES

From the times of the early church, the Bible was always considered the most important book, and every monastery and cathedral had a copy, but it was not usually available outside of those places. The leaders of the church thought it was better this way. The Fourth Lateran Council described the church as "mother and teacher," encouraging believers to put their trust in its care. In other words, they said, if you do what the church tells you to do and believe what it tells you to believe, everything will go well.

In some cases, good preachers could make up for the people not having the Bible in writing. Some, such as Bernard of Clairvaux, preached for over an hour, keeping up the ancient habit of working through whole books of the Bible. Some who were not trained well enough to preach chose to read the few published sermons of Augustine, Gregory the Great, and other church fathers. But many priests were not even able to find these texts and ended up reading the Bible in Latin without adding any explanation, or limited their sermons to good advice.

That's how the orders of friars started. Preaching initially in the open air, many of these friars enabled the people to hear the Bible more fully than they could in a church.

Great Questions of the Church

MAY PRIESTS MARRY?

In 1139 the Second Lateran Council confirmed a rule that some people had suggested before: priests should not marry. Monks, friars, and nuns had already adopted that rule voluntarily in order to spend more time in prayer and meditation, but priests, who were always around people, had been free to marry. Now all this was going to change. What's more, the council decided that all existing marriages of priests were no longer valid. That meant that married priests were expected to leave their wives and children.

Why did the church make this rule mandatory? One practical reason was that some priests, like most fathers do, passed on their titles and lands to their sons. As a result, many boys became priests just to keep their fathers' properties and not because they wanted to serve God. Another reason was to free the priests from responsibilities and help them to focus on their spiritual tasks. This didn't always work because some priests—and even popes—continued to have lovers, even though they didn't call them wives.

WHAT HAPPENS IN THE LORD'S SUPPER?

What did Jesus mean when He broke bread and wine with His disciples and said, "This is My body…. This is My blood" (Matthew 26:26, 28)? This question puzzled Christians for centuries. Some people believed that when the priest raised the bread and wine, these objects became in reality (or substance) the body and blood of Christ, even though they still looked and tasted the same. This teaching became known as **transubstantiation**, meaning "a change of substance."

Other Christians thought it couldn't possibly be so. When Jesus spoke those words, He was standing in His body with His disciples. There was an obvious difference between the actual body and blood of Jesus, as He was standing there, and the bread and wine He held in His hands—just as there is a huge difference now between the true and living resurrected body of Christ in heaven and the bread and wine that are passed out in the Lord's Supper. Already in the ninth century, a well-respected monk named Ratramnus of Corbie (800–868) suggested that Jesus might have been using a figure of speech as He did when He said, "I am the vine, you are the branches" (John 15:5).

No one doubted that Jesus was present at the Lord's Supper. The question was, how? In 1215 the Fourth Lateran Council made transubstantiation an official teaching of the church. In the Roman Catholic Church, this teaching continues today.

By that time, however, the Lord's Supper had already lost some of the original meaning of a meal shared by believers, so much so that people didn't even have to be present to benefit from it. A person could ask a priest to perform the ceremony, also known as the **Mass**, for them in their absence, with the hope that it would merit them God's favor. This practice became so common that in some Roman Catholic churches there are still a few small **altars** on the sides of the walls where priests can stand alone and perform a short Mass for people who may not be there.

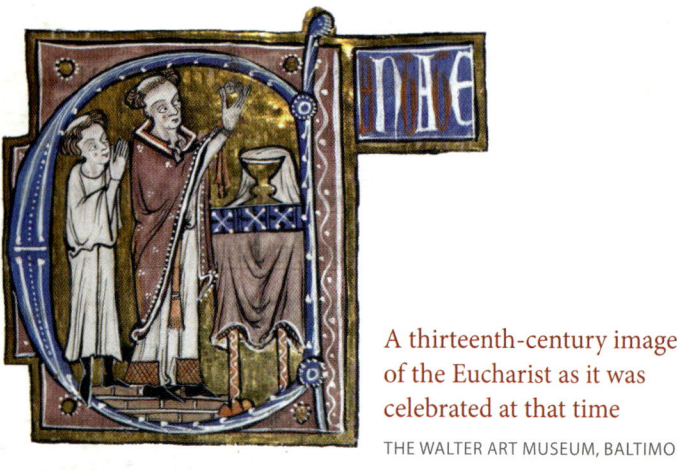

A thirteenth-century image of the Eucharist as it was celebrated at that time

THE WALTER ART MUSEUM, BALTIMORE

> *Think about It*
>
> How does your church celebrate the Lord's Supper? If you don't know the answer, ask your pastor what your church believes about this subject, and why.

More Men of the Church of the High Middle Ages

SCHOLARS AND WRITERS

In the Middle Ages, **theology**, the study of the nature and being of God, was considered the queen of all subjects. It was often taught with a method of questions and answers. A teacher would present a question and ask students to give contrasting answers, encouraging them to see for themselves which answer was best. Because of this, many books were written in the form of a dialogue between two people.

> **ANSELM OF CANTERBURY** (1033–1109) was an important scholar. Besides explaining why God had to become man, he wrote two books to prove the existence of God as perfect goodness, truth, mercy, justice, wisdom, love, and anything good. If one can think of perfection in all these things, that is God, he said. Even those who have found this explanation unconvincing have had a hard time finding proof against it. Anselm also wrote a book of prayers that shows his great devotion to God.

A book of hours showing a picture of a Dominican friar studying the Bible

THE WALTERS ART MUSEUM, BALTIMORE

> **PETER LOMBARD** (ca. 1100–1160) was the first person to compile the writings of previous theologians into subjects. This collection became a reading requirement for students in medieval universities.

> **THOMAS AQUINAS** (1225–1274) is probably the most famous scholar of this period. When as a young man he decided to join the Dominican order, his parents sent someone to kidnap him to make him change his mind. He escaped, joined the friars, and went on to study and teach in the best universities in Europe. He is famous for his conviction that faith and reason can go together. His lengthy book *Summa Theologica* (*The Sum of Theology*) is still foundational for the Roman Catholic Church. Protestants also have recognized his clarity and have benefited from many of his explanations.

THE FIRST UNIVERSITIES

Until the eleventh century, the families who wanted their children to learn more than the basics that they could teach them and who could afford to pay would hire private tutors or send their children to schools overseen by monasteries. The eleventh century saw the rise of a new type of school for higher education called a university (from the Latin *universitas*, meaning "totality"), because it taught a broad variety of subjects. Since Christians believed that the knowledge of Christ is the highest form of wisdom, theology continued to be the basis of education in Europe.

The first school of this kind might have been the Al-Azhar University in Cairo, founded around 970. The oldest university in Europe started in 1088 in Bologna, Italy. After these, important universities started in Padova, Italy; Salamanca, Spain; Paris and Montpellier, France; and Oxford and Cambridge, England. While these universities offered degrees, many students entered them just to increase their knowledge.

Restless Times

Many of the problems that afflicted the church intensified in the fourteenth and fifteenth centuries. At the same time, Europe suffered the effects of a terrible plague that killed over a third of the entire population. As the Continent recovered, people explored new ideas and asked new questions.

Constantinople

1245–1517

- **1245** — Pope Innocent IV sends a series of missions to the Mongols.
- **1274** — The Second Council of Lyon defines the teaching on purgatory.
- **1309** — Pope Clement V moves the papal court to Avignon, France.
- **1325** — Marsilius of Padua is condemned as a heretic for suggesting that the church should not claim political power and should be governed by councils and not a pope.
- **1377** — Pope Gregory XI brings the papacy back to Rome.
- **1378** — Two men claim to be pope at the same time.
- **1409** — The Council of Pisa tries to end the dispute over where the papacy should be located by electing another pope. Neither pope resigns, and the church is left with three popes.
- **1414–1418** — The Council of Constance decides that a council has greater authority than the pope. It also rejects Wycliffe's writings and burns at the stake the Czech theologian Jan Hus as a heretic.
- **1438–1445** — The Council of Florence declares that the church has seven sacraments. It also declares reunion with the Orthodox churches, but they don't agree. Eugene IV reclaims the authority of the pope over councils.
- **1439** — Johannes Gutenberg invents the printing press, which results in a great spread of information.
- **1453** — Ottoman sultan Mehmed II conquers Constantinople.
- **1478** — The Spanish government institutes a special court, which later was known as the Spanish Inquisition.
- **1492** — Christopher Columbus arrives in the Americas, opening the way for Europeans to travel there.
- **1493** — Pope Alexander VI gives the kings of Spain and Portugal the responsibility to bring Christianity to the new lands their subjects were discovering.
- **1516** — Desiderius Erasmus publishes the Greek New Testament, making it accessible to all those who can read it, and a new and more accurate Latin translation of the New Testament.

THE HIGH MIDDLE AGES • 69

MISSIONS TO THE EAST

While Europe was engaged in the Crusades, a new threat emerged from Asia: the Mongols, a fearsome population that became organized into a powerful empire by the talented warrior Genghis Khan (1162–1227). At the time of his death, the empire had become the largest ever, stretching from Eastern Europe to the Pacific Ocean and from Siberia to what is now Afghanistan. The Mongols allowed different religions in their empire. Many Christians from the conquered countries lived there, and even a daughter-in-law of Genghis Khan was a Christian.

In 1245 the pope sent two Franciscan friars, John of Pian del Carpine (ca. 1180–1252) and Benedict of Poland (1200–1280), to deliver a letter to the Grand Khan Güyük (1206–1248), a grandson of Genghis Khan. The khan, who was acquainted with the churches of the East, was not impressed by the pope's claim to be the head of all true Christians.

The main missionary to China at this time was the Franciscan John of Montecorvino (1247–1328), who lived in China until his death. In 1368, however, the rise of the Ming dynasty of China produced intolerance toward Christians, and missionaries were no longer welcome there.

EXPLORATIONS, MISSIONS, AND CONQUESTS

In some cases, explorations and missions went hand in hand. John of Pian del Carpine, for example, wrote an important book on the Mongols, and the famous merchant Marco Polo (1254–1324) and his family acted as messengers in the correspondence between khans and popes.

Some explorations were followed by both missions and conquests. Prince Henry of Portugal (1394–1460), known as Prince Henry the Navigator, is considered the greatest promoter of what became known as the Age of Discovery. He sent explorers to Western Africa and the islands of the Atlantic Ocean in search of valuable products and new routes. For this purpose, he promoted the invention of a faster and lighter ship, the caravel.

In 1492 Queen Isabella I (1451–1504) and King Ferdinand II (1452–1516), who ruled parts of modern Spain, agreed to sponsor a journey west led by Christopher Columbus (1451–1506), who arrived at an island in the Bahamas, opening a door to the European exploration of the Americas.

In both cases the exploration was followed by conquest and missionary efforts. In 1493 Pope Alexander VI (1492–1503) gave Isabella and Ferdinand the responsibility of taking Christianity to the lands their subjects were discovering. The missions didn't always go well because many of the conquerors ended up mistreating the native people. The loudest protest came from the missionary Bartolomé de Las Casas (ca. 1474–1566), who wrote a shocking account of these abuses. In 1535 Pope Paul III (1468–1549) issued an official paper condemning the teaching, held by many conquerors, that the native people of the Americas were not fully human.

Almost a century later, a strong accusation made by the Angolan prince Lourenço da Silva Mendouça (1620–1698), who had witnessed the terrible conditions of African slaves in Brazil, led to the 1686 condemnation of slavery by Pope Innocent XI (1611–1689). In spite of these efforts, however, slavery continued because traders and owners found ways to justify their actions.

The Papal Palace in Avignon, where the popes stayed from 1309 to 1377
JEAN-MARC ROSIER, HTTP://WWW.ROSIER.PRO

THE POPE IN FRANCE

In 1302 Pope Boniface VIII (1235–1303) made a bold claim: as pope, he was to rule over all earthly matters on behalf of Christ, and kings and emperors were to submit to him. What's more, he said that "it is absolutely necessary for salvation that every human creature be subject to the Roman Pontiff [pope]."

This didn't go over well with King Philip IV of France (1268–1314), who already had many complaints about the pope. When Boniface excommunicated the king and other officials for keeping some bishops from coming to Rome, the king fought back and sent some of his men to Rome to arrest the pope.

With the help of a powerful Roman family, the pope was captured, held prisoner, and mistreated until he was rescued by some of his supporters. He died two weeks later of a violent fever.

His successor, Benedict XI (1240–1304), was pope for less than nine months. The next pope, Clement V (1264–1314), was a Frenchman who wanted to stay in France and build a good relationship with King Philip. In 1309 he moved his papal court to Avignon, in the south of France. It was supposed to be a temporary move. In reality, the popes stayed there until 1377. During that time there were seven popes, one after the other, and all were French.

A three-crown tiara sitting on top of two keys that symbolize the keys of God's kingdom is still the symbol of the pope.

FABRIZIO ROSTICCI

Many Christians complained. Can a pope who calls himself bishop of Rome live in France? Some named this period the Babylonian Captivity because it reminded them of the exile of ancient Israel in Babylon. It was also clear that the popes were now serving the programs of the kings of France. One influential Italian woman, Catherine of Siena (1347–1380), visited the pope in Avignon and wrote him repeated letters, telling him to conquer his fears of Italy. In 1376 this pressure from the people convinced Pope Gregory XI (1329–1378) to return to Rome.

THE POPE'S TIARA

Like many of his predecessors, Pope Boniface VIII wore a **tiara** with two crowns. Some people say they symbolized the pope's power over the church and over the world. Boniface's tiara was enriched by forty-five emeralds, forty-eight rubies, seventy-two sapphires, and sixty-six large pearls and had a large ruby on top. A third crown was added to the papal tiara later, probably while the popes were in Avignon.

PICK A POPE

When Gregory died, the cardinals were divided over their choice of the next pope. The Italian cardinals wanted an Italian, and the French cardinals wanted a Frenchman. Eventually, an Italian was elected who took the name Urban VI (1318–1389). He was, however, so bossy that in 1378 a group of cardinals declared him deposed, returned to Avignon, and elected a different man, Clement VII (1342–1394).

Urban was not going to resign, so both he and Clement claimed to be pope at the same time. It was not the first time this had happened, but this time they had both been chosen by cardinals, and each election was legitimate in its own way.

Europe was split down the middle. To make things worse, Urban excommunicated everyone who was following Clement, and vice versa. This meant that everyone in Europe was excommunicated by one pope. This period of sharp division in the church is known as the Great Western Schism.

In 1409 a council at Pisa tried to resolve this matter by deposing the pope in Rome and the pope in Avignon (successors of Urban and Clement) and by electing a third man, Alexander V (1339–1410). Since neither of the popes accepted this decision, Europe now had three popes.

Finally, the Council of Constance (1414–1418) deposed two popes, convinced one to resign, and elected a new one, Martin V (1369–1431). Because of the confusion these popes had created, the same council proposed that ecumenical councils (councils that included bishops from every region) should oversee the actions and decisions of the popes. This suggested that councils were superior to popes—something that no council had ever proposed before. In fact, a philosopher who had made this suggestion earlier, Marsilius of Padua (ca. 1275–1342), had been condemned as a heretic.

If this system had continued, the church might have been quite different, but it didn't. Martin's successor, Eugene IV (1383–1447), found enough support to reclaim the authority of the papacy, stating that only popes could call a council, and every council had to submit to the pope.

At the Council of Constance, the newly elected Pope Martin V blessed the Jews. This was an important gesture because at that time the Jews were persecuted in many countries.

BPK BILDAGENTUR. FROM THE CHRONICLE OF THE COUNCIL OF CONSTANCE, 15TH CENTURY (FACSIMILE), ART RESOURCE, NY

INCREASE IN KNOWLEDGE

Throughout the High Middle Ages, Europeans had been able to gain access to ancient Greek texts that had been preserved by Byzantines and Arabs but had been forgotten in the West. These included important works of philosophy, medicine, mathematics, and science. This renewed interest in the Greek language encouraged Christian scholars to study the original version of the New Testament, which had been written in Greek. Some scholars also became interested in learning Hebrew, the language of the Old Testament. *Ad fontes*, which means "back to the sources," became a favorite motto.

After 1439, when the German Johannes Gutenberg (d. 1468) invented the printing press, scholars were able to pass on their information, old and new, with greater ease and speed. Study of the Bible became easier in 1516 when the Dutch scholar Desiderius Erasmus (better known as Erasmus of Rotterdam, 1466–1536) produced the first printed edition of the Greek New Testament.

A monument to Erasmus in Rotterdam, Netherlands

FEICO HOUWELING, WIKIMEDIA COMMONS

The printing press, which had been invented about eighty years earlier, made books like this easier to produce and circulate. Arranging the characters for a page on a printing press still took a long time, but once that was done, the same page could be printed hundreds of times.

Erasmus also produced a new Latin translation of the New Testament and placed it next to the Greek text. This was very useful to anyone who wanted to study the Bible. Until then, for over a thousand years, the Western church had used the Latin translation by Jerome without raising many questions. Erasmus's Latin translation was much more accurate and reliable.

Not all the church leaders were happy about this new version, especially since it challenged the interpretation of some words. For example, in Matthew 4:17, Erasmus translated Jesus's command as "Repent" instead of Jerome's translation "Do penance." It was an important change because over time, the word *penance* had come to mean something different from simple repentance, so people thought that what the church considered acts of repentance, such as long prayers, donations to the church, or avoiding pleasures, were necessary for salvation.

Erasmus's work was later used by scholars in many countries who translated the Bible in the language of the people where they lived.

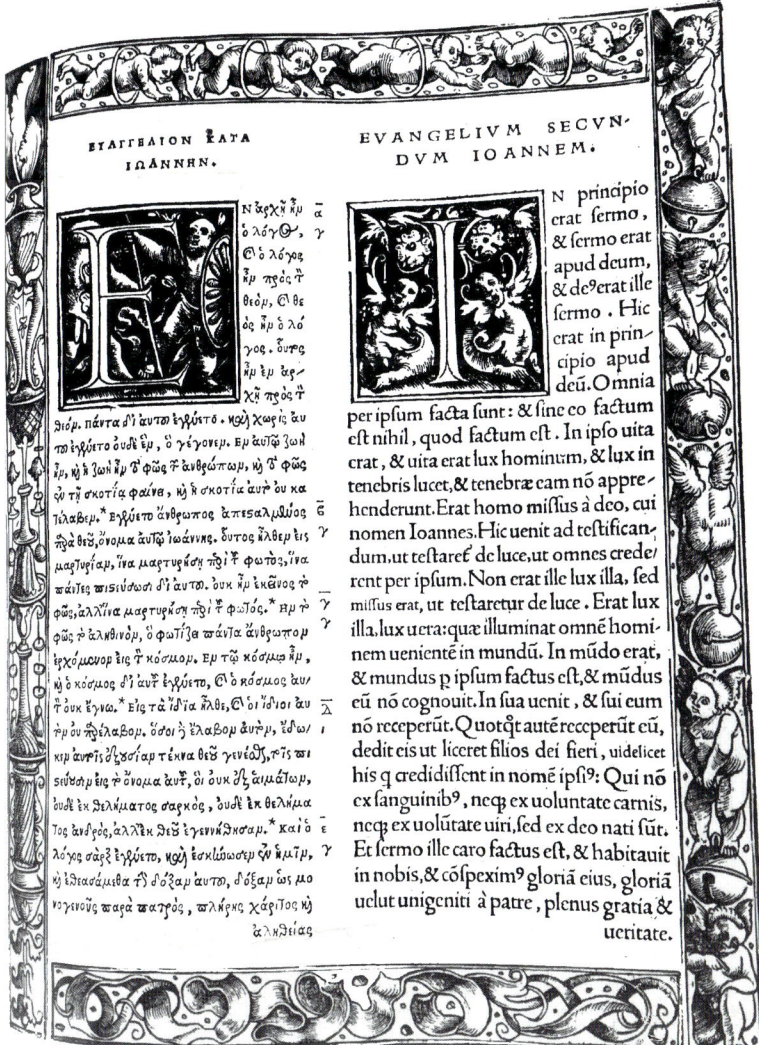

A page from Erasmus's Greek and Latin New Testament

CEDARVILLE UNIVERSITY, DIGITAL COMMONS

RELIGIOUS PRACTICES OF MEDIEVAL CHRISTIANS

In spite of this increase in learning, only men who had time and financial means could attend universities. A few women were able to study at home if their families encouraged education. Those who joined abbeys or convents had greater opportunities. Most of the population, however, could not read or write and could learn the Bible only through their preachers. That's one reason why the Western medieval church encouraged the use of images in their buildings. They hoped these images would help people who couldn't read remember the Bible stories they had heard.

While preaching was spoken in the language of the people, the rest of the church service was spoken in Latin, and people were encouraged to learn a few sentences so they could respond to the priest. Singing was usually done by a choir, using a set of Latin **chants** that were written for particular times of the year or of the day.

At home people were encouraged to repeat some set prayers, particularly the Our Father, the prayer Jesus taught to His disciples, and the Hail Mary, which included the words of the angel's announcement to Mary in the Bible, plus some words added by the church. During the Middle Ages, the practice of using beads to keep count of the number of recited prayers became increasingly popular, giving way to what we now call the Rosary.

Those who could read made use of prayer books, which included the Psalms and prayers for different occasions and different times of the day. These prayer books were also called books of hours and included many illustrations.

A page from a fourteenth-century book of chants, known as an antiphonary

THE WALTERS ART MUSEUM, BALTIMORE

Many prayer books included images of skeletons or dying people to remind their readers that life is short and death can come at any time. This prayer book belonged to Bonne of Luxembourg (1315–1349), a Bohemian princess who married the future king of France, who would be known as John the Good (1319–1364).

THE MET MUSEUM

74 • THE HIGH MIDDLE AGES

A seventh-century silver spoon used to stir the wine in the chalice

THE WALTERS ART MUSEUM, BALTIMORE

A thirteenth-century straw used by the priest to sip the wine during the Lord's Supper

THE CLOISTERS COLLECTION, 1947, THE MET MUSEUM

A fifteenth-century ceremonial cup for the wine, called a chalice

THE CLOISTERS COLLECTION, 1947, THE MET MUSEUM

HOW MANY SACRAMENTS?

In the Bible Jesus commanded His disciples to keep two ceremonies as means of grace and signs of spiritual realities: baptism (Matthew 28:19) and the Eucharist (Matthew 26:26–28), also known as the Lord's Supper or Holy Communion. The church called these ceremonies *sacraments*, meaning "sacred acts."

Later, however, the church began to give the name sacrament to other ceremonies. The Council of Florence (1438–1445) confirmed a total of seven: baptism, the Eucharist, penance (including confession to a priest and acts of repentance), confirmation (an act by a bishop that is said to impart the Holy Spirit), **ordination** of priests, extreme unction (the anointing of people who are about to die), and the wedding ceremony. Both the Roman Catholic Church and the Orthodox Church still keep these seven sacraments. Nearly all Protestants keep only the two that have been directly instituted by Christ: baptism and the Lord's Supper.

In the early church, believers who celebrated the Lord's Supper shared both bread and wine. Over time, however, some priests began to offer only the bread to the congregation while they kept the wine for themselves. They believed that Jesus is present in both bread and wine, so people didn't have to take both in order to receive Him. The Council of Constance confirmed this belief, and the practice of giving the congregation only the bread became common in the Roman Catholic Church.

A woman holding a rosary

THE WALTERS ART MUSEUM, BALTIMORE

THE HIGH MIDDLE AGES • 75

A statue of Meister Eckhart sharing some of his writings with a student
LOTHAR SPURZEM, WIKIMEDIA COMMONS

LOOKING FOR GREATER KNOWLEDGE OF GOD

From the earliest times, some Christians have desired to know God more closely than they could by simply reading the Bible. In the Middle Ages, this tendency became more frequent, especially in monasteries. Some people wrote down their experiences and their new thoughts about God and found others who were eager to read them. People who try to discover God directly through experiences or intuitions are called **mystics**.

In the fourteenth century, a German Dominican friar named Eckhart von Hochheim, better known as Meister Eckhart (ca. 1260–ca. 1328), recorded not only his experiences but also suggestions on how others should look for God. God, he said, is like a spark of fire inside a piece of wood. As the wood burns, it takes on the properties of the fire. Eckhart thought that human beings should let go of any knowledge and thought and let God burn inside them. He also thought that everything in the world includes a part of God. Pope John XXII (1244–1334) formally condemned some of Eckhart's teachings.

Other famous medieval mystics included Catherine of Siena, Hildegard of Bingen (1098–1179), and Julian of Norwich (ca. 1342–after 1416). All three claimed to have received revelations from God. They were particularly influential during their time.

> ### Think about It
>
> - If it's true, as the Bible teaches, that "the testimony of the LORD is sure, making wise the simple" (Psalm 19:7), while "the heart is deceitful above all things, and desperately wicked" (Jeremiah 17:9), which of the two (the Bible or the heart) is safer to trust?
>
> - The Protestant **Reformers** warned that mystics moved onto dangerous ground when they placed their intuition above the Bible. But the Reformers still admired the mystics' ability to show how God is great and holy and how His ways are not our ways. They believed it is possible to combine this sense of God's awesomeness with proper teaching that is firmly founded on the Bible. What do you think? Can you remember a book, poem, or hymn that shows God's awesomeness while staying faithful to the Bible?

> INDVLGENTIA · PLENARIA · PERPETVA
> QVOTIDIANA · TOTIES · QVOTIES
> PRO · VIVIS · ET · DEFVNCTIS

This inscription on the Church of St. John in Laterano, Rome, still promises "perpetual everyday plenary [full] indulgence on every occasion for the living and the dead."

JASTROW, WIKIMEDIA COMMONS

LOOKING FOR GREATER COMMITMENT TO GOD

As time went on, more Christians began to see a need to move away from the corruption and heartless service to God that were present in much of the church, where many priests and bishops seemed to be interested only in living a comfortable life.

To remedy this, some Christians started a movement that became known as *devotio moderna* (Latin for "modern devotion," or "a modern way of showing devotion to God"). The purpose was to encourage other Christians to live a life of greater commitment to God. One of its founders, the Dutch Geert Groote (1340–1384), began a society called **Brethren** of the Common Life, where people lived like monks and nuns but did not take vows.

The most famous follower of the *devotio moderna* was Thomas à Kempis (ca. 1380–1471). His book *The Imitation of Christ* became one of the most popular devotional books in the Middle Ages. It was meant to teach Christians how to reach perfection by following Christ's example. Although many people were inspired to try, many also discovered it was impossible to reach perfection in this life.

Other authors influenced by the *devotio moderna* were the German John of Wesel (ca. 1420–1481) and the Dutch Wessel Gansfort (1419–1489), who wrote against the practice of **indulgences**—papers signed by the pope that guaranteed less time in **purgatory** for those who bought them or for their relatives. Wesel and Gansfort thought that the pope didn't have the authority to make this promise. Wesel also stated that only the Bible—not human institutions—had any authority over the **conscience** of Christians. In the sixteenth century, the Church of Rome placed Wesel's writings on the Index of Forbidden Books (a list of books the church considered dangerous to the faith or morals of Roman Catholics).

Above: Wessel Gansfort
INTERNET ARCHIVE BOOK IMAGES

Below: A twentieth-century portrait of Thomas à Kempis
WIKIMEDIA COMMONS

PURGATORY

The Bible talks about heaven and hell, also described as life eternal and everlasting punishment, as the two destinations of human beings after this life. It explains that all humans deserve hell because of their sinful condition, but they can be saved from it through Christ's redeeming work (John 3:36).

Over time, some people began to think that most human beings will not be fit enough for heaven at the end of their lives. They imagined a third place after death where the souls of sinners would be purged, or cleansed, of their sins by fire and other punishments. It wasn't as bad as hell and lasted only for a time. This idea started early in church history. Later, this third place became known as purgatory ("purging place"). Since it was a temporary place, people started to pray for the souls of their loved ones who had died and to find ways, such as buying indulgences, to shorten their time in purgatory.

While popular, this idea never became official until 1274, when it was confirmed by the Second Council of Lyon. Protestants rejected this teaching, and the Eastern Orthodox Church never accepted it.

LOOKING FOR A REFORMATION

A general feeling of discontent continued to grow within the church. Many people realized that the church had to reform its ways, meaning change them for the better.

John Wycliffe

In England a priest and professor named John Wycliffe (ca. 1330–1384) shared many of the common concerns about a corrupt and divided church. He thought the church, with all its riches, had drifted far from the message and example of Christ. At a time when popes and councils were arguing over who should have the final say, he reminded Christians that the ultimate authority is the Bible. In fact, he promoted the first complete translation of the Bible from Latin into English so that everyone could read it.

Church leaders tolerated some of these thoughts, partially because Wycliffe had some powerful friends. They reacted only when he began to attack the church's teaching on the Lord's Supper.

Wycliffe disagreed with the church's teaching on transubstantiation. He based his reasons on simple logic. If bread and wine look like bread and wine and taste like bread and wine but we say they are no longer bread and wine, then we can't trust anything that our eyes see or our tongues taste. Instead of calling the Lord's Supper a transformation of true bread into true body, Wycliffe thought the church should teach the people to see Christ in the bread spiritually and by faith.

Wycliffe's followers were later called Lollards, from a Dutch word meaning "to mutter," probably because their worship included long readings of the Bible. They were considered dangerous heretics. After Wycliffe's death, many of them were burned at the stake, and their English copies of the Bible were also thrown to the flames.

A memorial showing Wycliffe preaching to villagers. The two men behind him might be the Franciscan friars he exposed for their riches, which were contrary to their order's original vision.

NIGEL STOLLERY. WITH KIND PERMISSION OF ST. MARY'S LUTTERWORTH CHURCH, CHURCH GATE, LUTTERWORTH, UK, HTTPS://WWW.LUTTERWORTHCHURCH.ORG/

Jan Hus

Wycliffe's teachings spread to other countries where people had entertained similar thoughts. In Prague (Bohemia, in today's Czech Republic), they inspired a man named Jan Hus (1369–1415), who was already involved in a reformation of the church, giving priority to preaching and insisting on the use of the local language in worship. Hus also wrote many books exposing the problems in the Roman Catholic Church.

The bishop of Prague tried to stop Hus from preaching but didn't succeed because Hus was supported by the king, the queen, and the local people. Frustrated, the bishop convinced the pope to punish the whole city by

This huge statue in the middle of Prague depicts Jan Hus and some of his followers, who fought against the Church of Rome and were forced into exile two hundred years after his death. The memorial, unveiled in 1915, was designed by Ladislav Šaloun (1870–1946) and paid for by public donations.

JIM GOOD

forbidding people to receive the Lord's Supper or to be buried on church grounds as long as Hus was there. To lift the punishment, Hus left Prague and went to live with some friends while he wrote books of instruction to his countrymen.

In 1414 he accepted an invitation to appear at the ecclesiastical Council of Constance. It was a dangerous move, but Holy Roman Emperor Sigismund (1368–1437) promised that Hus would be safe. Instead, Hus was arrested, imprisoned, and tried as a heretic without a chance to defend himself. He was burned at the stake in 1415.

Hus's execution backfired, as the people of Bohemia organized a military revolt against the established church. Between 1419 and 1434, the pope sent four consecutive crusades against them, and the Bohemians defeated them all. Eventually, the pope allowed Bohemia to practice its own version of Christianity, which included the duty for priests to give up all worldly possessions so they could not become as rich and corrupt as many did in those days. Today's **Moravian** Church is a descendant of the followers of Jan Hus.

More Men and Women of the Church of the High Middle Ages

OTHER QUESTIONING VOICES

THOMAS BRADWARDINE (1290–1349) was a theologian and mathematician who strongly defended the writings of Augustine of Hippo at a time when the Western church seemed to favor the teachings of Pelagius. In his writings he explained that the followers of Pelagius, by giving much importance to their own actions, were making Christ's sacrifice useless and robbing God of His glory.

At a time when many people thought that women were inferior to men, **CHRISTINE DE PIZAN** (1364–1430) reminded Christians that is not what the Bible teaches. In fact, it is what the pagan nations believed before Christ. She became the first woman in Europe to support herself and her family by writing.

GIROLAMO SAVONAROLA (1452–1498) was a Dominican friar who preached strongly against the materialism of his times and the church's love for riches. At a time of political instability, he took charge of Florence. His followers went to an extreme, raiding homes and burning what they considered vanities. This included many works of art. Savonarola was eventually arrested, tortured, and executed by order of the pope.

PART 5
THE PROTESTANT REFORMATION

A Reforming Church

Throughout history many people tried to make changes in the church to bring it closer to the teachings of the Bible. Some of these changes had to do with the people's laziness in worship or with the immoral behavior of church leaders. But the movement for change that took place in the sixteenth century was different. It had to do with the way the church interpreted the Bible and was so radical and widespread that it became known simply as the Reformation. It's also known as the Protestant Reformation because the people who promoted it were protesting some basic teachings the church had adopted because of tradition.

1517–1600

1517 — Luther posts ninety-five propositions to the door of the church in Wittenberg. Some historians consider this the start of the Protestant Reformation.

1521 — Pope Leo X excommunicates Luther. At an imperial meeting, Luther is asked to deny his teachings and refuses.

1523 — The first two Lutheran martyrs die in Brussels (in today's Belgium).

1534 — King Henry VIII breaks with Rome and is declared supreme head of the English church.

1535 — The Anabaptist rebels who took over the city of Münster, Germany, are defeated and killed.

1536 — John Calvin publishes *Institutes of the Christian Religion*, a clear explanation of Reformed teachings.

1540 — The statutes of the Jesuit order are approved by the pope, making the order official.

1545–1563 — The Roman Catholic Church examines its practices and teachings in what is known as the Council of Trent.

1549 — The English archbishop Thomas Cranmer publishes the Book of Common Prayer.

1553–1558 — Mary I of England tries to restore Roman Catholicism in the nation. She executes three hundred Protestants.

1555 — Emperor Charles V signs the Augsburg Settlement, allowing each prince to choose the religion his subjects should follow.

1558 — Elizabeth I of England restores Protestantism in the nation.

1559 — John Calvin founds the Academy of Geneva.

1560 — The Scottish Parliament declares Scotland a Protestant nation.

1568 — Start of the Eighty Years' War for Dutch independence from Spain.

1572 — A Roman Catholic mob kills thousands of Protestants in Paris and other parts of France.

1598 — The Edict of Nantes gives French Protestants some freedom of worship.

THE PROTESTANT REFORMATION • 81

The Start of the Protestant Reformation

October 31, 1517, the day the German friar Martin Luther (1483–1546) nailed his Ninety-Five Theses (or propositions) to the church door in Wittenberg, Germany, is often considered the start of the Protestant Reformation. In reality he wanted only to discuss some questions with other local priests and scholars. He was especially concerned with a practice that had become frequent in the church: the sale of indulgences. At that time, Luther was not questioning the authority of the pope. He was concerned that money was taking the place of true repentance.

He thought Pope Leo X (1475–1521) would agree with him, but he was wrong. The pope's secretary told Luther that popes have to be obeyed without question, even if they lead people "by crowds into the possession of hell."

Luther had always taken sin seriously. But he knew he couldn't avoid sinning, no matter how hard he tried, and that all the penance and offerings in the world could never remedy this problem. Finally, by studying the Bible, he understood that God's grace and forgiveness are gifts that God gives freely in Jesus Christ to all who believe. He explained this finding in some books that were quickly translated in other languages.

This was similar to what Augustine of Hippo had taught eleven centuries earlier, but the pope could not accept it. In 1520 the pope sent an official paper to Luther, giving him sixty days to repent. Luther was troubled because he had never meant to leave the church but couldn't deny what he believed was the truth. He burned the papal document in the public square. The next year, he was officially excommunicated.

Emperor Charles V (1500–1558) called Luther to an official imperial meeting known as the **Diet** of Worms. There, church authorities asked Luther to deny everything he had written. Luther could not do it, so he was condemned as a heretic and declared an outlaw. Unlike Sigismund of Hungary, who broke his promise not to harm Jan Hus, Charles kept his word and allowed Luther to leave the meeting unharmed.

But as an outlaw, Luther was still at risk of being arrested, and anyone helping him could be charged with a criminal act. In spite of this, his friends hid him in a castle where he worked on translating the New Testament into German. The first four thousand copies of this translation sold within two months. Eventually, he translated the whole Bible.

A statue of Martin Luther in Worms, Germany

AD MESKENS, WIKIMEDIA COMMONS

LUTHER'S CONTRASTS

Luther used many contrasts in his writings. They help us understand his teachings.

Law and gospel. The law includes all the commandments of God, and the gospel includes all the promises of salvation in Christ. The law says, "Do this, and you shall live." The gospel says, "Christ has done this for you." The law tells us how we should live but doesn't give us the power to do it. The gospel gives both the power and the right motivation, which is thankfulness to the God who saved us.

Faith and works. God gives His forgiveness, favor, and eternal life as a free gift to those who believe. At the same time, good works are a necessary part of the Christian life. God saves us through faith so that we may work for the good of others.

External and internal. The gospel is preached and the sacraments are performed outside of us but produce a change inside. Unlike many medieval writers who tried to find God by looking inside themselves, Luther said that the only reliable description of God is found in the revelation He has given of Himself in His written word, the Bible.

Righteous and sinful. Christians in this life are at the same time righteous and sinful. They are declared righteous by God because of Christ but still have a sinful nature. That's why they must continue to fight against sin, even though their salvation has already been accomplished in Christ.

A treasure chest used to collect the money from the sale of indulgences

RENÉ, FLICKR

The European Reformations

The message of the Reformation spread quickly throughout Europe, either by word of mouth or by books and pamphlets. Some of the first Reformers in each country were people who had studied in either Germany or Switzerland, where the Reformation first took shape. Some were killed for their faith.

The Reformation took different forms in the various countries. Much had to do with the attitude of the local rulers, who usually imposed their religion. In the end, some of the countries remained Protestant, and some returned to the Church of Rome or remained in it.

HOLY ROMAN EMPIRE

The Reformation continued to grow in the German regions, at that time known as the Holy Roman Empire, where many local rulers employed Lutheran preachers to instruct their people. For a while, the conflict between these rulers and Roman Catholic princes became so fierce that it led to an actual war. Finally, in 1555 Emperor Charles V signed a peace treaty known as the Augsburg Settlement, allowing each ruler to decide what religion his people would follow without interference from other rulers or even the emperor himself. Those who disagreed had the choice to convert or leave the country, which was difficult, especially for farmers. They could also stay and keep their religion but had to make compromises.

Martin Bucer (1491–1551), one of the main Reformers in the Holy Roman Empire, was exiled in 1549 for disagreeing with some regulations imposed by Charles V in the emperor's effort to find a compromise between Protestants and Roman Catholics. Bucer moved to England, where he helped to strengthen the Reformation.

Ulrich Zwingli began the Reformation in Zurich, Switzerland.

REFORMATION ART

SWITZERLAND

The Reformation in Switzerland started in Zurich under the leadership of Ulrich Zwingli (1484–1531), who by studying the Bible came to many of the same conclusions as Luther. Unlike Luther, Zwingli didn't have a prince to protect him. He died during a military battle between Swiss states controlled by the Protestants and other Swiss states controlled by Roman Catholics.

After Zwingli's death, a man named Heinrich Bullinger (1504–1575) continued his work. Bullinger strove to bring unity among the different Protestant reformations. He summarized the Reformed faith in a document called the Second Helvetic Confession, which is still used today.

Another Swiss city, Geneva, became an important center of reformation, particularly after 1541 when the city council invited a Frenchman named John Calvin (1509–1564) to be the main minister. Calvin's clear teachings on the Bible and his organization of the church drew many people to Geneva to learn how to reform the church in their countries. The academy (or college) he founded in 1559 trained many pastors and served as a model for schools in other countries. His *Institutes of the Christian Religion*, originally written to explain the reasons for the Protestant Reformation to King Francis I (1494–1547) of France, has been reprinted in many languages.

Another important work by Calvin, *The Necessity of Reforming the Church*, was addressed to Charles V. According to Calvin, everyone could agree that the church had many problems. The question was, how long should the church continue to just talk about them without taking action? He believed that the church had spent too much time talking about a change. He thought that a reformation was urgent because the problems affected "the whole substance of the Christian religion."

Theodore Beza (1519–1605) is considered Calvin's successor. With Calvin, he was cofounder of the academy in Geneva and its first director. He wrote a biography of John Calvin, a history of the Reformation in France, and many books explaining Reformed teachings.

John Calvin was one of the most important Protestant Reformers.

REFORMATION ART

FRANCE

The French Reformation was greatly influenced by the writings of Calvin and the preaching of ministers who had studied under him. By 1559 there were so many Reformed churches in France that they were able to organize their first official meeting, called a **synod**. French Protestants were often called **Huguenots**.

By 1562 there were over two thousand Reformed churches in France. This large number worried Roman Catholics, who often reacted in anger. Influential families took sides, turning their differences into a political and military struggle, with each faction trying to rise to the throne.

The marriage of the Protestant Henry of Navarre (1553–1610) and the Roman Catholic Marguerite of Valois (1553–1615) was supposed to bring peace. Instead, it became the occasion for an attempted murder, followed by the unexpected massacre of thousands of French Protestants in Paris on August 24, 1572, and in the weeks following, throughout France. Since August 24 is St. Bartholomew's Day, it became known as the St. Bartholomew's Day Massacre.

Some peace was restored in 1598 when Henry, who had become king of France under the name Henry IV, became Roman Catholic and declared that Protestant worship should be tolerated. This declaration, known as the Edict of Nantes, remained in effect for almost ninety years.

THE NETHERLANDS

The Netherlands (literally, Low Countries) included a large portion of Europe, equivalent to today's Holland, Belgium, Luxembourg, and parts of northern France. In the first part of the sixteenth century, the Netherlands were ruled by Emperor Charles V. They were among the first lands to receive the message of the gospel and the first to execute Lutheran believers in 1523. Over time, they had more Protestant martyrs than any other European nation.

The worst persecution happened under Charles's son, Phillip II (1527–1598) of Spain, who ruled over the Netherlands beginning in 1555. Phillip caused much discontent for many other reasons, such as the high taxes he demanded. In 1566 the people rose in protest. This included raids on Roman Catholic churches, stripping them of all images, which were considered a sign of idolatry.

Phillip's armed intervention started an actual war. William I, Prince of Orange (1533–1584), led the Dutch forces to some major victories but couldn't prevent the country from becoming divided into a southern Roman Catholic region under Spain and a northern, independent, Protestant region. In 1584 a Roman Catholic man murdered William, hoping to receive the large reward Philip II had promised. He was instead captured, tortured, and executed.

An artist's view of the St. Bartholomew's Day Massacre

MORPHART CREATION, SHUTTERSTOCK (FROM *POPULAR FRANCE*, 1869)

Archbishop Thomas Cranmer

BY KIND PERMISSION OF THE ARCHBISHOP OF CANTERBURY AND THE CHURCH COMMISSIONERS

> *Blessed Lord, who hast caused all holy Scriptures to be written for our learning: Grant that we may in such wise hear them, read, mark, learn, and inwardly digest them, that by patience and comfort of thy holy Word, we may embrace and ever hold fast the blessed hope of everlasting life, which thou hast given us in our Saviour Jesus Christ.*
>
> —BOOK OF COMMON PRAYER

ENGLAND

The teachings of Wycliffe (see p. 78) in the fourteenth century prepared England for the Reformation. The event that catapulted the country in that direction was a decision by King Henry VIII (1491–1547) to **annul** (or cancel) his marriage to Catherine of Aragon (1485–1536), who, after giving birth to a daughter, Mary (1516–1558), seemed incapable of having other children. Henry wanted a son to be his heir.

In those days marriages could be annulled only by the pope in rare circumstances. Since the pope in this case delayed his answer, Henry appointed as archbishop of Canterbury a man who knew how to proceed: Thomas Cranmer (1489–1556). In 1534, under Cranmer's guidance, the English **Parliament** declared Henry supreme head of the Church of England, with no more ties to the pope. Cranmer granted Henry's divorce.

After a brief marriage to Anne Boleyn (d. 1536), who gave birth to another daughter, Elizabeth (1533–1603), Henry married Jane Seymour (ca. 1508–1537), who gave him the son he had always wanted, Edward (1537–1553).

Henry had never meant for the English church to depart from Roman Catholic teachings, but Cranmer and other people in his court supported the Protestant Reformation and encouraged the king to make small changes. One of the first changes was the translation of the Bible into English, even though Henry allowed only people with a good education to read it. He thought everyone else would misread it.

Since many monks had become rich and corrupt, Henry decided to close down all monasteries and sold them for a low price. The income went to help his government.

Apart from this, Henry remained faithful to most Roman Catholic beliefs. Most of his son's tutors, however, brought up the young prince according to Protestant teachings. When Henry died, the ten-year-old boy became King Edward VI. He and his counselors made great changes to the church. Cranmer called to England some of the best Protestant teachers to instruct university students and future pastors.

Since few of the existing pastors had received that training, Cranmer produced a manual to lead them step-by-step in Reformed worship. This manual, called the Book of Common Prayer, first authorized for use in 1549, has been used in England, with some revisions, for centuries. In 1552 Cranmer oversaw the compilation of an important statement of faith for the English church known as the Forty-Two Articles.

Edward died unexpectedly in 1553, leaving the throne to his cousin, the Protestant Lady Jane Grey (1537–1554). But many people rejected Jane as queen. They thought Edward should be succeeded by one of his half sisters, Mary or Elizabeth. Mary took advantage of this popular feeling to raise a large army and take over the throne as Mary I.

Since Mary was Roman Catholic, she reversed many of Edward's changes. She also ordered that some of Edward's counselors, including Cranmer, be executed, together with Lady Jane Grey, her husband, and many others. Altogether, about three hundred Protestants were burned at the stake. This cruelty, as well as her marriage to the Spanish ruler Philip II, caused her to lose many supporters because people were afraid that England would be ruled by Spain.

When Mary died, Elizabeth took the crown as Elizabeth I, and went back to the Protestant teachings of Cranmer, revising his Forty-Two Articles into Thirty-Nine Articles, which are still used by the Church of England. To avoid making drastic changes, she continued to organize the church with a system of priests, bishops, and archbishops, culminating with the king or queen as supreme governor.

Engraving of Queen Elizabeth I, created during her reign
THE MET MUSEUM

> *I affirm that faith only saves. But it is meet for Christians, in token that they follow their master Christ, to do good works, yet may we not say that they profit to salvation. For, although we have all done all that we can, yet we be unprofitable servants, and the faith only in Christ's blood saveth.*
>
> *I ground my faith upon God's Word and not upon the church. For if the church be a good church, the faith of the church must be tried by God's Word, and not God's Word by the church.*
>
> —LADY JANE GREY

> *But now, what makes me so bold and strong, to presume to come to the Lord with such audacity and boldness, being so great a sinner? Truly, nothing but His own Word.… For this is life everlasting, Lord, that I must believe You to be the true God, and Jesus Christ whom You did send.*
>
> —KATHERINE PARR, King Henry's sixth wife and the first woman in England to publish a book under her name. This book, *The Lamentation of a Sinner*, was a bold proclamation of how God saves sinners only by grace and through faith.

THE PROTESTANT REFORMATION

THE ENGLISH PURITANS

Some Christians objected to Elizabeth's compromises. For example, some opposed the use of vestments for members of the **clergy** (priests, bishops, and archbishops) and certain ceremonies, such as kneeling to receive the Lord's Supper and lighting candles. Their main argument was that the church didn't have the right to impose customs that were not required in the Bible.

These men and women were often called **Puritans** because they wanted greater purity of worship and life. Some were later called Nonconformists because they refused to conform to the Church of England's pattern of worship. Basically, the Puritan movement sought to reform the church so that it was completely faithful to the Bible and promoted models of godly living.

One of the first men to object to the use of vestments was John Hooper (1495–1555), who was imprisoned during the reign of Edward VI for refusing to wear the prescribed clothes during his ordination as bishop. Many ministers felt the same way and were punished for their disobedience. Later, Richard Hooker (1554–1600), one of the main theologians of the Church of England, tried to put this matter to rest by arguing that wearing or not wearing vestments is not an essential matter of Christian faith.

But there was more to the Puritans' protest. They were concerned that many preachers neglected the study of the Bible and read other people's sermons, using the Book of Common Prayer as a formula instead of a guide to worship. The Puritans wanted better training for preachers. William Perkins (1558–1602), who lived and ministered under Queen Elizabeth, wrote one of the most influential books on this subject.

Queen Elizabeth didn't understand the need for more preachers. In fact, instead of increasing their number, she reduced it, thinking that a smaller number would be easier to supervise. The archbishop of Canterbury Edmund Grindal (1519–1583) opposed this decision in a six-thousand-word letter. "Christ told us to pray for more laborers, not fewer," he said. He was suspended from his duties, and a man who was intolerant of Puritans was appointed in his place.

Today, the Puritans are remembered for their sincere devotion to God and their commitment to a godly life.

A monument to John Hooper at St. Mary's Square, Gloucester, England

GRAHAM SHAW, FLICKR

> *But surely I cannot marvel enough how this strange opinion should once enter into your mind, that it should be good for the Church to have few preachers. Alas, Madam! Is the Scripture more plain in any one thing, than that the gospel of Christ should be plentifully preached, and that plenty of labourers should be sent into the Lord's harvest, which, being great and large, standeth in need, not of a few, but of many workmen?… Bear with me, I beseech you, Madam, if I choose rather to offend your earthly Majesty than to offend the heavenly majesty of God.*
>
> —EDMUND GRINDAL, in a speech to Queen Elizabeth

SCOTLAND

When the Roman Catholic authorities began punishing those who spread Reformed teachings in Scotland, they stirred up the people's curiosity instead. The first Protestant martyr in the country was Patrick Hamilton (1504–1528). His courage in the flames, where he burned for six hours, was a great testimony of his faith and brought many people to consider his teachings.

Another important martyr was George Wishart (ca. 1513–1546), who preached in different parts of Scotland for almost three years before his arrest and execution. His death provoked a strong reaction in his followers. Eighteen of them managed to enter the bedroom of the Roman Catholic cardinal David Beaton (ca. 1494–1546), killed him, and hung his body on his castle's wall for all to see. The castle became a Protestant fortress, where the rebels formed what might be described as the first congregation of the Church of Scotland.

Eventually, the Scottish government, with the help of the French, freed the castle. Many Protestants were imprisoned or forced to row in the French **galleys**. In spite of this, the Scottish Reformation continued to grow.

Many promoters of the Reformation were noblemen who had the means to buy books and influence others. They invited some Scottish preachers who had found refuge in Europe. The most famous of these is John Knox (ca. 1513–1572), who had been freed from the galleys by the English government and had lived for some time in England, Germany, and Switzerland. He was invited back to Scotland in 1559.

By this time most Scottish Protestants had come to believe that when rulers ask their subjects to disobey God's word, Christians not only may rebel but they must. This conviction led to an actual revolution so powerful that the Scottish ruler Mary of Guise (1515–1560), who reigned in the place of her underage daughter, Mary Stuart (1542–1587), had to ask France for military support. In return, the Protestant lords asked England to come to their rescue. Knox encouraged the Scottish revolution with his powerful sermons.

Finally, in March 1560, the English army defeated the French. In June, Mary of Guise died and Mary Stuart, now the official queen, allowed the Scottish lords to form a new parliament. Since at that time each government determined the country's religion, Scotland became officially a Protestant country. Knox and five other preachers, all named John, wrote a **confession of faith** and a book of discipline that set some rules for both church and state. One of the benefits of the Scottish Reformation was the building of schools to make sure that everyone could read the Bible.

John Knox
INTERNET ARCHIVE BOOK IMAGES

Mary Stuart's position as Roman Catholic queen of a Protestant country was quite uncomfortable. Most people were willing to work with it until some scandals at court brought the country to the brink of a **civil war**. Eventually, she was imprisoned, and the Scottish Parliament forced her to resign. Her young son James, who was just a little more than one year old, was crowned King James VI (1566–1625) of Scotland.

Mary escaped from prison and moved to England, where she was executed for her involvement in a plot to kill Queen Elizabeth I.

EASTERN EUROPE AND SCANDINAVIA

Like in other places, the Reformation in Eastern Europe and Scandinavia was dependent on the favor of the rulers. In both areas, the Reformation spread quickly, but in the end, most of the rulers of Eastern Europe restored their countries to the Roman Catholic Church for political reasons.

Poland

In the sixteenth century, Poland was one of the largest and most powerful kingdoms in Europe, including other countries in Eastern Europe. Most rulers of Poland refused to have one national church and were tolerant of other forms of Christianity. This good policy created some problems by attracting teachers who were considered heretics in other countries, including some who doubted the Trinity and that Jesus is truly God.

As the number of Protestant churches kept growing, some Polish noblemen asked John Calvin for help. He suggested a Polish Reformer who had been living in England, Jan Laski (1499–1560). Laski moved to Poland in 1556, where he worked to organize the Protestant churches and to protect them from false teachings.

In the meantime, the Roman Catholic leaders in Poland continued to fight the spreading of the Reformation. In 1564 they invited a militant religious group known as the **Jesuits**, who did much to return the country to obedience to the pope. By the seventeenth century, Protestant books and churches were banned.

A commemorative medal of Jan Laski

NATIONAL MUSEUM IN POZNAN, PIOTRUS, WIKIMEDIA COMMONS

Hungary and Romania

Luther's ideas arrived in Hungary, which included Romania, as early as 1519 and continued to be spread throughout the country both by merchants and by young men who studied in Wittenberg and Geneva. In 1559 the church adopted the Hungarian Confession of Faith.

The town of Debrecen housed so many Reformers that it became known as the Hungarian Geneva. One of these, Matthias Biro Dévai (ca. 1500–1545), suffered frequent imprisonments for his faith and became known as the Hungarian Luther.

Another important Hungarian, Leonhard Stöckel (1510–1560), brought the Reformation to his native Bardejov, in today's Slovakia. He also founded a school that became so famous that other cities in Slovakia adopted its program.

In 1541 armies from the Ottoman Empire invaded Buda, then the capital of Hungary, and occupied the central and southern regions. To avoid Ottoman rule, some northern regions pledged allegiance to the Austrian Hapsburg family and followed their religion, Roman Catholicism.

Some regions, such as Slovakia and the independent principality of Transylvania (now in Romania), were able to keep the Protestant faith.

A monument to Leonhard Stöckel in the city park in Bardejov, Slovakia

ANTEKBOJAR, WIKIMEDIA COMMONS

A monument to Olaus Petri in front of Storkykan (the Great Church) in Stockholm, Sweden
NICNAC1000, FLICKR

SWEDEN AND DENMARK

King Gustav Vasa (1523–1560) made the Lutheran church the official church in Sweden, which at that time included Finland. To do so, he promoted the work of two Swedish brothers, Olaus (1493–1552) and Laurentius Petri (1499–1573), who had studied in Wittenberg.

In Denmark, which included Norway, Iceland, and parts of today's Sweden, the establishment of the Lutheran Reformation was due to King Christian III (1503–1559), who had first seen Luther at the Diet of Worms. Christian married a Lutheran and kept a frequent correspondence with Luther; with Philipp Melanchthon (1497–1560), who was Luther's closest assistant; and with a man named John Bugenhagen (1485–1558), known as the Reformer of the North. Bugenhagen earned that nickname for introducing the Reformation in northern Germany and Poland. Christian invited him to do the same in Denmark.

A monument to Olaus and Laurentius Petri outside the old Olaus Petri Church in Orebro, Sweden
GEORGE CHAMOUN, FLICKR

John Bugenhagen
UNIVERSITÄTS BIBLIOTHEK, LEIPZIG

FEEDING BODIES AND SOULS

Following Luther's appeals to care for the poor, Bugenhagen started important programs for the needy in his community. Most churches already had a chest where people dropped money to support the church. He suggested that they add another for the benefit of the poor. He reminded believers to include everyone and even "gladly serve those who have offended us, if they need us in their need, as Christ teaches us in [Matthew] 5:44 and as we are often admonished otherwise in Scripture." Today, some churches have kept the tradition of collecting two offerings: one for the church and one for the poor.

SOUTHERN EUROPE

The Protestant Reformation encountered many obstacles in southern European countries like Spain and Italy, which were strongly under the power of the pope.

A portrait of Cardinal Fernando Niño de Guevara (1541–1609), Grand Inquisitor of Spain, by the Spanish artist El Greco

THE MET MUSEUM

Spain

In Spain, Martin Luther's message met the immediate and fierce opposition of both the Roman Catholic Church and the Spanish rulers Ferdinand II and Isabella. To repress it, they already had a powerful tool at hand: a special religious court called the Tribunal of the Holy Office of the Inquisition. This court was first established in 1478 primarily to determine through intense interrogation if converts to Roman Catholicism from Islam and Judaism were sincere. It became particularly active after 1492, when Spanish forces defeated the last Muslim stronghold in Spain, the kingdom of Granada.

In time, this court became strict and cruel toward anyone who believed something different from the Church of Rome. If those who had embraced the gospel wanted to save their lives, they had to flee the country. Sometimes if people escaped, Spanish authorities made life-size puppets that looked like the fugitives and burned them in a public square as a warning to others.

Italy

The Protestant Reformation was greeted with interest in Italy but was not allowed to grow. In 1542 the pope reinstated an Italian version of the Inquisition, which the church had used in the past to question people who spread Reformed teachings. It was not as harsh as the Spanish Inquisition, but it caused many Italians to be imprisoned or to leave the country. A few were executed.

Peter Martyr Vermigli was one of the most respected Reformers. He became particularly important for his teachings on the Lord's Supper.

WITH PERMISSION BY MICHAELFINNEY.CO.UK

Some Italians who left the country went on to become pastors and teachers in other parts of Europe. The most famous of these were Peter Martyr Vermigli (1499–1562) and Jerome Zanchi (1516–1590), who wrote important books and trained other pastors.

A best seller of the Italian Reformation was *The Benefit of Christ*, a book written by a monk named Benedetto Fontanini (1495–1556). It was the first document to clearly explain in Italian God's free gift of salvation through faith in Christ. It sold forty thousand copies, a huge number at that time, within three months just in the city of Venice but was published without the name of the author. Fontanini's name was revealed only after his death during the trial of another Christian.

Jerome Zanchi was Vermigli's student in Lucca. He became particularly important for his explanation of how God keeps the faith of His children, staying faithful to them until the end.

COURTESY WWW.MICHAELFINNEY.CO.UK

BIBLE TRANSLATIONS AND GRAMMAR BOOKS

The Roman Catholic Church was suspicious of translations of the Bible in the languages of the people. For one thing, they feared the translations may have some mistakes. They were also afraid that the common people, who didn't have a good education, would misunderstand the Bible. They thought it was best for people to leave the study of the Bible to the clergy.

Instead, the Reformers believed it was important for all people to read the Bible in their language and worked hard to make sure they had suitable translations. In doing so, they also promoted reading and education by establishing print shops and schools. In some regions where there was no written language, they had to write spelling and grammar books. That's what Matthias Biro Dévai did in Hungary and Primož Trubar (1508–1586) did in Slovenia. Today, Slovenia is a Roman Catholic country, but it still celebrates Trubar for creating their written language.

Translating the Bible was a dangerous task, and most translators had to leave their country to do it. Some were killed for it, like William Tyndale (ca. 1494–1536), an English scholar at the time of King Henry VIII. Since Henry, like the pope, opposed all translations of the Bible, Tyndale moved to Germany, where he translated the New Testament from Greek into English. He was arrested before he could complete an Old Testament translation and was executed in 1536. By that time, thousands of copies of the English New Testament had already been printed. His translation became the basis for other versions, including the version that King Henry finally allowed in 1539.

Bringing translated Bibles into a country was also extremely risky. For many years, the Spanish Julián Hernández (d. 1560) smuggled into Spain the New Testament and Psalms translated by Juan Pérez de Pineda (ca. 1500–1567), a Spaniard who had escaped to Geneva. In the end, Hernández was betrayed, arrested, tortured, and burned alive. Like many Reformers, he sang as he was carried to the stake.

A bust of Primož Trubar in Lendava, Slovenia
SILVERIJE, WIKIMEDIA COMMONS

William Tyndale
INTERNET ARCHIVE BOOK IMAGES

Title page of the New Testament translated by Juan Pérez de Pineda from the original Greek into Castilian (a variety of Spanish) and published in 1556
BRIDWELL LIBRARY SPECIAL COLLECTIONS, SOUTHERN METHODIST UNIVERSITY

The Council of Trent
WOLFGANG SAUBER, WIKIMEDIA COMMONS

THE ROMAN CATHOLIC RESPONSE

The Protestant Reformation caused the Roman Catholic authorities to take seriously requests for changes. From 1545 to 1563, a group of bishops, archbishops, and cardinals assembled three different times in the Italian city of Trent to discuss the problems of the church and how to fix them. Some hoped for a middle way between Protestants and Roman Catholics so that the church wouldn't be divided. This meeting is known as the Council of Trent.

In the end the Roman Catholic leaders could not accept the Protestant proposals. In fact, they wrote an official document stating that anyone who shared the Protestants' ideas was cursed by God. This document is still valid in the Roman Catholic Church.

They all agreed, however, that many leaders of the church had been terrible examples, breaking the same commandments they gave others. To remedy this problem, they instituted better training and supervision of their priests.

A major Roman Catholic reformer was Ignatius Loyola (1491–1556), a Spanish soldier who founded a new religious group and organized it like an army. The group, officially approved by the pope in 1540, was called the Society of Jesus, and its members became known as Jesuits. Loyola had a double mission: encouraging his members to take religion more seriously and recruiting more people into the Roman Catholic Church—including some European countries that had become Protestant. To do so, the Jesuits went throughout the world as missionaries, reaching faraway places like India, Indonesia, the Philippines, China, Japan, and the Americas.

In many ways the Roman Catholic Church went the opposite direction from the Reformers. While Protestant churches emphasized simplicity, Roman Catholic churches emphasized magnificence and splendor. While Protestant preaching emphasized the authority of the Bible and the wonders of God's unmerited grace, Roman Catholic preaching emphasized the authority of the pope and tradition, the importance of good works, and stories of saints.

Did You Know?

The Council of Trent confirmed that the Old Testament should include the books of Baruch, Judith, 1 and 2 Maccabees, Sirach, Tobit, and Wisdom. Protestants disagreed because these books were never recognized as God's word by the Jews, by some of the church fathers (including Jerome, who translated the Bible into Latin), or even by a pope (Gregory I). Like in other matters, the Roman Catholics kept them because they had become part of their tradition.

A Summary of Reformation Teachings

Many Protestants today use five expressions as a summary of the teachings of the Protestant Reformation. These expressions, in Latin, include a form of the word *solus*, meaning "only." You can see what a difference that little word can make.

SOLA GRATIA— *Only by Grace*

- ROMAN CATHOLICS—We are saved by God's grace with our free cooperation. God first gives this grace at baptism, but in order to receive eternal life in heaven, Christians must increase this grace by praying, receiving the sacraments, and doing good works for the rest of their earthly lives (and, in most cases, after years of purification in purgatory).

- PROTESTANTS—We are saved *only* by God's grace, from beginning to end. It's true that Christians must grow spiritually over time, but this is a work of the Holy Spirit, who uses ordinary means like preaching and the sacraments to communicate and confirm God's grace to make Christians willing to obey and to give the strength and power to do it.

SOLA FIDE— *Only through Faith*

- ROMAN CATHOLICS—We are saved through faith *and* good works. Roman Catholics quote Galatians 5:6 about "faith working through love." To them, good works are essential for salvation.

- PROTESTANTS—We are saved *only* through faith, which includes trust in Christ and what He has accomplished for us. Faith is like the hand that accepts God's gift of salvation. Protestants quote Ephesians 2:8 to show that even faith is a gift of God, so men and women can never take credit for any part of their salvation. They believe it's important for faith to produce good works, but those are a result of and not a condition for salvation.

SOLUS CHRISTUS— *Only Christ*

- ROMAN CATHOLICS—Jesus Christ gained our salvation on the cross, but the saints (especially Mary, mother of Jesus), the priests and bishops, the pope, and the church as institution are **mediators** that are necessary to take our prayers to Christ and to impart the grace that God provides.

- PROTESTANTS—Jesus Christ is the *only* Mediator between God and mankind (1 Timothy 2:5). We are saved by trusting *only* in Him and His sacrifice. He accomplished everything necessary for our salvation, and there is nothing left for us or others to do.

SOLA SCRIPTURA— *Only the Scriptures*

- ROMAN CATHOLICS—God's truth is found in the Scriptures *and* in the official teachings of the church, which is known as apostolic tradition. The Roman Catholic Church is the only authority for interpreting the Scriptures.

- PROTESTANTS—Only the Scriptures contain the truth we need to know for salvation. Studying what the church has taught in the past and consulting with other Christians is important, but people can make mistakes. Only the Scriptures are inspired by God, and the church cannot impose anything that is not taught in the Scriptures.

SOLI DEO GLORIA— *To God Alone Be Glory*

- ROMAN CATHOLICS—All honor and glory ultimately belong to God.

- PROTESTANTS—All honor and glory belong *only* to God. This is related to *solus Christus*. The Reformers thought the Roman Catholic Church was assuming too much glory and honor by saying that the pope was the representative of Christ on earth and by claiming a spiritual power over believers, so much so that it could decide who was a saint in God's eyes. They also thought that priests assumed too much power by stating that through their ceremony they could turn bread and wine into the body and blood of Christ.

Changes in Worship

The Protestant Reformation changed the way people worshiped. Protestant churches emphasized the preaching of God's word. This meant that the **pulpit** became the focal point of every church. Also, Protestant sermons were usually longer than those preached in Roman Catholic churches. Because of this, Protestant churches began to build benches, later known as pews, for people to sit down.

While Lutheran and **Anglican** churches allowed some images in their buildings, most Reformed churches took them out and whitewashed their walls so that people could concentrate on the preaching of God's word. Roman Catholics continued to encourage the use of images in their churches as a way to teach those who couldn't read. Protestants instead tried to open more schools in order to teach everyone to read.

The Reformation also changed the way people sang in church. Protestant churches emphasized the singing of psalms in the language of the people instead of using chants. Protestants used simpler tunes, which made it easy to memorize the words, and encouraged everyone to sing. Most of the time, they didn't use instruments to accompany the singing.

Some of these changes were difficult for the people, who were used to the sense of mystery in ceremonies and Latin prayers and to the candles, pictures, colors, and smells of wax and incense that filled the churches in the past. Also, most people like what is familiar to them and have a difficult time accepting new ways. That's why Protestants put a strong emphasis on training pastors who could in turn help their people to understand why things were different.

In *The Necessity of Reforming the Church*, John Calvin explained that following the instructions God has given in the Bible is the only safe way to worship Him without disrespecting Him, offending Him, or creating idols. At the same time, Martin Luther advised his friends to go slow in making changes. He believed that people should just be offered the gospel, not forced to accept new regulations. "The matter should be left to God," he said. "His word should do the work alone."

The Protestant church in Lyon, France, called the Paradise was built in 1564 but was demolished three years later during the religious wars. This painting, probably a work of the Protestant artist Jean Perrissin, shows the pulpit in the middle of the church, placed there so that everyone could hear the preacher. The hourglass near the preacher helps him keep track of the time.
ERICH LESSING / ART RESOURCE, NY

The closure of English monasteries, ordered by King Henry VIII, was a sudden decision that left many people without the support of monks and nuns and without offering an immediate alternative. Many people also objected to Henry giving the lands he took from the church to noblemen. This image shows the ruins of Neath Abbey in Glamorgan, Wales.
MARTYN SMITH, FLICKR

Catechisms and Confessions

By the end of the sixteenth century, the Protestant churches had written many **catechisms** and confessions to help believers understand biblical teachings. The most commonly used catechisms were Luther's Catechisms (1529) and the Heidelberg Catechism (1563), and the most common confessions were the Augsburg Confession (1530) and Formula of Concord (1577) for the Lutheran churches, the Gallic Confession (1559) for the French churches, the Scots Confession (1560) for Scottish **Presbyterians**, the Belgic Confession (1561) for most Reformed churches, and the Second Helvetic Confession (1564), which was used in Switzerland and Eastern Europe. Most of these documents are still used today in many churches around the world as clear explanations of what Protestants believe.

The frontispiece of a 1563 copy of the Heidelberg Catechism

SILVERIJE, WIKIMEDIA COMMONS

An engraving of Philipp Melanchthon by the German artist Albrecht Dürer

THE MET MUSEUM

The Heidelberg Catechism was written mostly by Zacharias Ursinus (1534–1583) and Kaspar Olevianus (1536–1587), with the support of Frederick III (1515–1576), **Elector** Palatine, who put together a team to bring the Reformation to his capital, Heidelberg.

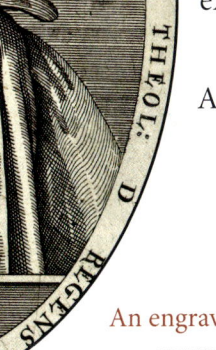

The Gallic Confession (or French Confession of Faith) was initially written by John Calvin and modified at a French synod in 1571. The Belgic Confession was mostly written by the pastor Guido de Brès (1522–1567), who was executed for his faith. The Second Helvetic Confession was written by Heinrich Bullinger.

The Augsburg Confession was largely composed by Philipp Melanchthon, Luther's closest assistant, and was presented to Emperor Charles V in the German city of Augsburg in 1530. When the emperor rejected it, Melanchthon wrote a longer explanation in its defense.

The Formula of Concord clarified many points in the Augsburg Confession, especially regarding the Lord's Supper.

An engraving of Zacharias Ursinus

UNIVERSITÄTSBIBLIOTHEK LEIPZIG

WHAT'S IN A NAME? LUTHERAN AND REFORMED

Initially, Protestants were called by different names. Many were called Lutherans because Luther's writings became the main spark of the Reformation. They were also called Evangelicals, from the Greek word *euangelion*, which means "good news." *Reformed* was initially a general term. For example, the Italian Reformer Peter Martyr Vermigli mentioned many Protestant leaders, including Luther, Zwingli, and Calvin, as "heroes of the Reformed religion."

Later, when the differences between Luther, Zwingli, and Calvin were emphasized, the term *Lutheran* was used specifically for the followers of Luther, and the term *Reformed* for those who agreed with Zwingli or Calvin. While both Lutherans and Reformed agreed on most teachings of the Reformation, they disagreed on a few, such as the meaning of the Lord's Supper.

For the Reformed, Jesus is present in the Lord's Supper in spirit and unites the believers spiritually with His true presence in heaven. For the Lutherans, He is truly present with the bread and wine, even though the nature of the elements doesn't change, as the Roman Catholics believe. To some people, this might not seem like a big difference, but it changes the way in which the Lord's Supper is performed and experienced.

Other Religious Groups

In the sixteenth century, some small groups earned the disapproval of both Protestants and Roman Catholics. Some taught things that were openly contrary to biblical teachings about the Trinity and the authority of the Scriptures Christians had upheld for centuries.

THE ANABAPTISTS

Some Christians were given the name Anabaptists (meaning "rebaptizers") because, unlike Roman Catholic, Lutheran, Reformed, and Eastern Orthodox believers, they didn't baptize their infant children and rebaptized people who had been baptized as infants. They believed baptism should be only for those who professed faith in Christ, while those who baptized infants believed that baptism was God's sign of His promise and should not be grounded in someone's faith.

The Anabaptists thought that Christians should separate themselves from the rest of the world and churches should not work together with city councils. The first recorded time when an Anabaptist group separated from an established church was in 1525 in Zollikon, Switzerland.

These views caused some government officials to worry because rulers at that time assumed that having one state religion was the only way to keep the peace. Their worries seemed to come true when a group of radicals started an armed revolution in the German city of Münster in 1534–1535. The occupation failed, and many Anabaptists were imprisoned. Their leaders were tortured, executed, and hung in cages from the steeple of St. Lambert's Church as an example to all.

The cages that held the bodies of Anabaptist leaders still hang from the steeple of St. Lambert's Church in Münster.

PTWO, FLICKR

Menno Simons
RIJKSMUSEUM, AMSTERDAM, NETHERLANDS

Most Anabaptists, however, were peaceful. One of their leaders, Menno Simons (1496–1561), was particularly careful to preach a message of nonviolence. Today's Mennonites, who are peaceful descendants of the Anabaptists, owe their name to Menno Simons. They too believe in keeping separate from the world.

In spite of being illegal, the Anabaptist movement continued to grow. By the late 1520s there were many groups of Anabaptists in different parts of Europe. A few Anabaptists depended on special revelations apart from the Bible that they said they received from God. Other Christians thought this was a problem because anyone could say they have heard a new message from God and others couldn't deny it.

Today's **Baptists** also believe that baptism is only for those who profess their faith in Christ. Some trace their roots to the Anabaptists. Reformed Baptists came out of **Congregational** (Puritan) churches in the seventeenth century.

UNITARIANS AND SOCINIANS

Around this time, some people brought back old doubts about the Trinity (see p. 18). Those who didn't believe in the Trinity were known as Unitarians. Their teachings became particularly widespread in Poland, where the government allowed them; other governments banned these teachings as heresies.

Some famous Unitarian leaders in Poland were the Italian Laelius Socinus (1525–1562) and his nephew Faustus Socinus (1539–1604). Along with denying the Trinity, these men taught that Jesus was simply a man, even though He never sinned, and that His death on the cross was simply meant to teach others how to suffer patiently.

They also taught that God only knows "all that is knowable," which includes the past and the present, not the future. Writing in the seventeenth century, the English theologian John Owen (1616–1683) explained that this is a terrible teaching. Not only does it contradict the Bible, but it robs Christians of any peace and comfort in God's loving wisdom and providence.

Over time, the followers of Laelius and Faustus Socinus became known as Socinians. The Socinians became popular when they began to print their own papers.

Faustus Socinus
RIJKSMUSEUM, AMSTERDAM, NETHERLANDS

THE PROTESTANT REFORMATION • 99

PART 6
A TROUBLED CENTURY

The Church Organizing, Defending, and Spreading

The seventeenth century was a time of struggles. The Thirty Years' War, fought between 1618 and 1648, was one of the most destructive conflicts in European history. It began with a Protestant rebellion in Bohemia against the Holy Roman Emperor Ferdinand II (1578–1637) and spread through much of Europe. The worst episode was the 1631 Sack of Magdeburg, Germany, with a loss of about twenty thousand lives.

In the meantime, the British Isles fought a series of civil wars (1638–1651), which included the execution of King Charles I (1600–1649). On the Continent, King Louis XIII of France (1601–1643) captured the last Protestant stronghold in his country, while the Netherlands continued to fight their eighty-year war of independence from Spain (1567–1648).

In spite of this, Protestants worked hard to organize their churches, defend the teachings of the Reformation, and explain them clearly in official documents, while Roman Catholics continued to refine their guidelines and send missionaries all over the world.

EUROPE, 1600–1700

1611 — A group of translators completes an English translation of the Bible known as the King James Version.

1618 — The Thirty Years' War between the Catholic Habsburg rulers and the Protestant princes begins.

1618–1619 — A group of theologians from European countries meets at Dordrecht, Netherlands, to discuss questions related to eternal salvation.

1620 — Around seven hundred Protestants are killed in the Valtellina region in northern Italy.

1627–1628 — The Siege of La Rochelle, France, marks the final military victory of the Roman Catholic king over French Protestants.

1631 — The Catholic armies' attack on Protestants in Magdeburg, Germany, marks the worst loss of lives of the Thirty Years' War.

1638 — Representatives of Scottish churches sign the National Covenant.

1642–1651 — The forces of King Charles I and those of his Parliament fight each other in what is known as the English Civil Wars.

1643–1653 — A group of British theologians composes the Westminster Standards as new confessional documents of the Church of England.

1648 — The Peace of Westphalia puts an end to the Thirty Years' War and to the Eighty Years' War of Dutch independence from Spain.

1649 — Charles I is convicted of treason in a court of law and sentenced to death.

1655 — Waldensians are massacred in northern Italy.

1662 — Charles II of England orders all pastors and preachers to follow government-mandated rules of worship. About two thousand Puritan pastors have to leave their ministries.

1685 — King Louis XIV of France revokes the Edict of Nantes, ending religious freedom for Protestants.

1688–1689 — William III of Orange and his wife, Mary, overthrow James II of England in what is known as the Glorious Revolution.

1689 — Exiled Waldensians return to Italy in what is known as the Glorious Return. Baptists in England issue the Baptist Confession of Faith to show they agree with most of the Westminster Standards, although they don't baptize babies.

Charting the Reformation

Two of the most important documents of the Protestant church—the **Canons** of Dort and the Westminster Standards—were composed during the seventeenth century.

THE CANONS OF DORT

Some pastors in Leiden, Netherlands, were concerned. The sermons of one of their university professors, Jacob Arminius (1560–1609), seemed to contradict the Belgic Confession, which every Dutch preacher had promised to follow. Arminius said it wasn't so, but after his death, his followers repeated his teachings.

In 1610 forty-two of these followers asked the Dutch government for permission to teach these things freely. This step was necessary because, as it was in most countries, the government ruled over the church.

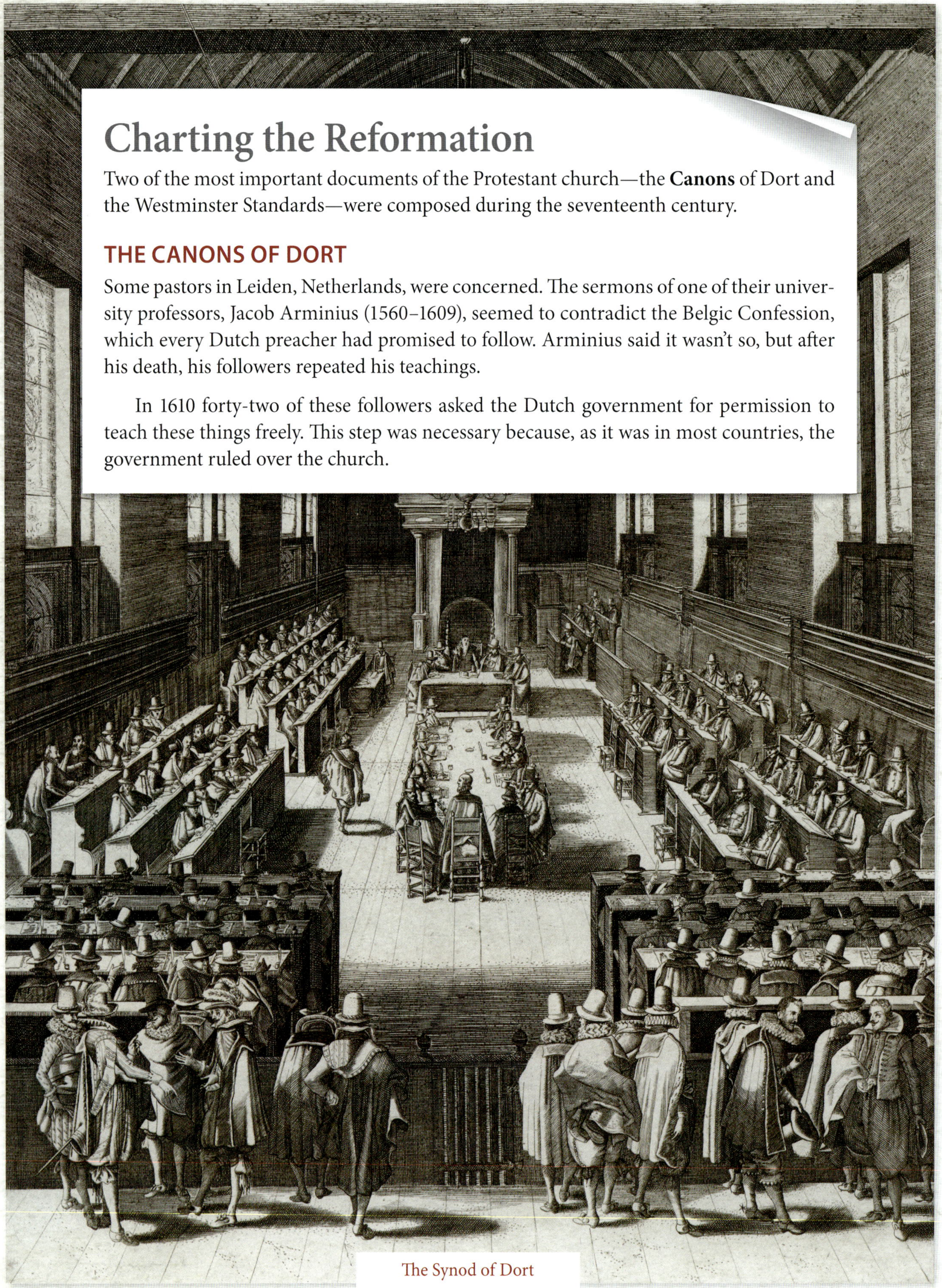

The Synod of Dort

RIJKSMUSEUM, WIKIMEDIA COMMONS

Their letter, called a remonstrance (protest), listed their beliefs through five points:

1. God chooses to give eternal life in heaven to those He knows will believe and obey.
2. Jesus died for everyone, but only those who believe and obey until the end are saved.
3. Human beings are born in sin and must be born again of God's Spirit.
4. A person can choose to resist and reject God's grace.
5. A person who has received God's grace might be able to lose it through rebellion or disobedience.

The Reformed pastors objected to most of these points. To discuss these matters, they asked the government for permission to hold an official meeting, called a synod, and invited pastors from different European countries, making this the first Protestant council held at an international level.

The representatives met in the Dutch city of Dordrecht (Dort) from November 1618 to May 1619. In the end, they gave a reply to the five points:

1. God's choice of those who will be saved is *not* conditioned by what people may or may not do.
2. Jesus died for those God has chosen to save. He didn't just make salvation possible; He gave it.
3. Human beings are born in sin and incapable of choosing to believe in Christ, so God has to save them supernaturally. (This was similar to what the **Remonstrants** said, but their conclusions, in the next point, were different.)
4. All those who are called by Christ come to Him because God's Spirit frees them from the sinful nature that would cause them to reject God's grace.
5. When Jesus said that no human being can take someone out of His hand (John 10:28), He meant no one, not even that person. When God chooses to save a person, that person will be kept until the end, and nothing will separate him or her from God's love.

These points were explained in a document called the Canons of Dort. Together with the Belgic Confession and the Heidelberg Catechism, they became part of the Three Forms of Unity, the confessional standards for many Reformed churches.

After the Synod of Dort, the ruler of the Dutch Republic, Maurice of Orange (1567–1625), determined that the teachings of the Remonstrants were not to be allowed in any Dutch church. Many Remonstrant pastors left the country. The restrictions began to be lifted in 1630, and Remonstrant churches were officially recognized by 1798. In the English-speaking world, the Remonstrants are often called **Arminians**.

Some Men of the Seventeenth-Century Church

SOME PARTICIPANTS AT THE SYNOD OF DORT

FRANCIS GOMARUS (1563–1641), a major participant at the synod, was one of the first to confront Arminius. He is remembered for challenging another representative to a duel because he took the opponent's comments on Christ's sacrifice as a personal offense. The duel never happened, but this shows how seriously Gomarus took this issue.

JOHANNES BOGERMAN (1576–1637) was the president of the synod. When the Remonstrants tried to delay the synod, he told them to leave. He was one of the translators of the new version of the Bible commissioned by the synod.

WILLIAM AMES (1576–1633) was Bogerman's adviser. Born in England, he chose to live in the Netherlands. He thought Arminianism could lead to heresy. He wrote an important book on modeling worship after the examples of the New Testament and avoiding any new inventions. His writings had a great influence on the Puritans in North America.

JOHN DIODATI (1576–1649), one of the representatives of the church of Geneva, produced the first complete translation of the Bible from its original sources into Italian. At Dort, he was one of the reasonable voices that helped the synod reach an agreement while preserving the essential teachings of the Protestant Reformation.

SIMON EPISCOPIUS (1583–1643) was the spokesman for the Remonstrants. He gave the longest speech. Later, he became head of a Remonstrant college in Amsterdam.

Assertion of Liberty of Conscience by the Independents of the Westminster Assembly of Divines. Oil painting by John Rogers Herbert.
© PARLIAMENTARY ART COLLECTION, WOA 652 HERITAGECOLLECTIONS.PARLIAMENT.UK

THE WESTMINSTER STANDARDS

In 1643 the English Parliament called an official meeting of 121 Puritan pastors to define the beliefs of the Church of England and unify a nation divided by civil war and religious differences.

The English Civil Wars (1642–1651) were fought between the armies of King Charles I and the Puritan armies of Parliament. By law, the king was supposed to consult with Parliament about major decisions, but Charles had often neglected this duty. What's worse, he used his power for his own interests, making dangerous alliances with other nations against his own people and, in the eyes of the Puritans, moving England, Wales, and Scotland back to Roman Catholic teaching.

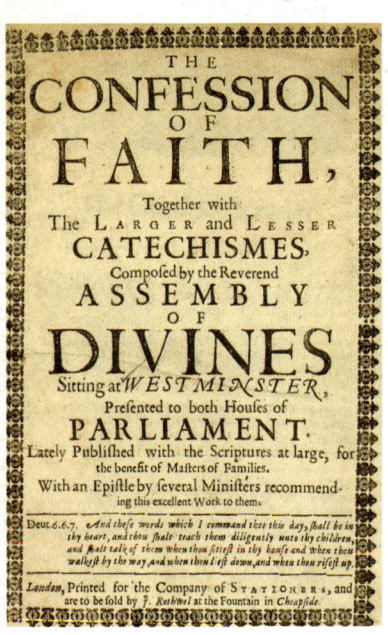

Title page of 1658 printing of Westminster Standards

WIKIMEDIA COMMONS

In 1649, after almost seven years of battles, Charles was accused of treason in a court of law and sentenced to die. It was the first time a legitimate head of state was put on trial and executed in the name of the people. Europe was stunned.

The assembly met during these difficult times and continued until 1653. For over ten years, the representatives worked hard, day after day, with hardly any time off. They had disagreements, but it was a good thing because it forced them to consider every issue more thoroughly and to decide which teachings were essential for all and which could be left to the choice of each church.

They also spent time examining new preachers to make sure they didn't live immoral lives or preach questionable doctrines. They wanted preachers who could preach and not just read other people's sermons from the pulpit.

The resulting documents, the Westminster Standards, provide a good and accurate summary of the conclusions of the Protestant Reformation. These include the Westminster Confession of Faith, the Larger Catechism, and the Shorter Catechism. They also provided the basis for the Baptist Confession of 1689, which follows them closely, differing mainly on church government and infant baptism.

More Men of the Seventeenth-Century Church

SOME PARTICIPANTS AT THE WESTMINSTER ASSEMBLY

WILLIAM TWISSE (1578–1646) was chosen as chairman at the Westminster Assembly and preached a three-hour opening sermon. At a time when people could hardly lift their thoughts from the civil war that was raging around the country—a war that was affecting the properties and families of many delegates to the assembly—he chose as his text John 14:18: "I will not leave you comfortless; I will come to you." In 1645 his health forced him to retire from his post.

SAMUEL RUTHERFORD (1600–1661) was one of six Scottish ministers who were invited to the assembly as advisers who had no voting powers. He is often remembered for his book *Lex Rex*, which means "the law is king." He meant that each nation should be directed by its laws, not by the whims of a ruler. Charles II's government had the book publicly burned in 1660. They also called Rutherford for a hearing, but he was ill and died a few days later. Throughout history, many Christians have found comfort in Rutherford's letters and writings on the beauty and perfection of Christ.

THOMAS GOODWIN (1600–1680) had to flee to the Netherlands when Charles I toughened his restrictions on the Church of England. After the assembly, he and five other men created a confession for Congregational churches. He was valued for his sermons and writings that pointed people to Christ. He told people who thought that God couldn't possibly love them to stop looking at their own faults and look to Christ, who died for them.

Thomas Goodwin
REFORMATION ART

WHAT'S IN A NAME? EPISCOPALIAN, PRESBYTERIAN, AND CONGREGATIONAL

One of the main issues discussed by the assembly was the organization of the Church of England. Until then, the churches in the country had been organized by bishops, who were in turn overseen by archbishops, as it was in the Roman Catholic Church. We call this type of church **Episcopalian**, from the Greek *episkopos*, meaning "bishop." Today, the Church of England (or Anglican Church) still has the same organization, with the king or queen as supreme governor on earth under God. The Episcopalian churches outside England don't have to answer to the king or queen.

Other churches in Europe, especially in Switzerland and Scotland, were overseen by individual groups of elders. Today, we call these churches Presbyterian, from the Greek *presbyteros*, meaning "elder." Elders had equal status and could make decisions for their local church. Decisions affecting all Presbyterian churches in an area were made in official meetings with each church sending elders as its representatives.

Some Christians thought it was best for decisions to be made directly by the congregations without having to answer to a bishop or to elders. This type of church is known as Congregational. Most of today's Baptists have this type of church government.

Think about It

What are the advantages and disadvantages of a national church overseen by the government as there was in England and in other European nations during the seventeenth century?

Some of the pastors who were ejected from their churches began to preach in homes or in the open, but the government added a new law forbidding meetings of more than five people.

ROGER GRIFFITH, WIKIMEDIA COMMONS

The Great Ejection

After the death of Charles I, England established a republican government headed by Oliver Cromwell (1599–1658). But Cromwell couldn't solve all the problems of a deeply divided country, and these problems became worse under his son Richard (1626–1712). This situation forced Parliament to invite Charles's son, Charles II, to reclaim the throne. Initially, Charles II promised fair treatment of the Puritans. Later, his Parliament pressured him to take back some of his promises.

In 1662 all pastors and preachers were required to follow the Book of Common Prayer and other set regulations during worship. Those who refused were fined and forbidden to preach. On August 24, close to two thousand pastors preached their last sermon to their congregations. Some of them later left the country. This is known as the Great **Ejection**.

More restrictions followed. Since Christians had started to worship privately in homes, the government passed a law (the Conventicle Act) that punished anyone "who met in greater numbers than five." Later, they forbade any pastor to preach within five miles of a place where he had already preached. This last rule was especially cruel because it was largely directed at the Puritan preachers who were in London during the 1665 plague, ministering to people in the midst of death. It was cruel for the government to think they should abandon those people.

In 1672 Charles II eased his rules, allowing the Puritans to preach on condition that they obtain a license. The large number of licenses issued, more than sixteen hundred, showed how many preachers preferred to be independent from the Church of England in spite of the king's efforts to have everyone worship the same way. The king went back on his word the following year, but by that time the Puritans were stronger.

In 1689, when the Protestant Mary II of England (1662–1694) and her Dutch husband, William III of Orange (1650–1702), became corulers of England, Wales, Scotland, and Ireland in the so-called Glorious Revolution, the Puritans were given freedom to meet for public worship.

More Men and Women of the Seventeenth-Century Church

ENGLISH PURITANS

JOHN OWEN (1616–1683) is considered the greatest English theologian. He led an adventurous life as pastor, army **chaplain**, and vice-chancellor of the University of Oxford. His writings were appreciated by pastors who wanted to defend their congregations from false teachings. Today, he is especially known for his book *Mortification of Sin* about the importance of fighting sin and temptation.

JOHN BUNYAN (1628–1688) was an unschooled fixer of pots who was imprisoned for preaching without the authorization of the Church of England. In prison he wrote *The Pilgrim's Progress*, an imaginary story describing the life of a Christian as a difficult journey to the Heavenly City. This immediately became one of the most popular books ever published and has been translated into many languages.

John Owen
RIJKSMUSEUM

MATTHEW HENRY (1662–1714) is best known for his **commentary** on the Bible, which has been used by Protestant churches ever since it was published.

LUCY HUTCHINSON (1620–1681) is especially known for her biography of her husband, who died in prison after he was arrested for supporting the execution of King Charles I. Her long letter to her daughter and her poem on the book of Genesis (the first epic poem written by a woman in the English language) clearly communicate the beauty of the gospel.

John Bunyan
INTERNET ARCHIVE BOOK IMAGES

> *In the crystal mirror of God's grace*
> *All things appear with a new lovely face.*
> *When that doth Heaven's more glorious palace show*
> *We cease to admire a Paradise below,*
> *Rejoice in that which lately was our loss,*
> *And see a Crown made up of every Cross.*
> —LUCY HUTCHINSON

Some people say the Scottish rebellion against the Book of Common Prayer started when a woman, Jenny Geddes, threw a stool at the preacher.

WIKIMEDIA COMMONS

The Covenanters

The demands of the English kings were particularly difficult for the people in Scotland. From the time of John Knox, their church had been organized differently from the Church of England. They believed Christ, not a king or queen, is the head of the church. But they lost their independence when King James VI of Scotland inherited the English throne and united the two countries. From then on, Scotland had to submit to English interests.

Eventually, many Scots rebelled. Some say the rebellion started on July 23, 1637, when a woman named Jenny Geddes (ca. 1600–1660) threw the stool on which she was sitting at an English preacher who was reading for the first time from the Book of Common Prayer. It was a Protestant book, but some of its rituals and ceremonies (especially kneeling during the Lord's Supper) seemed too close to the Roman Catholic Church (see p. 88). The Scots especially disliked that these things were imposed on them by the king. Soon, other people in Jenny's church joined in her protest until the preacher and the local bishop had to run for their lives.

In 1638 representatives of almost every church in Scotland signed the National **Covenant**, formally rejecting any form of worship and teaching that seemed close to those of the Roman Catholic Church. They also insisted on keeping their presbyterian type of church, ruled by elders instead of by a pyramid of bishops and archbishops. Apparently, about half of the Scottish population signed the National Covenant. Today, those signers are known as Covenanters.

The Covenanters suffered much for their convictions, especially during the reign of Charles II. When a group of radical Covenanters called Cameronians took arms, the Anglican government reacted harshly, killing many of them and extending persecution to all Presbyterians.

After the Glorious Revolution of 1688–1689, Scottish Presbyterians reestablished themselves as the Church of Scotland, adopting the Westminster Standards as their official confession of faith.

Quakers, Seekers, Ranters, Diggers

The main reason the English government opposed the Puritans and Nonconformists was fear of disunity. In those days, religious disunity could create sharp divisions in a country. Also, as heads of the English church, kings and queens felt they had a responsibility to keep out of their country any teachings they considered unbiblical. In fact, during the period when England didn't have a king, a few unconventional groups started.

A group of people most English Protestants found unbiblical were the **Quakers** (also known as the Society of Friends). The Quakers rejected any formal creeds, church structures, and sacraments, emphasizing instead a search for "inner light." Their worship meetings were times of silence and meditation, interrupted when people thought the Spirit was speaking to them. There were no priests or pastors.

People called them Quakers because sometimes their personal experience of God made them tremble or quake. Their founder, the Englishman George Fox (1624–1691), believed his group represented a purer church.

George Fox
LIBRARY OF CONGRESS

John Bunyan wrote two papers against the Quakers. His main concern was that they kept talking about Jesus born, crucified, and resurrected inside of them instead of looking at the Jesus who was born, crucified, and resurrected in history—the only true Savior.

The Seekers believed that no true church existed in the world, so they waited for God to bring about a new, true church.

The Ranters were never an organized group. They believed that God is present in all creatures, but mostly in humans, and that those who cared for this god inside them could not sin. Because of this, some Ranters felt free to go out dancing, drinking, smoking, and swearing.

The Diggers believed that God made the earth to be a common treasury and that private property was a result of Adam and Eve's fall into sin. They were called Diggers because they dug public property to build houses for themselves and others.

The Muggletonians were the followers of Lodowicke Muggleton (1609–1698) and his cousin John Reeve (1608–1658), who claimed to be the two witnesses mentioned in Revelation 11:3. They didn't believe in the Trinity, so they said that when God came down to earth in the body of Jesus, He left Elijah in charge of heaven. Their meetings included a reading of the writings of the two founders and songs set to popular tunes so that others wouldn't know they were having a religious meeting.

> *Think about It*
>
> - Why would new revelations that are not in the Bible create a new religion?
> - What problems can we encounter when a religion puts the Bible on the same level as people's feelings and intuitions?

> *Though the fruits of the Spirit be excellent, and to be owned where they are found, yet have a care you take not away the glory of the blood of Christ shed on the cross without the gates of Jerusalem.*
>
> —JOHN BUNYAN

Religious Persecution in Other Countries

The Scottish Covenanters and English Puritans were not the only ones to suffer persecution in the seventeenth century. The Augsburg Settlement, which since 1555 had allowed rulers to determine the religion their people would follow, didn't work well for those who were not willing to give up their convictions or leave their countries. Sometimes, this provoked rebellions that governments felt compelled to put down.

While some acts of persecution were limited to specific situations, some were meant to put an end to particular religious groups. These included, among others, the persecutions of Waldensians in the Italian Alps, Roman Catholics in Japan, and Huguenots in France.

THE WALDENSIANS

During the Protestant Reformation, the Waldensians, who had survived waves of persecution since the Middle Ages, adopted the teachings of the Reformed church. This didn't help their chances of survival in Roman Catholic Italy.

In January 1655 Duke Charles Emmanuel II of Savoy (1634–1675)—ruler of the northwestern Italian region where many Waldensians lived—ordered members of the group to attend Mass or move further up the Alps. Because it was winter, he probably thought they would choose the first alternative, but they didn't. The duke, eager to earn the favor of the pope, sent troops to attack them.

On Easter day, his troops burned entire villages and brutally killed or captured men, women, and children. The men and women were imprisoned while the children were sent to Roman Catholic families to be raised in their religion.

Only a few managed to flee. These included a farmer named Joshua Janavel (1617–1690), who had led a short-lived but fierce resistance, and a young Waldensian pastor, Henri Arnaud (1643–1721). These men wrote letters to encourage the persecuted Italians and to raise support from other European Protestants.

In 1655, under pressure by other European rulers, the duke signed a document titled Patents of Grace, allowing the Waldensians some religious freedom as long as they stayed within a limited area in the Alps.

Henri Arnaud
LAURA FERRARIS

But the peace didn't last long, and there were still occasional rebellions and government interventions. In 1686 the new duke of Savoy, Victor Amadeus II (1666–1732), banished Waldensian pastors, forbidding public worship and forcing parents to give their children a Roman Catholic baptism. Those who rebelled were killed or imprisoned.

Only three years later, the new king of England, William III of Orange, took the Waldensian cause to heart and promoted the return of their exiles to their lands. And the Waldensians were ready. For some time Janavel and Arnaud had been engineering this mission, which became known as the Glorious Return.

In 1689 nine hundred Waldensians engaged in a long march across the Alps. After a fierce fight against the French armies, they settled in the small village of Sibaud, Italy, where they held a worship service and promised loyalty to God and to their leaders.

A similar persecution against Waldensians happened on another part of the Italian Alps called Valtellina, above Lake Como. There, on July 19, 1620, an army gathered by Roman Catholic noblemen and clergy went from town to town attacking the Waldensian communities, who were attending church, and killing about seven hundred of them. Many Waldensians managed to escape to Protestant countries. In this case, however, they never reclaimed their lands.

The martyrs of Nagasaki

FR. LAWRENCE LEW, O.P., WITH KIND PERMISSION OF THE CHURCH OF ST. FRANCIS XAVIER IN NEW YORK

THE MARTYRS OF JAPAN

In the meantime, the Jesuits had spread their missions as far as Japan, where they were initially well received. In Nagasaki, the main center of Roman Catholicism in the country, up to five hundred thousand people professed to be Christian at one point.

The authorities became concerned that this fast-spreading religion would divide the country. They were also worried that foreign missionaries could open a door for foreign invasions.

In 1597 twenty-six missionaries in Nagasaki were executed by crucifixion. This was just the start. In 1614 Christianity became officially banned, and foreign missionaries were expelled from the country. But Japanese Roman Catholics remained and continued to worship in secret.

The government then came up with an idea to find out who was a secret Roman Catholic. They put on the ground images of Jesus and asked every person in Nagasaki to step on them. Those who refused were terribly tortured until they either died or renounced their faith. Altogether, it seems that two thousand people were killed. Many ended up renouncing Christianity but later repented and went back to worship secretly with other Roman Catholics.

Only in 1868, with the so-called Honorable **Restoration** by Emperor Meiji (1852–1912), Christianity was again allowed in Japan.

A TROUBLED CENTURY • 111

THE HUGUENOTS

While the French Reformed churches enjoyed some peace under the Edict of Nantes (see p. 85), problems started again when the French king Henry IV died and his only son, Louis XIII, rose to the throne, ruling through his mother until he came of age.

While Louis and his advisers left the edict in place, they were careful not to give Protestants too much influence. When the Synod of Dort invited French representatives, the king allowed a small commission but quickly changed his mind and ordered them not to leave.

The king's ultimate goal was to see the Roman Catholic religion established throughout France. In 1627 he sent his troops to bring to submission the last Huguenot stronghold in France, the port city of La Rochelle in the south.

A commemorative stone in memory of the persecuted Huguenots. The cross is the symbol of the Huguenots, who were said to be suffering "under the cross." The dove represents the Holy Spirit; the grid, the prisons; and the ship, the galleys where many Huguenot men were condemned to row for the rest of their lives.

EVELYNE RENOULEAU

After this he began to slowly take away the Huguenots' rights by making their lives difficult. For example, he allowed the Huguenots to have their own schools only if these schools were built next to their churches. But many Huguenot children lived far from their churches, making their daily attendance impossible.

The king also put an end to national meetings of pastors and tried to limit the Huguenots' communication with Reformed churches outside of France. And even though the Edict of Nantes allowed Huguenots to serve in the government, Louis would not appoint them. Other people followed his example and avoided hiring Huguenots as lawyers or doctors.

Huguenot homes became favorite places for traveling bands of soldiers who needed a place to stay. Staying at people's homes was a common practice, and people were expected to give hospitality. But soldiers knew they could take advantage of Huguenots, mistreating them and stealing their food, and the government wouldn't do anything about it.

Eventually, the king gave permission to Huguenot children, at the age of seven, to choose their religion. If they chose to be Roman Catholic, they would be taken from their families and placed in Roman Catholic homes at their parents' expense. He was hoping that children could be easily convinced.

Finally, in 1685, the next king of France, Louis XIV (1638–1715), abolished the Edict of Nantes altogether, depriving Huguenots of whatever rights they had left. Huguenot churches were closed, and Huguenot pastors had two weeks either to leave the country or become Roman Catholics. If they chose the second option, they would receive a raise of one-third of their salary. Most pastors chose to leave. Those who resisted or didn't leave on time were sent to the galleys for forced labor.

The king forbade those who were not pastors to leave and sent soldiers to their homes to force them to become Roman Catholics. From 1560 to 1760, more than two hundred thousand Huguenots left France. Many found refuge in the Netherlands, England, Ireland, and present-day North and South Carolina. This was a great loss to their native country because most of them were excellent workers and had been faithful citizens.

Some of those who stayed kept their faith without telling others about it, while some prepared to fight back. They eventually created what they called the Church of the Desert, with secret meetings in caves or private homes. Those who attended these meetings ran terrible risks. If they were caught, the women were sent to jail and the men to the galleys, where they were forced to row.

Most likely, the Huguenots used some caves by the Ardèche River in France for meetings and worship.

JVB, WIKIMEDIA COMMONS

Did You Know?
HOW THE HUGUENOTS LEFT FRANCE

The Huguenots who chose to leave their country faced many dangers. Those who had money could pay a smuggler. It was a considerable expense because smugglers placed their lives at risk. After a while, some Huguenots created handwritten manuals with advice on how to escape.

Most people left by ship because borders were heavily guarded. To reach the harbors, they often traveled by night and hid during the day. Some died during the trip from exhaustion, hunger, or cold. Then they had to get used to a new country and find accommodations in countries that were already receiving a large number of refugees from northern Italy and the Spanish-ruled region of the Netherlands. Thankfully, they could usually find a French-speaking church, often pastored by other Huguenots, where they could be reminded of God's unfailing promises.

The Huguenots were not the only ones who had to worship in caves. This was also the case with Protestants who lived in the Spanish-ruled region of the Netherlands.

INTERNET ARCHIVE BOOK IMAGES

A TROUBLED CENTURY • 113

The Academy of Geneva is now called Calvin College. Originally, it had only one building. More buildings were added in the course of time.

AMIN, WIKIMEDIA COMMONS

The Academies

The seventeenth century saw a flourishing of Protestant colleges, also known as academies. These included the academy founded by John Calvin in Geneva and many that were built on that model. As well as teaching theology, biblical languages, and general education, most of the teachers in these schools wrote important books that helped others to better understand the Protestant Reformation, why it happened, and what it meant. This was, in some ways, similar to what the early church had to do—clarifying Christian teachings and warning against those who taught something different.

To make things especially clear, these teachers wrote very carefully, weighing their words so that there wouldn't be any misunderstandings. They wrote mostly in Latin, which was taught to everyone who kept studying after elementary school. Because they devoted much of their lives to the academies, or schools, these teachers are often known as scholastics. One of the main Reformed scholastic thinkers of the seventeenth century was Francis Turretin (1623–1687). His grandfather had moved to Geneva from Italy during the Protestant Reformation, when Protestants were persecuted. Francis Turretin led the Academy of Geneva, the same school that Calvin had founded, and was a pastor in the local Italian church. His main book, the *Institutes of **Elenctic** Theology*, was used as a textbook in Reformed seminaries for more than one hundred years. His writings address many theological errors that are still common today.

Other important Reformed scholastic thinkers were Gisbertus Voetius (1589–1676) of the University of Utrecht, Netherlands, and John Owen of the University of Oxford, England. Among Lutherans, Johann Gerhard (1582–1637), of the University of Jena, Germany, wrote a lengthy overview of Christian teachings and many devotional works.

The most important scholar in the Roman Catholic Church was the Italian cardinal and inquisitor Robert Bellarmine (1542–1621). He opposed Protestant teachings but studied them carefully and respectfully, so Protestants took his objections into consideration as they explained their convictions. He was also critical of giving the pope too much power and condemned several faults of the Roman Catholic administration.

Around the same time, a Roman Catholic bishop in the Netherlands, Cornelius Otto Jansen (1585–1638), condemned the church for becoming closer in its teachings to Pelagius than to Augustine of Hippo. He taught that it is impossible to do good works without God's grace and this grace is irresistible. His teachings were condemned as heretical by Pope Innocent X (1574–1655) but continued to spread in the next century, especially in France and Italy.

The Pietists

While pastors and theologians worked hard to define what true Christians should believe, they were also concerned about how they should live. Since in most countries going to church was mandatory (those who didn't attend had to pay a fine), some people went just because they had to and didn't pay much attention, which was a problem.

Most pastors continued to preach as usual, believing that the gospel would work faith and gratitude in people's hearts. Others tried to find new ways of stirring hearts. They were often called Pietists, from the word *piety*, which means "devotion to God."

Pietist authors wrote detailed manuals on how to obey God. These books became popular because people like specific instructions. Their authors didn't mean to replace the gospel with rules, but many of the readers ended up doing just that. For example, the book *True Christianity*, written by the German Johann Arndt (1555–1621), became so widely read and popular that pastors had to remind their congregations to read the Bible too.

Johann Arndt
WIKIMEDIA COMMONS

In time, this emphasis on piety brought some changes early authors may not have intended. For example, while Arndt, like Luther, kept encouraging people to look outside themselves and to Christ for answers, some Pietists did the opposite, looking at their own hearts, feelings, and impressions.

Because of this, many people started to replace church attendance with personal devotions or gatherings outside churches. Philip Jacob Spener (1635–1705), who is considered the father of **Pietism**, wrote books that promoted this habit.

Johann Sebastian Bach
LIBRARY OF CONGRESS

One opponent of Pietism was Erdmann Neumeister (1671–1756), a German pastor and poet who wrote many of the words for the cantatas composed by the famous musician Johann Sebastian Bach (1685–1750). Like Martin Luther, Neumeister believed that God communicates His grace primarily through the preached word and sacraments, which cannot be abandoned for private meditations or searching the heart. Bach was also, like Neumeister, a traditional Lutheran.

DUTCH MISSIONS

The wars in Europe kept most European Protestants from engaging in missions. One exception was the Dutch, who included missionaries in their expeditions to find new routes. Peter Plancius (1552–1622) was a promoter of missionary work and a mapmaking pastor who created more than one hundred maps. He also played a major role in the discussions that led to the Synod of Dort. Some important Dutch missionaries were George Candidius (1597–1647), Robert Junius (1606–1655), and Abraham Rogerius (1609–1649). Candidius was the first missionary to be stationed in Taiwan. Junius, who arrived later, opened the first school on the same island. Rogerius spent ten years among the Tamil people of India and five more in Indonesia. His book about the culture of India became a main source of information about **Hinduism**.

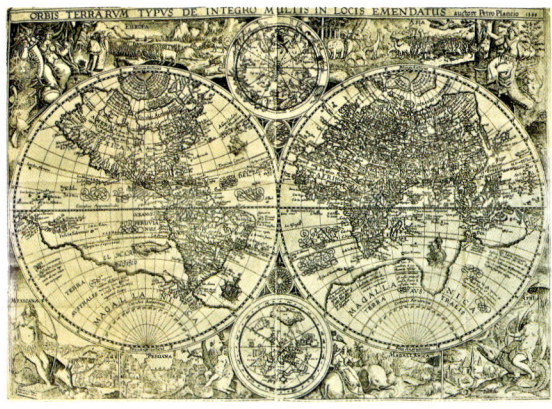

Map of the world by Peter Plancius
INTERNET ARCHIVE BOOK IMAGES

All music ... should have no other end or aim than the glory of God and the refreshment of the soul.

—JOHANN SEBASTIAN BACH

Great Questions of the Church

HOW DO WE KNOW WHAT'S REAL?

In the middle of the seventeenth century, a French-Dutch philosopher and mathematician named René Descartes (1596–1650) caused a great stir by saying philosophy should begin by doubting everything. Even things that seem real, he thought, could simply be a dream. Ultimately, he wanted to find a solid foundation for truth. He concluded that he could doubt everything except for the fact he was doubting. If he was doubting, that means he was thinking, and if he was thinking, he existed. He summed up this discovery in the phrase "I think, therefore I am." That was the foundation of certainty on which he thought philosophy and science should build—the self.

Christians were divided about Descartes's teachings. Some thought it was a good way to prove God's existence by using their reason. For others, this logic was problematic because it made human reason the judge of God's existence and character.

The Dutch theologians Gisbertus Voetius and Petrus van Mastricht (1630–1706) were some of the strongest voices of their time against the teachings of Descartes and especially of his followers. Voetius and van Mastricht taught that God's revelation should always be above reason.

René Descartes
WIKIMEDIA COMMONS

THE ENLIGHTENMENT

Descartes's teachings were part of a shift of ideas that is often called the **Enlightenment** because it was seen as an effort to rediscover the light of reason that—according to Enlightenment thinkers—was appreciated in ancient Greece and Rome and forgotten in the Middle Ages. Modern historians, however, don't think this is correct because during the Middle Ages, an age of great discoveries, reason was highly valued.

Inspired by Descartes's method of doubt, some Enlightenment thinkers questioned anything people had generally accepted, including the miracles and prophecies in the Bible, and refused anything that couldn't be accepted by reason. Since this was also a time of great scientific discoveries, many people thought the human mind could find answers even to things the Bible presents as mysteries.

Others, inspired by a Dutch philosopher named Baruch Spinoza (1632–1677), believed that God and nature are really one thing and God is in everything that is created. In both cases, the authority of the Bible was challenged as it had never been before.

Francis Turretin
RIJKSMUSEUM

Gisbertus Voetius
RIJKSMUSEUM

Petrus van Mastricht
RIJKSMUSEUM

IS THEOLOGY PRACTICAL?

As scholars worked hard to explain biblical teachings, some tried to answer a question that had been asked since the Middle Ages: Is theology practical? In other words, why do we want to know more about God? Will this knowledge help us in our daily lives? Or are we just trying to know more, whether it helps us or not?

Francis Turretin said it is a little of both. We want to know God more because the Bible encourages us to do so and because we are naturally interested in the One who made us, saved us, and is keeping us from day to day. But the more we know who God is and what He has done and is doing, the more we want to love and worship Him.

A biblical knowledge of the doctrine of the Trinity is a good example of how learning about God moves us to action. In a book called *Communion with the Triune God*, John Owen showed how this knowledge can help Christians have a clearer idea of the God they worship and can make their prayers, their reading of the Bible, and their daily lives much more meaningful.

Think about It

- Some people, like the Socinians, wanted to make theology completely practical by focusing on what Christians must do and avoiding the mysteries of God's Word, such as the Trinity and the two natures of Christ. Explain how it would be difficult to really love and obey God if you don't know anything about Him.

- If you erased from the Bible any teaching that makes God mysterious and hard to understand and kept only the portions that seem most practical in your daily life, could you call yourself a Christian? Why or why not? What kind of God would be left?

- If you start by doubting everything, how could there ever be an end to your doubting? What would be a better foundation for knowing truth?

- Why would God's revelation be more reliable than our own minds?

What God says deserves more credit than the musings of humans whose rational abilities are fallible.
—PETRUS VAN MASTRICHT

A TROUBLED CENTURY • 117

Settlers in the New World

Until the sixteenth century, most explorers and conquerors of Central and South America were sponsored by the Spanish government. They also moved north, as far as the regions of today's California and Florida. In time, however, other Europeans moved to the Americas, particularly North America, founding settlements or colonies.

Many of these settlers came to America for business and trade. Some looked for a place where they could worship freely and raise their families without the problems, pressures, and wars they had experienced in Europe.

SPANISH EMPIRE

NORTH AMERICA, 1601–1700

1607 — A group of 104 Englishmen start a colony in Virginia. They name it Jamestown after King James I. This became the first permanent English settlement in North America.

1620 — A group of Christians, later known as Pilgrim Fathers, leaves England on a ship named the *Mayflower*. They land in Plymouth, Massachusetts, where they found a colony.

1624 — Dutch settlers found the colony of New Amsterdam, which the British renamed New York in 1664.

1630 — John Winthrop leads a group of Puritans to found the Massachusetts Bay Colony, the second major New England settlement.

1634 — English settlers are the first to arrive on St. Clements Island, Maryland.

1636 — Roger Williams founds Providence, Rhode Island.

1663 — John Eliot publishes the first Bible in the language of the Native Americans of Massachusetts. This is also the first complete Bible published in America.

1681 — William Penn founds the Province of Pennsylvania.

A TROUBLED CENTURY

The landing of the Pilgrims at Plymouth
WIKIMEDIA COMMONS

LOOKING FOR A NEW START

The first Europeans to arrive in North America for religious reasons were probably Huguenots, who settled in Fort Caroline (near modern Jacksonville, Florida) in 1564. Their colony didn't last long because the Spanish, who had taken over most of Florida, destroyed their fort and hung everyone they found inside. Then the Spanish founded a colony named St. Augustine, which became the oldest permanent settlement in what is now the United States. The Spanish commander gave King Philip II (1527–1598) two reasons for this massacre: the Huguenots had built the fort without the king's permission and "were scattering the despicable Lutheran doctrine in these Provinces." The natives, who had been fascinated by the French psalms the Huguenots sang, continued to sing portions of them as "code words" to determine whether foreigners who arrived on their lands were French, whom they considered friendly, or Spanish, who had so far acted violently.

The most famous group of immigrants who moved to America for religious freedom arrived in Plymouth, Massachusetts, in 1620. They are often known as the Pilgrim Fathers. A second, similar group of Puritans settled in the Massachusetts Bay Colony in 1630, led by John Winthrop (1606–1676). Their goal was to be an example to others by building a biblical Christian community that they described as "a city on a hill." They encountered many obstacles to that dream not only because humans are sinners no matter where they are but also because they didn't all agree on how the church should be governed. For example, some people wanted to be completely separate from the Church of England, and some didn't. After a while, some of the people started to move to colonies where other people shared their ideas.

The Pilgrims in Massachusetts were Congregationalists. Most Christians in Virginia, North and South Carolina, and Georgia were Anglicans. The Scottish settlers in Nova Scotia, Canada, were Presbyterians; and some of the Germans in Pennsylvania were Lutheran. Most settlers were Protestants. Only Maryland was founded as a refuge for Roman Catholics, who couldn't worship freely in Protestant England.

Rhode Island was an unusual colony. It was founded by a Puritan minister, Roger Williams (ca. 1603–1683), after he had some disagreements with the Massachusetts settlers about the nature of government. The colony became a refuge for other dissenters, such as the Quakers. Williams welcomed them, even though he disagreed with their beliefs. He also helped to establish the first Baptist church in America and was committed to bringing love and the gospel to Native Americans. Williams's writings on religious freedom and the separation of church and state became very influential.

A colony founded specifically for Quakers was Pennsylvania, established in 1681 by William Penn (1644–1718). Over time, they became instrumental in the abolition of slavery.

More Men and Women of the Seventeenth-Century Church

PURITANS IN THE NEW WORLD

JOHN COTTON (1585–1652) was one of the most influential Puritan pastors in New England. His children's catechism, *Milk for Babes*, was commonly used until the end of the nineteenth century. One of his main contributions in New England was his emphasis on God's grace.

WILLIAM BRADFORD (1590–1657) was one of the founders of the Pilgrim settlement in Plymouth, Massachusetts, and one of the main drafters of the Mayflower Compact, the first independent constitution in America. His *History of Plymouth Plantation* is important to help people understand the Pilgrims' difficult sea voyage to America and the challenges they had to face in their new lands.

JOHN ELIOT (1604–1690) was one of the first missionaries to the Native Americans. He devoted his whole life to this cause, learning the language of the natives of Massachusetts so he could preach and translate. He translated the Bible into that language and compiled a grammar book. This was the first version of the Bible in a Native American language. He established fourteen villages of Christian Native Americans for a total of about eleven hundred people and defended them against those who tried to rob them of their lands. He also trained Native American pastors. The **tracts** he published about his missionary work did much to inspire other Christians to take up the same task.

ANNE BRADSTREET (1612–1672) was an English poet who immigrated to Massachusetts. She was the first woman to publish a book of poems in America. Many of her poems describe her faith in God's providence that continues to uphold Christians during troubles and difficulties.

A plaque placed in front of John Cotton's house in Boston, Massachusetts

DADEROT, WIKIMEDIA COMMONS

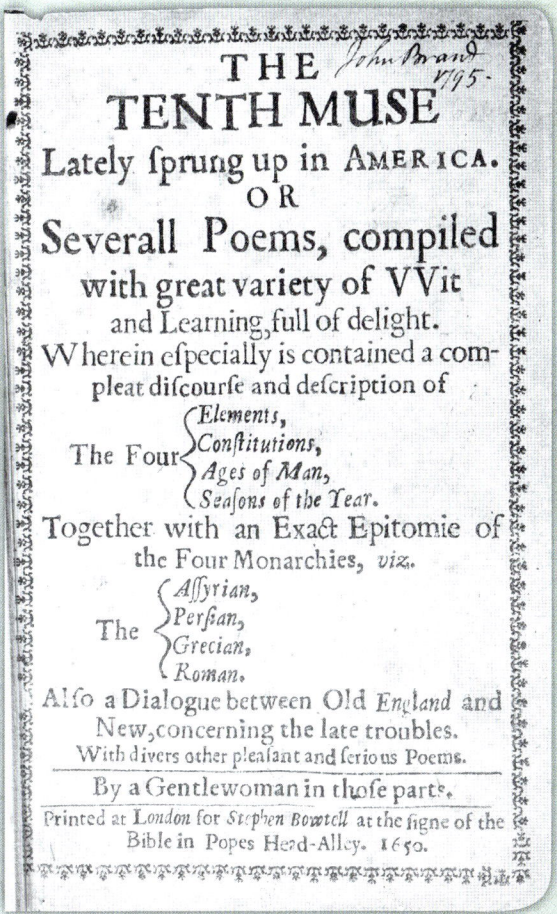

The frontispiece of Anne Bradstreet's book of poems, *The Tenth Muse*

BEINECKE RARE BOOK & MANUSCRIPT LIBRARY, YALE UNIVERSITY

A TROUBLED CENTURY

Revivals and Reason

For Protestants, the eighteenth century was marked by religious revivals—times when God's Spirit seemed to work in an extraordinary way to bring a group of people to a greater commitment to God. This happened in different ways in many countries.

But it was also a time of new challenges to the church—a time when many turned away from God's revelation and tried to explain life on the basis of human reason.

ROMANIA

EUROPE, 1700–1789

1701	The Church of England founds the Society for the Propagation of the Gospel in Foreign Parts.
1702–1704	Some Huguenots fight a war of rebellion and self-defense against the government.
1715	Taking advantage of a change of rulers, some Huguenot pastors meet to discuss the future and unity of the French churches.
1718	The republication of *The Marrow of Modern Divinity* causes a controversy in the Church of Scotland.
1721	Czar Peter I of Russia replaces the Orthodox patriarch with a synod of bishops supervised by a government official.
1722	Count Nikolaus Ludwig von Zinzendorf starts a Moravian community of faith.
1733	Some Scottish pastors start a new branch of the Church of Scotland. This separation is called the First Secession.
1737	Howell Harris and Daniel Rowland become leading preachers in the Welsh revival.
1757	Pope Benedict XIV allows a translation of the Bible into Italian for the first time since the Council of Trent. But the church doesn't encourage reading it, and most Italians don't know how to read.
1764	Empress Catherine the Great of Russia strips the Orthodox church of all its properties and turns it into a government institution.
1773	Pope Clement XIV ends the religious order of the Jesuits and removes them from the countries where they had founded missions.
1788	The British government sends a group of over one thousand settlers, including 778 prisoners, to New South Wales, on the east coast of Australia. This is the first official British colony in that continent. The colonists build a church under the guidance of their chaplain, Richard Johnson.

A TIME OF REVIVALS

French Revival—Huguenots and Camisards

In 1702 some of the Huguenots who had stayed in France after the Edict of Nantes was canceled started a war of rebellion and self-defense against the government. They were known as Camisards because they wore white shirts (*camisa* means "shirt" in the language of a certain French region) so that they could recognize each other at night.

The Camisards were few in comparison with the king's troops, but they knew their areas and were ready to die for their freedom. To fight back, Roman Catholic authorities formed their own group of revolutionary fighters. The war caused many losses on both sides. It ended in 1704, but uprisings continued until 1710, after the Camisards' main leaders had died.

King Louis XIV died in 1715, leaving the throne to his five-year-old great-grandson Louis XV (1710–1774), who ruled through a relative until he came of legal age. Taking advantage of this time of change, some Huguenot pastors met secretly to discuss the future of the French churches. The main leader was nineteen-year-old Antoine Court (1696–1760).

Court promoted a reformation without violence. He wanted the churches to be well organized, each supervised by a group of elders who would meet at regular times. He also wanted to have well-trained pastors instead of preachers who relied on messages they believed they received from God. To this purpose, he founded a college for French pastors in Lausanne, Switzerland.

The Tower of Constance in Aigues-Mortes, France, where many Huguenot women, including Marie Durand, was imprisoned for thirty-eight years

INGO MEILING, WIKIMEDIA COMMONS

Some Men and Women of the Eighteenth-Century Church

OTHER EIGHTEENTH-CENTURY HUGUENOTS

PIERRE DURAND (1700–1732) was a Huguenot pastor and friend of Antoine Court. He trained in Switzerland and returned to France to preach to the churches that met in secrecy. The authorities finally caught him and executed him in 1732.

MARIE DURAND (1711–1776), Pierre's sister, was imprisoned for thirty-eight years simply for being related to a pastor. She had many opportunities to leave the prison. All she had to do was become Roman Catholic, something she refused to do. From prison, she wrote many letters and helped some influential Frenchmen understand the injustice done to Protestants.

PAUL RABAUT (1718–1794) was one of the main pastors of the French church. He had to live in hiding for thirty years, preaching in different places and encouraging the churches. He talked to many influential men to convince them to allow Protestants to worship freely. He also defended the Reformed catechisms and confessions against those who tried to make them more appealing to modern philosophers.

> *I will not reject a mystery for the only reason that it cannot be understood.*
> —PAUL RABAUT

A German Revival—The Moravians

Since 1618, Bohemia (in today's Czech Republic) had been a Roman Catholic country. Some groups of Protestants, however, continued to survive. One of them, known as the Hidden Seed, had been living secretly in a northern area of the region known as Moravia.

In 1722 Count Nikolaus Ludwig von Zinzendorf (1700–1760), a follower of Lutheran Pietism, helped some of these Moravians to settle in his lands and form the community of faith he had always envisioned. They called it *Herrnhut* (the Lord's watch). Soon, other people joined them, and other communities tried to follow their example.

Nikolaus Ludwig von Zinzendorf
HAMBURG STATE AND UNIVERSITY LIBRARY

After a revival in 1727, the Moravians became committed to missionary work. In 1732, in answer to a plea from Anton Ulrich, who was born a slave in the Caribbean and had siblings and friends enslaved there, *Herrnhut* sent its first missionaries, Johann Leonhard Dober (1706–1766) and David Nitschmann (ca. 1695–1772), to the island of St. Thomas in the West Indies to present the gospel to the African slaves.

Another important Moravian was Rebecca Protten (1718–1780), who is remembered as the first African American female missionary. A freed slave from the Caribbean Islands, she brought the gospel to other female slaves. She was mistreated by slave owners who feared that missionaries would encourage the slaves to rebel. Later in life, she and her husband ran a school on the Gold Coast of Africa. To best communicate with the slaves, Dober and Nitschmann were willing to become slaves themselves. Although they were never taken as slaves, they lived with them in a hut on the plantation.

By the time Zinzendorf died in 1760, 226 missionaries had been sent to 28 mission fields. Unlike previous missionaries, these were not pastors or monks but ordinary people with ordinary jobs who often continued their professions wherever they went and spent the rest of their time talking to people about Christ.

They often inspired other Christians by their example. In one situation, when the Moravian George Schmidt (1709–1785) arrived as a missionary to South Africa, he found that the Dutch preachers who were there were ministering only to their Dutch community, without reaching out to the local Khoisan people. In fact, the Dutch objected to his presence and to his methods of praying in public. After six years of ministering alone to the Khoisan, he returned to Europe. But seven years later, another group of Moravians founded a mission in the same place where he had lived.

Like the Pietists, the Moravians encouraged deep feelings and emotions. But they didn't stir these up by looking inside themselves—at least not in the beginning. They did it by frequent reminders of Christ's sacrifice, which moved them to quiet tears of devotion.

The Moravians left a wonderful example of love and concern for those who had not heard the good news of the gospel and inspired many missionaries after them. By the end of the century, more Christians recognized the importance of bringing the gospel to other parts of the world and to be more organized in their efforts.

The Moravians started to produce these beautiful Christmas stars in the nineteenth century—initially as a school project. They are now popular all over the world. This image is from a Moravian star sale in Erfurt, Germany.

WIKIMEDIA COMMONS

The Welsh Eighteenth-Century Revival

The conversion of two young preachers, Daniel Rowland (ca. 1711–1790) and Howel Harris (1714–1773), in 1735 is usually considered the start of the eighteenth-century Welsh Revival. Because of their strict discipline and their emphasis on personal faith, those who joined this revival were nicknamed **Methodists**. It was not meant as a compliment. It was like calling someone picky.

Rowland and Harris were powerful preachers who encouraged people to repent of their sins, meditate on God's love in Christ, and let His Spirit move in their lives instead of simply going to church out of habit or upbringing. They stressed the need for faith in the heart as well as the head. Like the Pietists, they organized local meetings, called societies, to encourage each other in studying the Bible and growing in their Christian lives.

Welsh Methodists stayed faithful to the Reformed confessions. They also placed great importance on singing, so much so that over three thousand hymns were composed in Welsh during this period.

For the most part, they remained within the Church of England. They formed a separate **denomination** in 1811 only because the Church of England was reluctant to ordain Methodists.

Daniel Rowland, from an illustration in the *Gospel Magazine*, July 1778
WIKIMEDIA COMMONS

William Williams
INTERNET IMAGE ARCHIVE

Thomas Charles
INTERNET IMAGE ARCHIVE

More Men and Women of the Welsh Revival

GRIFFITH JONES (1684–1761) was a Welsh minister of the Church of England and a powerful preacher. He founded a system of circulating schools to teach people to read the Bible in Welsh. Each school stayed in one place for three months. At the time of Jones's death, over two hundred thousand people—nearly half the population of Wales at that time—had learned to read through this system.

WILLIAM WILLIAMS (1717–1791), also known as Pantycelyn, composed over eight hundred beautiful and moving hymns in Welsh. The most famous of these translated into English is "Guide Me, O Thou Great Jehovah." He is considered one of the greatest poets in Welsh history.

ANN GRIFFITHS (1776–1805) was also a poet and hymn writer. Her poems express well the Welsh Methodists' love for Christ and desire to know Him better.

THOMAS CHARLES (1755–1814), pastor at Bala, continued the work of the early revivalists in both preaching and establishing schools. He was one of the founders of the Bible Society, overseeing the publication of a Welsh Bible and making sure it was distributed among the people.

MARY JONES (1784–1864), being poor, had to save money for six years to buy a Bible. At age fifteen, she walked twenty-six miles to purchase a copy from Thomas Charles. Her story became an inspiration.

The English Revival

By the eighteenth century, many Christians in England had drifted from both the passion of the Reformers and the devotion of the Puritans. Some people thought it was time for a religious revival.

One of these people was John Wesley (1703–1791), son of a minister in the Church of England. In 1729 he took over the leadership of a group of Christians that had been formed by his brother Charles Wesley (1707–1788) and who shared his concerns. They studied the Bible and encouraged one another to be faithful to the Lord. Like in Wales, they were given the name Methodists. Charles wrote hundreds of hymns. "Hark! The Herald Angels Sing" and "And Can It Be That I Should Gain" are particularly famous.

Later, John Wesley wrote that despite all these efforts, he had not really understood his salvation in Christ. He came to this understanding in 1735 during a short missionary journey to the Native Americans in Georgia, when he was influenced by a group of Moravians he met on his way. Wesley's beliefs were confirmed when in 1738 he heard someone read Luther's commentary on Romans and felt his heart "strangely warmed."

Wesley began to preach with conviction. After meeting George Whitefield (1714–1770), who preached in the open air, he decided to follow his example. This practice allowed him to reach people who would rarely go to church.

Once when Whitefield prepared to take a trip to North America, he asked Wesley to take over his tasks. Wesley was moved by the reaction to the gospel of a group of miners. It was a message they rarely heard since they lived far from any church. From then on, for the next fifty years, Wesley traveled thousands of miles, mostly on horseback, to bring the gospel to other people in similar circumstances. He never left the Church of England but saw his work as a supplement and a revival. After his death, however, the Methodists became a separate denomination.

John Wesley
LIBRARY OF CONGRESS

Charles Wesley
NEW YORK PUBLIC LIBRARY

George Whitefield
NEW YORK PUBLIC LIBRARY

THE WORLD IS MY PARISH

When a man asked John Wesley why he didn't teach in a college or pastor a church, he replied, "The world is my **parish**." What he meant is that he wanted to be free to take the gospel anywhere. Like the Pietists, he thought Christians everywhere had to be inspired to a greater devotion to Christ. During his ministry, he rode over 250,000 miles on horseback. That's like going around the equator ten times.

Great Questions of the Church

CAN WE BE PERFECT IN THIS LIFE?

In spite of their friendship, John Wesley and Whitefield had some sharp disagreements. Following the Reformed confessions, such as the Canons of Dort and the Westminster Standards, Whitefield taught that God chooses who will be saved. Wesley, instead, followed the teachings of the Arminians, insisting that God would not be loving if He chose to save only some people. He also thought that if God makes the choice, there is no point in living well or in telling others about the gospel.

In 1741 John Wesley preached a sermon with an unusual proposition. He said that the goal of this life is to reach Christian perfection. He didn't mean to say that Christians could not make mistakes. To him, perfection is reached when a person loves as God loves—so much that there is no room for evil. He called this perfection a second blessing after salvation and believed it could be reached in this life.

This was different from what Luther and other Protestant Reformers had taught, who believed that Christians are at the same time sinful and righteous in this life—sinful in themselves and righteous in Christ—and that perfection will occur only in the life to come. Some Christians, such as Whitefield, von Zinzendorf, Augustus Toplady (1740–1778), and Anne Dutton (1692–1765), believed Wesley's teaching on this issue was not biblical.

Like Whitefield, Toplady was often attacked by John Wesley for believing that God chooses the people He wants to save. When writing his famous hymn "Rock of Ages," Toplady reminded Christians that no matter how well they might behave, they are still sinners and even on their deathbed will need to cry, "Foul, I to the fountain fly; / Wash me, Savior, or I die."

John Wesley and Whitefield could have worked together much better if Wesley had not preached and published a sermon condemning Whitefield's teachings as works of the devil. Charles Wesley was saddened by this disagreement. He thought this disunity was the devil's work. But even though they didn't work together, John Wesley and Whitefield remained friends and respected each other.

Augustus Montague Toplady
INTERNET IMAGE ARCHIVE

Think about It

John Wesley thought that striving for perfection (or perfect love) was a good way to prevent laziness. Those who disagreed with him believed that gratefulness for what God has done without our help is a better motivator than duty and doesn't produce discouragement. Do you agree with Wesley or with his critics? Give an example of what best motivates you to obey.

WHAT MAY WE SING IN CHURCH?

While most people appreciated the hymns written by Charles Wesley, Isaac Watts, and John Newton, not everyone agreed about what to sing during church services. Following some of the original Protestant Reformers, some people claimed that worship should include *only* psalms and songs that are in the Bible. Since Jesus and His disciples sang psalms, the church should do the same and sing nothing else.

Other churches believed that worship can include elements that are not in the Bible as long as God didn't specifically forbid them. John Newton even wrote hymns to accompany his sermons.

Another question was raised when the German Lutheran George Frideric Handel (1685–1759) composed *Messiah*, an oratorio (musical composition) whose text was taken entirely from the Bible. As people crowded the theaters to hear it, some wondered if the words of the Bible should be sung in places of entertainment. John Newton wondered if the audience would pay more attention to the music than to the words. To remedy this problem, he preached a series of sermons based on the Bible passages included in *Messiah*.

More Men and Women of the Eighteenth-Century Church

SOME MEN AND WOMEN OF THE ENGLISH REVIVAL

ANNE DUTTON (1692–1765) saw her writing as her calling to encourage others and help them to understand God's free grace. She left behind fifty volumes of poetry, letters, hymns, treatises, and an autobiography.

Isaac Watts
UNIVERSITÄTSBIBLIOTHEK LEIPZIG

ISAAC WATTS (1674–1748) is one of the most famous hymn writers. He thought the psalms that people usually sang in churches didn't talk about Christ as clearly as the New Testament does. He based his hymns on the Bible but called them an imitation and included more mentions of Jesus. Two of his best-known hymns are "O God, Our Help in Ages Past" and "Joy to the World."

William Cowper
INTERNET IMAGE ARCHIVE

JOHN NEWTON (1725–1807) was a slave trader who became a pastor. His autobiography, *An Authentic Narrative*, is a story of God's grace that conquers even the most reluctant hearts. Later in life, he fought for the abolition of the slave trade. He and the poet **WILLIAM COWPER** (1731–1800) wrote many hymns together. Newton's best-known hymn is "Amazing Grace."

Selina Hastings
SMITHSONIAN AMERICAN ART MUSEUM, TRANSFER FROM THE ARCHIVES OF AMERICAN ART

SELINA HASTINGS, Countess of Huntington (1707–1791) was probably the most famous evangelical woman of her time. She supported many preachers, particularly George Whitefield, and financed foreign missions. She also built chapels and founded a theological college.

Olaudah Equiano
INTERNET IMAGE ARCHIVE

OLAUDAH EQUIANO (1745–1797) was taken from his African home and sold as a slave. As he was passed on from owner to owner and from country to country, he was able to study the Bible and to understand the meaning of Jesus's sacrifice for sinners. His autobiography, full of appreciation for God's providence and protection, became a best seller and helped to convince many people of the evils of slavery.

The Marrow Men

Some small things cause big changes. In 1717 the elders of the town of Auchterarder, Scotland, examined a man named William Craig to see if he was qualified to be a pastor. As usual, they asked him if he agreed with the creed of the church. They brought up a specific point in the creed that said, "It is not sound and orthodox to teach that we must forsake sin in order to our coming to Christ."

Craig said he agreed, but later he was no longer sure. Shouldn't people be willing to give up their sins before coming to Christ? So he changed his answer. Surprised by his response, the elders brought up the question to the general assembly (a group of elders and pastors chosen to make decisions that affect the whole church). The assembly agreed with Craig and changed that portion of the creed.

Thomas Boston
INTERNET IMAGE ARCHIVE

Thomas Boston (1676–1732), one of the pastors present at the assembly, disagreed with this decision. He recommended that the pastors and elders read a book he had just discovered called *The Marrow of Modern Divinity* (the words in the title mean "the main point of modern theology"). The book, published about fifty years earlier and simply signed E. F., explained the importance of letting the gospel work in people's hearts.

The following year, Boston's friend James Hog (d. ca. 1736) helped in republishing the book, which was read by many pastors. But most pastors were afraid of giving their support. They feared that people who thought that repentance and obedience were not necessary for salvation would call themselves Christians and continue to live in sin. Boston, Hog, and ten others tried to explain that there was a difference. Yes, Christians should repent of their sins and try to obey God's laws, but repentance and obedience are the *fruits* of salvation, not *conditions* people had to meet before they can come to Christ.

Still, the general assembly banned the book and started to look with suspicion at the twelve men who had supported it, later known as the Marrow Men.

The Scottish Secession

At the same time, the Church of Scotland had another serious problem. Normally each church was supported by a local family who owned the property the church was on, and these rich families thought they had the right to choose the pastors for the churches. Because of this, many pastors were simply the favorites of some family and not the best for their churches.

In 1733 one of the Marrow Men, Ebenezer Erskine (1680–1754), decided that the only way to preserve the pure preaching of the gospel was to start a separate branch of the Church of Scotland. His brother, Ralph Erskine (1685–1752), who was both a pastor and poet, joined him later, as did other pastors.

It was not an easy decision. In those days, people didn't just start their own denomination, at least not in Europe. The Church of Scotland was supposed to include every Christian in that nation. But Erskine and others were convinced that the problems had become too serious.

The pastors who left the Church of Scotland lost their financial support and had to continue on their own. This break is now known as the First **Secession** because a Second Secession happened in 1761 for some of the same reasons.

Ebenezer Erskine
INTERNET IMAGE ARCHIVE

Protestant Missions to India

Like the Moravians, other European Protestants began to travel to different parts of the world to spread the gospel. Some were sponsored by rulers, as in the case of the German Lutherans Bartholomäus Ziegenbalg (1682–1719) and Heinrich Plütschau (1676–1752), who were sent by King Frederick IV of Denmark (1671–1730) to be the first Protestant missionaries to India. In spite of initial opposition (they were imprisoned for four months), Ziegenbalg and Plütschau set up printing presses and schools and trained local evangelists in the Tamil Nadu state. The first ordained Indian preacher was named Aaron.

Another Lutheran, Christian Frederick Schwartz (1726–1798), continued the work in Tamil Nadu, training local missionaries and sending them to other parts of India. Some of his most famous disciples are Satyanathan Pillai, who became a pastor in Thanjavur, Tamil Nadu; Rasa Clorinda (ca. 1750–ca. 1806), a widow who built a church and a school in the same town; and Vedanayagam Sastri (1774–1864), who became the official court poet for Prince Serfoji II (1777–1832), also a student of Schwartz. Vedanayagam's beautiful presentation of the gospel story in verse was often sung to well-known Tamil tunes.

First Church in Australia

In 1788 eleven British ships arrived in New South Wales, on the east coast of Australia, carrying about one thousand settlers. Of these, 778 were prisoners shipped to Australia by the British government as a solution to the problem of overcrowded prisons. The settlers raised a British flag, formally establishing the first European colony on the continent.

The group's chaplain, Richard Johnson (1753–1827), held the first worship service under some trees in Sydney Cove, where the group had settled. The ship's captain who became governor, Arthur Phillip (1738–1814), named the place after the British home secretary. The native people, the Aborigines, called it Warrane. Today it is the city of Sydney.

Building a church took a long time because the lieutenant governor who took Phillip's place didn't see it as a priority. Eventually, Johnson and some of the prisoners were able to build a church out of wood, and the following governor, John Hunter (1737–1821), refunded him for his expenses. Besides preaching and taking care of other common duties of chaplains (such as performing baptisms, marriages, and burials), Johnson worked toward the education of the prisoners and took care of the sick. One of the prisoners described him as "a physician both of soul and body."

Both Johnson and Phillip established a good relationship with the native population, preached the gospel to them, and gave help to those in need. Johnson and his wife named their first daughter Milbah, a name used by the native people.

A monument to Bartholomäus Ziegenbalg in Tranquebar, in today's Tamil Nadu, South India, commemorating the three hundredth anniversary of his mission. Ziegenbalg produced a valuable translation in Tamil, built a church that is still standing, and trained and ordained the first Indian pastor, Aaron.

CHRISTA GÄBLER-KAINDL, WIKIMEDIA COMMONS

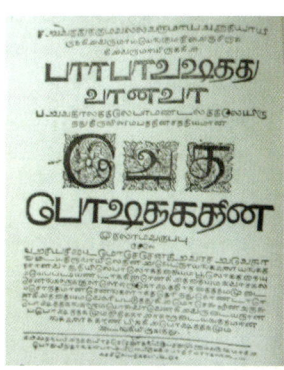

First page of a Tamil New Testament printed in Tranquebar by Bartholomäus Ziegenbalg. The missionaries thought that Tamil was a difficult language and gave thanks to God for allowing them to learn it quickly.

WIKIMEDIA COMMONS

Great Questions of the Church

HOW CAN GOD ALLOW PAIN AND SUFFERING?

In 1755 a terrible earthquake destroyed most of the city of Lisbon, Portugal. It was followed by a tsunami. Together, these disasters killed at least ten thousand people. The French philosopher Francois-Marie Arouet, better known as Voltaire (1694–1778), had already been wondering how a good God could allow catastrophes and wars, and this tragedy was the last straw. He didn't understand other philosophers who insisted that this is the best of all possible worlds, where some evil is necessary to bring out the good. There is just too much evil, he thought.

He published a novel, *Candide*, in which he made fun of those optimistic philosophers. The novel ends with Candide's conclusion that instead of trying to understand things, "we must cultivate our garden." What was important for Voltaire is to do good to others.

This went along with the teachings of some people who said that God had simply created the world, put its laws in place, and then let it run by itself. If that's true, no one can blame God for the evils in this world, and each person has to work hard to make a better world. People who believe that God is indifferent to the world are known as **deists**.

The German Immanuel Kant (1724–1804), who is considered the most influential philosopher of the Enlightenment, came to a similar conclusion. Born to a Pietist family, he summarized Christianity as a set of rules for acting well. In fact, the only way to know God, he said, is through our inner sense of duty, which he called "the moral law within." To him, that was the important thing—not a revelation God gave outside of us. He thought people should do what is right simply because it is right.

Immanuel Kant
WELLCOME LIBRARY, LONDON

French philosopher Jean-Jacques Rousseau (1712–1778) agreed that human beings could follow a moral law inside of them. In fact, he believed that people are basically good. If someone grew up alone in a forest, Rousseau said, that person would never learn to envy others or try to take what they have. "Man was born free, and everywhere he is in chains," Rousseau wrote at the beginning of one of his books. The only way to be free in a society is to live where everyone wants to do what's best for the community. This sounded good, but what if someone refused to do what is best? Rousseau thought they should be forced to do it—"forced to be free." While he meant well, when his ideas were put into practice after the French Revolution, they resulted in what is known as the Reign of Terror.

Rousseau influenced many people who began to see heroes as men and women who fought every boundary of society. He also promoted the idea that populations who live far from civilization are kinder and purer than others.

All these men asked important questions. Sadly, the church was not always ready to answer, as we read in one of Rousseau's writings: "It is asked, he says, of the citizens of Geneva, if Jesus Christ is God. They dare not answer. It is asked if He is a mere man. They are embarrassed and will not say they think so. They are alarmed, terrified, they come together, they discuss, they are in agitation and often earnest consultation and conference. All vanishes into ambiguity [lack of clarity], and they say neither yes or no."

A bust of Voltaire, created two months before his death

WALTERS ART MUSEUM, BALTIMORE

An eighteenth-century portrait of Jean-Jacques Rousseau by French artist Pierre Michel Alix

THE MET MUSEUM

Think about It

- It's natural to feel confused when we see much pain and evil in the world. It's also natural to feel annoyed at people who insist on being optimistic without acknowledging the depth of someone's pain. Even the Psalms are full of difficult questions to God, begging Him to put an end to suffering (for example, see Psalm 2:1 or Psalm 13:1). How can these psalms become a model for our prayers? How can they help us to be more compassionate toward others?

- Why do you think there is so much evil and suffering in the world? Read the first three chapters of Genesis. How did God create human beings? Where did evil come from? What remedy did God provide?

- Looking at all the pain and evil in the world, Voltaire concluded that God has chosen to step back and leave it all to us. Find some passages in the Bible that show the opposite.

- If you could travel back to Geneva in Rousseau's day, how would you answer his questions about Jesus?

- The people in Geneva who didn't seem to know what they believed about Jesus ended up agreeing with the philosophers that the Bible is only a manual on how to be good and avoiding anything that cannot be explained by reason. Either they were right, or the Bible is a story of how God has been saving a people who have lost the ability to be truly good. Which of these two answers do you find in the Bible? Which one gives you more comfort? How do people who agree with the first answer read the Bible differently from those who agree with the second one?

- Do you agree with Rousseau's statement that every human being is born free? In explaining your answer, think about the following questions: Are babies free? Are they naturally good? Are most children naturally willing to share, or is it something that parents have to teach them? Give some other examples that prove or disprove Rousseau's ideas.

- Name another man in church history who taught that human beings are basically good.

- If you force someone to be free, is that person really free? Explain your answer.

A TIME OF REVIVALS • 133

Changes in the Russian Church

Until 1453 the city of Constantinople saw itself as the Second Rome. After the Ottomans took over Constantinople, Moscow, the capital of Russia, saw itself as the Third Rome and the protector of Christianity in Eastern Europe. The ruler of Moscow took on the title of czar, a variation of caesar, which was used by Roman emperors. Ivan IV (1530–1584), known as Ivan the Terrible, was the first Russian czar.

More than ever before, the church in Russia was faced with a question that had concerned the Western church: How can church and state work together? Most of the time, the czars wanted greater oversight over the church, while the church wanted to be independent. This created many arguments.

Czar Peter I
LIBRARY OF CONGRESS

Another problem had to do with finances. Like in other nations, the Russian government had to deal with many expenses, particularly to defend the country. The czars didn't think it was fair that the churches could collect money from believers and didn't give any to the state. They liked the way some Western nations were working, with rulers supervising the churches in their country.

Czar Peter I (1672–1725), known as Peter the Great, was particularly attracted to Western governments and thought that Russia could learn from them. In 1721, in the course of a series of church reforms, he replaced the Orthodox patriarch with a group of ten (later twelve) bishops supervised by a government official. The group became known as the Most Holy Synod.

Although the czar didn't claim authority in matters of faith, his synod controlled the bishops and had a say in how the church managed its organization and properties. As it often happened, the changes he imposed were for the good of the economy, the state, and the military and not for the well-being of believers.

In 1764 Empress Catherine II (1729–1796), also known as Catherine the Great, took the reform one step further and declared that all church properties belonged to the state. The church became a government institution supported by the state. If a church or monastery didn't seem profitable to the state, it didn't receive support and was forced to close. In the end, only one-third of the monasteries survived.

She allowed the Jesuits to stay in her country after Pope Clement XIV (1705–1774), pressured by other European rulers who feared they were becoming too powerful, put an end to their order in 1773 and removed them from the nations where they had founded missions.

She also invited a large group of German farmers to Russia by giving each family a large plot of land (about one hundred times the size of a football field) by the Volga River and a loan to get started. German by birth, Catherine believed that Germans were excellent farmers and could bring life to rough regions of the country. They did. But they also brought their Protestant worship, their Bibles, and their hymnals.

Catherine the Great
WELLCOME LIBRARY, LONDON

134 • A TIME OF REVIVALS

The Orthodox Church under Ottoman Rule

In the meantime, the Orthodox Church in what used to be the Byzantine Empire had to adapt to new conditions under the Muslim Ottoman rule. While the Ottomans allowed Orthodox Christians to keep worshiping, they were considered inferior citizens, were forced to pay heavy taxes, and were not allowed to share their faith with Muslims or speak negatively about Islam. If any of them converted to Islam, they were not allowed to turn back. Those who did were given three chances to repent, and if they persisted, they were put to death.

Still, the church continued to faithfully preach, week after week, understanding that diligent preaching and the distribution of Bibles and catechisms was essential to keep believers from yielding to the temptation to convert to Islam in order to live an easier life.

An important Christian at this time was Antim of Iberia (1650–1716), a native of the ancient kingdom of Georgia, who founded the first printing press in his land and printed the first translation of the gospel in Georgian. He then moved to Romania, where he set up a publishing center, supplying the Orthodox Church in different locations with Bibles and other books. When the prince who had invited him to Romania died, the new prince had Antim exiled. The Ottoman troops then drowned him in a river while he was on the way to his destination.

THE PRINCIPALITY OF TRANSYLVANIA

Sandwiched between the large Ottoman Empire and the strong Habsburg Empire was the small Principality of Transylvania, which struggled to stay independent in both politics and religion. Since the Protestant Reformation, it had been mostly a Reformed country, and its princes fought as long as they could to keep it this way. Eventually, however, it became absorbed first by the Muslim Ottomans and then by the Roman Catholic Habsburgs.

The Protestants, reduced to about one-third of the population, persevered in their faith. One example of this perseverance was the Countess Kata Bethlen (1700–1759), who, in spite of the opposition of Roman Catholic relatives and many other problems she had to endure, built Reformed churches and schools and supported Reformed pastors, authors, and scientists, such as Peter Bod (1712–1769). Bod's writings have helped other scholars understand the history of the church in Transylvania.

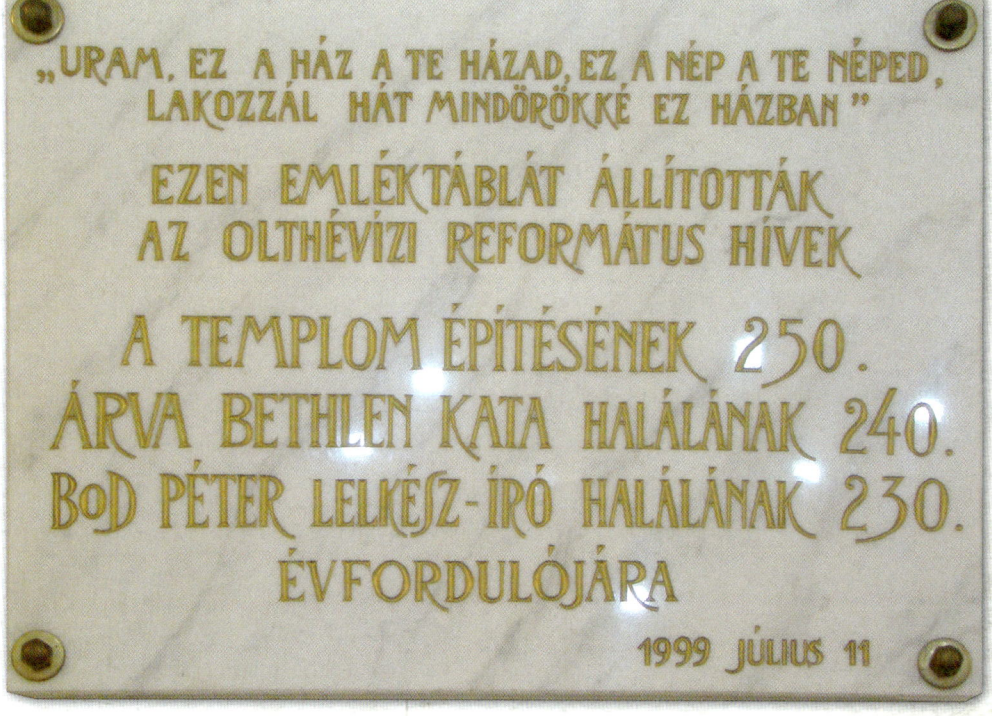

This plaque on the wall of the Reformed church in Hoghiz, Romania, marks the anniversary of the deaths of Kata Bethlen and Peter Bod. The inscription on the top says, "Lord, this House is your house, this people is your people, so dwell in this house forever."

ȚETCU MIRCEA RAREȘ, WIKIMEDIA COMMONS

NORTH AMERICA, 1701–1788

1737 — Jonathan Edwards writes *A Faithful Narrative of the Surprising Work of God*.

1740 — George Whitefield preaches in North America, creating a great stir.

1746 — Jonathan Edwards writes *A Treatise concerning Religious Affections*.

1749 — Jonathan Edwards's biography of the missionary David Brainerd inspires other missionaries in both North America and Europe.

1773 — Phillis Wheatley becomes the first published African-American woman.

1775 — The American Revolutionary War begins.

1776 — The American colonists sign the Declaration of Independence.

1777 — Vermont becomes the first independent state in the world to abolish slavery.

Atlantic Ocean

The Great Awakening

The American colonies, like England, experienced a time of great religious revival. Much of it was inspired by the preaching of pastors like Jonathan Edwards (1703–1758), one of the best-known American theologians and preachers of that time, and George Whitefield, probably the leading evangelist of his day, who made frequent visits from England.

A TIME OF REVIVALS • 137

Whitefield and Edwards tried to help people remember their sinful nature and their need for a Savior and then told them how God had met that need by sending His Son. Their sermons brought people to tears, and many were converted and became spiritually mature in their Christian lives.

Recognizing this as a work of God's Spirit, in 1737 Edwards wrote a booklet titled *A Faithful Narrative of the Surprising Work of God* in order to encourage preachers in other parts of the world. This revival in the American colonies became known as the Great Awakening. Edwards's book became influential because other pastors wanted a revival in their churches. Even John Wesley and other pastors in England read this book eagerly.

Not every pastor liked this type of revival. Some thought that people were getting too emotional. They were afraid that people would get excited over a new preacher and later go back to their old habits or that they would confuse emotions with real religion. In response to this, Jonathan Edwards wrote a booklet titled *A Treatise concerning Religious Affections*. He agreed that emotions are not always a sign of the work of God's Spirit, yet he strongly defended the revivals as a great and extraordinary saving work of God.

A bigger concern was that some preachers of the Awakening discouraged the people's faith in their pastors. One man, Gilbert Tennent (1703–1764), preached a sermon titled "On the Danger of an Unconverted Ministry." In his view, preachers who opposed the revival were not true Christians. This caused a lot of doubts and divisions.

Soon American Christians were split between supporters of the Awakening (known as New Side) and those who had some serious objections (Old Side). One of the leaders of the Old Side was a preacher named John Thomson (1690–1753). In addition to disagreeing with the unkind judgments that had been made about faithful preachers, he opposed some of the methods of New Side preachers, especially preaching in order to bring about a revival. He thought preachers should just preach the gospel and let God work in people's lives.

In spite of these arguments, the Great Awakening generated a large number of genuine conversions. It also encouraged some preachers to bring the gospel to groups of people who didn't always have a chance to hear it, such as the Native Americans and the slaves.

Along with an account of the revival in Northampton, Massachusetts, Jonathan Edwards wrote many other books, reminding people of the main themes of the Reformation, such as the power of sin and the need for God's grace.

YALE UNIVERSITY ART GALLERY

Missions to the Native Americans

Missions to the Native Americans flourished during the Great Awakening. One of the main missionaries was David Brainerd (1718–1747), who devoted his life to this cause until he died of **tuberculosis**. Brainerd was a good friend of Jonathan Edwards, who housed him in the last months of Brainerd's life and wrote a biography based on his diary. This biography, published in 1749, became Edwards's most popular book and inspired other missionaries in both North America and Europe.

Few people know that Edwards, near the end of his life, was also a missionary to the Native Americans. He served at a Mohawk mission for seven years and sent his ten-year-old son Jonathan (1745–1801), who lived for a while with Native Americans, became fluent in Mohican and Mohawk, and served as an interpreter for a missionary team, to the Onohquaga tribe, near New York.

Another important missionary was Samson Occom (1723–1792), a member of the Mohegan nation and one of the first ordained Native American pastors. He created a community of Christians from different Native American tribes called the Brothertown Indians. The community still exists today and celebrates Samson Occom Day every July 14.

The Battle of Lexington, one of the first battles in the American Revolution
LIBRARY OF CONGRESS

The American Revolutionary War

The American Revolutionary War began in 1775 after many years of protest by the American colonists against the high taxes the British government required them to pay. The next year, some representatives of the colonists signed the Declaration of Independence from Britain.

Not all Christians agreed with this war. Some people, known as Loyalists, thought it was not biblical because the Bible told Christians to obey those who have the rule over them. They were also afraid that the revolutionaries might not be able to keep the same orderly government the British were maintaining. Some of these people went back to England.

Their opponents, known as Patriots, believed the king of England had lost his right to rule because he had broken his royal oath of caring for his subjects. Some were also afraid that the Church of England might one day persecute Nonconformists again.

Along with these were the Quakers and the Mennonites, who were against any type of war, and many other people who didn't know what to think and just hoped the fighting would end soon.

The war continued until 1783. Four years later, a group of delegates wrote the Constitution, which became effective in 1789. The First Amendment to the American Constitution, added in 1791, established that the American colonies, unlike England, would not have only one type of church supported by the government.

This also meant that no church would be supported by the government. Each congregation had to raise its support. This freedom increased the number of denominations in the country. Christians from different denominations who agreed on the most important issues of Christianity learned to work together.

A TIME OF REVIVALS • 139

Great Questions of the Church

MAY CHRISTIANS ALLOW SLAVERY?

The combination of the revivals, which were directed to all people—rich and poor, slave and free—and the new ideas of freedom as a God-given right encouraged people to think seriously about slavery. Slavery had been around for thousands of years. When one nation conquered another, they took some people as prisoners and made them their slaves. In other cases, poor people gave themselves or their children as slaves in order to pay off a debt. Initially, slavery was not based on race or color. The ancient Romans, for example, enslaved some of the people from Northern Europe and valued their strength.

Some Christians, like Gregory of Nyssa, Patrick of Ireland, and Bartholomew de Las Casas understood slavery was wrong, but most people didn't think it could be abolished. People thought it was just one of the evils of this world—like war and sickness—that will only end in the next world.

By the eighteenth century, slavery had become a big business in both Europe and America. Especially in the southern American colonies, where some people owned large plantations, there was a great need for laborers. Some merchants would then go to Africa, where they encouraged some natives to kidnap other Africans—usually from rival tribes—and sell them in exchange for goods. Slaves were packed together in ships under terrible conditions. They were not treated like human beings.

More Christians began to speak out against slavery. In England, a group known as the Clapham Sect, which included politicians William Wilberforce (1759–1833) and Granville Sharp (1735–1813), ministers Zachary Macaulay (1768–1838) and Charles Simeon (1759–1836), and author Hannah More (1745–1833) wrote articles and tracts about it and pressured the English government to put an end to the slave trade. The Quakers were also vocal opponents of slavery.

Many slave owners justified slavery, saying that it was allowed in the Bible. Under the influence of the Enlightenment and its emphasis on reason, some said that Africans were not fully human because they had not produced great works of art and literature or scientific discoveries. Benjamin Rush (1746–1813), one of the signers of the Declaration of Independence and a medical doctor, provided scientific proof against these claims.

Phillis Wheatley, as she was pictured in the first edition of her poems
LIBRARY OF CONGRESS

Talented Africans also proved these claims wrong. For example, in 1773 Phillis Wheatley (ca. 1753–1784), the first African American published poet, gained fame in both England and North America for her abilities. She also pointed out to North Americans the absurdity of fighting for freedom from England without extending the same freedom to their slaves.

Most African American authors of that time, including Wheatley, Briton Hammon, and Jupiter Hammon (ca. 1711–ca. 1806), showed an impressive knowledge of the Bible. Some, such as Lemuel Haynes (1753–1833) and David George (ca. 1743–1810), were both authors and ministers. Haynes was the first African American to be an ordained pastor. George became pastor of the first all-Black Baptist church in America, planted the first Black Baptist church in Canada, and established the first Baptist church in Africa.

While England abolished the slave trade in 1807 and slavery in 1833, other nations took longer. For example, when British abolitionists tried to convince the authorities of Morocco to abandon the slave trade, they were told abolition was against Islam since slavery was allowed in the Qur'an and Muhammad had slaves. But most nations needed to keep a good relationship with Britain and eventually banned the slave trade.

Think about It

- It's true that the apostle Paul encourages Christians to accept their present situation, including being a slave (1 Corinthians 7:20). "But," he adds, "if you can be made free, rather use it. For he who is called in the Lord while a slave is the Lord's freedman. Likewise he who is called while free is Christ's slave. You were bought at a price; do not become slaves of men" (verses 21–23). Slave owners who insisted that the slaves stay in their condition often forgot that all men are created in God's image (Genesis 1:26) and that they, as free men and women, must be slaves of Christ in service to others.

- Today, in most nations, slavery is not accepted as it was in the past, but there is still a tendency to consider some groups of people less valuable than others. What are some examples in our society? What can we learn from the Clapham Sect and other Christians who fought against slavery?

A statue of William Wilberforce in front of the Wilberforce House, Hull, UK

FREDDIE PHILLIPS, FLICKR

Lemuel Haynes

NEW YORK PUBLIC LIBRARY

A TIME OF REVIVALS • 141

PART 8
A CHANGING WORLD

PRUSSIA

The Church in a Time of Questions and Doubts

The nineteenth century has often been called the long century, sandwiched between two events that changed the course of history: the French Revolution and World War I. Between these two events, the church had to face growing questions and doubts about its teachings, the Bible, and even the existence of God.

EUROPE, 1789–1914

1789	The French Revolution begins.
1793	The French Reign of Terror begins.
1796	Napoleon's troops invade Rome and take Pope Pius VI as prisoner to France.
1801	Napoleon gives Roman Catholicism a special status in France.
1804	The British and Foreign Bible Society is founded.
1807	The British Parliament votes to abolish the slave trade.
1809	Pope Pius VII excommunicates French officials, and Napoleon imprisons the pope.
1817	Frederick William III of Prussia tries to unite his Lutheran and Reformed subjects.
1820	The Church of England approves singing hymns in worship.
1833	A group of scholars at Oxford publishes some tracts that seek to bring the Church of England closer to the Roman Catholic Church. The same year, England abolishes slavery.
1834	A group of Christians leaves the Dutch church to start the Christian Reformed Church.
1843	A group of Christians leaves the Church of Scotland to start the Free Church.
1848	Charles Albert, king over a north-northwest portion of Italy, grants civil rights to Waldensians and Jews that are later included in the Italian Constitution.
1854	Pope Pius IX declares that Mary was born without sin.
1870	The First Vatican Council declares that the pope cannot make mistakes in his official speeches. The Italian army takes over the pope's territories and ends his political power.
1871	Charles Darwin publishes *The Descent of Man*, suggesting that human beings evolved from other species.
1886	Abraham Kuyper leaves the Dutch church with a group called the *Doleantie*.
1887	An article by Charles Spurgeon starts the Down-Grade Controversy about the decline of the church.
1892	The *Doleantie* unite with the Christian Reformed Church to form the Reformed Churches in the Netherlands.

A CHANGING WORLD

The French Revolution and the Church

The writings of philosophers and the American Revolution helped to convince the people of France that they should rise against the abuses of both church and state. The government's cruel persecution of Protestants had troubled many consciences, and the absurd display of riches by French kings, queens, nobles, cardinals, and bishops looked shocking next to the dreadful condition of the poor.

In 1789 a mob of revolutionaries stormed and destroyed the Bastille, a prison that had become a symbol of the king's power. This act, followed by the capture of the king, marked the start of the French Revolution.

Many people welcomed the revolution with hope for a new government based on liberty, **equality**, and brotherhood. In time, however, it became extremely violent. During the so-called Reign of Terror (1793–1794), the most radical rebels executed anyone they considered an enemy of the revolution, including hundreds of priests, monks, and nuns. Of those who survived, about thirty thousand were exiled, while the new government confiscated all church property.

French revolutionaries burning the royal carriages
LIBRARY OF CONGRESS

The Conciergerie, in Paris, France, where the revolutionaries kept their enemies before executing them. In 1794 sixteen nuns were imprisoned here.
KING OF HEARTS, WIKIMEDIA COMMONS

A POPE'S RISES AND FALLS

Most European governments were not pleased with the French Revolution. The tension between these governments and France escalated into the French Revolutionary Wars. During these wars, a French general, Napoleon Bonaparte (1769–1821), invaded Rome and took Pope Pius VI (1717–1799), who had sided with France's enemies, as prisoner.

Pius VI died in France, and for six months there was no pope. In 1800 the newly elected pope, Pius VII (1742–1823), had to be crowned with a papier-mâché tiara decorated with jewels because the French still had the official tiara in their possession.

Despite his differences with popes, Napoleon signed an agreement that recognized the Roman Catholic Church as "the religion of the great majority of the French people." The church wouldn't be mistreated as it was during the French Revolution but would be paid by the state and placed under its supervision. Also, all priests and bishops in France had to swear allegiance to the French government.

For a while, Pius VII and Napoleon managed to work together. In 1804 Napoleon asked Pius to recognize him as emperor, even though Napoleon placed the crown on his head himself, something the pope would usually do.

144 • A CHANGING WORLD

The relationship between emperor and pope changed again in 1809, when Napoleon, who was already ruling over much of Italy, decided to add to his empire the large portion of Italy belonging to the pope (known as the Papal States). When the pope refused and excommunicated some French officials, Napoleon took the Papal States by force and took the pope to France as a prisoner.

From prison, the pope refused to authorize the bishops Napoleon had appointed. This caused a lot of confusion, with the priests not knowing whom to obey. The pope was only able to return to Rome in 1814, after Napoleon's defeat.

NEW ROMAN CATHOLIC TEACHINGS

A few decades later, Pope Pius IX (1792–1878) decided to make official some teachings that had been circulating among the people, even though they were not in the Bible. For example, the Roman Catholic Church believed, as the Bible tells us, that Adam's sin in the garden of Eden caused every human being to be born a sinner (see Romans 5:12). In time, however, many Roman Catholics started to think that Mary, the mother of Jesus, was an exception. This is not in the Bible, but it had been part of the Roman Catholic tradition, so Pius IX confirmed it in 1854. The Roman Catholic Church calls this belief immaculate conception and celebrates it on December 8.

In 1863 Pius IX compiled a Syllabus of Errors—a list of things the Roman Catholic Church officially condemned. This included **Communism** and Bible societies. He also decreed that all public schools in Italy had to teach the Roman Catholic religion and be supervised by the church. These ideas were reinstated in the First Vatican Council (1869–1870)—the first major Roman Catholic council since the Council of Trent.

Portrait of Napoleon Bonaparte
PURCHASE, JOSEPH PULITZER BEQUEST, 1943, MET MUSEUM

Pius IX
LIBRARY OF CONGRESS

The same council also determined that the pope is infallible, meaning he cannot make mistakes when he declares official statements related to the Christian faith. For example, no one would consider the pope infallible if he said something privately to a friend or if he predicted sunny weather, but if he spoke in his official capacity, as he did when he said that Mary was born without sin, all Roman Catholics have to take his words as God's word.

This teaching can create some problems because each pope is bound to keep what a previous pope said, even though he might not agree with it.

A CHANGING WORLD • 145

RELIGIOUS PERSECUTION IN ITALY

While the pope, as head of the Roman Catholic Church, claimed spiritual authority over Roman Catholics all over the world, only in Italy did he have the power to oversee the programs of public schools and to ban the distribution of Bibles and the teaching of other religions.

The Roman Catholic Church opposed the distribution of the Italian Bible so firmly that most of the people considered it a Protestant book. Those who kept distributing Bibles were often arrested, imprisoned, and exiled. Still, from their new lands they corresponded with friends and smuggled Bibles into Italy—often shipped in commercial boxes or wrapped in waterproof material and moved underwater—under the nose of customs officials.

Once in the country, Italian Bibles and tracts were brought to the remotest regions by traveling salesmen. One of the worst incidents of persecution happened in 1866 when church officials in Barletta (in the heel of the Italian boot) encouraged the local population to raid the homes of evangelicals and drag them into the streets. Six evangelicals died that day.

The pope had so much authority in the country that an officer of the Inquisition was able to order that a six-year-old boy, Edgardo Mortara (1851–1940), be taken from his Jewish family. Why? Because Edgardo's nanny had secretly baptized him as a Roman Catholic, so the church decreed that he could not be raised a Jew. Edgardo was then raised by the church and became a priest.

> *My dear friend, pray earnestly for us, that God will allow us to honor and bless Him with all our hearts, in the place where He was pleased to put us. The Spirit is willing but the flesh attacks fiercely.*
> —ROSA MADIAI (1796–1871), from the Italian prison where she was kept for about two years for being a Protestant and for talking about her faith. She was exiled after her release.

THE END OF THE POPE'S POLITICAL POWER

Much of this changed on September 20, 1870, after Italy became a unified country, when the Italian troops marched on Rome and took it from the pope. This meant that he was still the head of the Roman Catholic Church but not of a state and had no official authority over the Italian laws. The pope, however, refused to accept the authority of the Italian government and declared himself a prisoner of the state.

For Italian Protestants, September 20 marked the day when the gospel could be preached freely. This new freedom was displayed by a man who marched in front of the troops with a cartload of Italian Bibles pulled by a dog named Pius IX. It was a powerful message. The long-forbidden Bible was now available to all.

A monument in memory of the Bersaglieri soldiers, a branch of the Italian army, who stormed Rome through a breach near Porta Pia (one of the official gates), taking the city from the pope

LUCE61, WIKIMEDIA COMMONS

Watanabe Gikai, **colporteur** of the American Bible Society, in Japan around the year 1900. Colporteurs were traveling salesmen bringing Bibles to the remote areas of their countries. It was a dangerous task.

GEORGE GRANTHAM BAIN COLLECTION (LIBRARY OF CONGRESS)

BIBLE SOCIETIES

The Bible societies the pope had condemned were groups of Christians devoted to the translation and distribution of the Bible. The first one was founded in Britain in 1804 and was named the British and Foreign Bible Society (BFBS). At that time, the Bible had been translated into only eighty languages. One hundred and fifty years later, thanks to the BFBS and other similar societies, it was translated into thousands of languages.

Pius VII was the first to openly condemn these societies. That's because the Roman Catholic Church believes that the Bible has been given specifically to them by the apostles and that the church has the duty of determining how it should be interpreted.

For example, in 1757 one pope, Benedict XIV (1675–1758), had allowed a translation of the Bible into Italian, but only with the addition of comments, explanations, and quotations. Pius VII, however, opposed the distribution even of this translation.

In 1824 Pope Leo XII (1760–1829) wrote, "It is to be feared that by false interpretation, the Gospel of Christ will become the gospel of men, or still worse, the gospel of the devil."

Twenty-two years later, Pius IX repeated the same warning, calling the Bible societies "crafty" for giving Bibles to everyone, "even the unlearned," so that "everyone in his own way interprets the words of the Lord, and distorts their meaning, thereby falling into miserable errors."

Think about It

- On the one hand, what are the dangers of giving the Bible to people who have never read it before without adding any explanation and without teaching them how to read each passage by taking into consideration what comes before and after and what other passages say on the same topic?

- On the other hand, what are the dangers of not allowing people to read the Bible for themselves and forcing them to accept the church's interpretation without giving them a chance to compare it with what the Bible says?

- If these are both dangers, what is the solution? Why might attending a faithful church and reading the history of the church and the historical creeds and confessions be helpful?

A CHANGING WORLD • 147

New Challenges to the Church

DARWIN'S SUGGESTIONS

Throughout the history of Christianity, scientists saw science as a tool to explore and understand God's creation. For example, the astronomer Johannes Kepler (1571–1630), who had a difficult life at the time of the Thirty Years' War, found in science a confirmation of a loving God who has a perfect and beautiful plan for His creation.

An understanding of this strong connection and cooperation between faith and science continued in the nineteenth century. Michael Faraday (1791–1867), who showed how magnetism can turn into electricity, was an active elder in his church and a champion of the gospel.

Despite this general agreement, some scientists, influenced by the idea that reason could lead us to understand God, began to present science as a supreme authority over the Bible.

The most famous scientific challenge to Christianity came from Charles Darwin (1809–1882). In his book *The Origin of Species by Means of Natural Selection*, he suggested that many animals are the result of a long process of **natural selection** and evolution. Natural selection means that all living things are in constant war against each other, and in the end only the fittest will survive. In a later book, *The Descent of Man*, he proposed the same theory about human beings. If he didn't mean to challenge Christianity, his suggestions did just that, and some people used them to that end.

Not everyone's faith was shaken. Many people continued to believe that serious scientific discoveries could only confirm God's written revelation. For example, the Scottish geologist Hugh Miller (1802–1856) and his wife and editor, Lydia Falconer Miller (1812–1876), who had to face Darwin's challenges in their field of study, believed that Darwin deserved respect only for theories he could support with valid, scientific facts. Beyond that, he could not speak with authority.

Charles Darwin
WELLCOME LIBRARY, LONDON

Dear children, let us remember that God made us only a little lower than the angels; that He has crowned us with glory and honour in giving us those souls which are within us, the incorruptible germs of an immortal life.
—LYDIA FALCONER MILLER, *Cats and Dogs*

Michael Faraday and his wife, Sarah Barnard Faraday
WELLCOME LIBRARY, LONDON

Hugh Miller
WELLCOME LIBRARY, LONDON

DARWIN AND A REIGN OF SELFISHNESS

Lydia Falconer Miller, who edited her husband's work after his death, was concerned that Darwin's idea of human beings developing from lower species instead of being created with specific and immortal souls could bring the world to a "reign of selfishness."

In a way, she was right. When in one of his letters Darwin suggested the survival of the fittest may apply to human history, with "the less intellectual races being exterminated" over time, people used this idea to suggest that some races or classes of people are more deserving of life than others. Like Scrooge in Charles Dickens's *Christmas Carol*, they said, "It's better that they should die."

The idea continued to spread, and people wrote books about the possibility of speeding up this survival of the fittest in order to produce a better race. In 1883 Sir Francis Galton (1822–1911), a well-respected scholar and cousin of Darwin, called this idea *eugenics*, from two Greek words that mean "well" and "born." Soon, the idea developed into a movement. Some American states tried to preserve a "better race" by limiting immigration and controlling births in order to ensure that the poor and disabled were not having children. In the twentieth century, about seventy thousand people in the United States were forced to adopt strict birth control programs. In Germany the **dictator** Adolf Hitler (1889–1945) took this idea to an extreme, killing entire groups of people in order to save what he considered the best race.

A CHANGING WORLD • 149

THE PHILOSOPHERS' CHALLENGE

Following the trend of giving priority to human reason, some philosophers questioned everything that reason could not explain, including the existence of God, the miracles described in the Bible, and that Jesus was both God and man.

In 1835 a German author, David Friedrich Strauss (1808–1874), tried to prove that Jesus was only a man by examining His life through historical documents other than the Gospels. He didn't believe that the Gospels told a true story and thought the Bible was just a book like many others.

His book sparked an interest in historical research of the life of Jesus. About seventy years later, another German author, Albert Schweitzer (1875–1965), denied that the

Albert Schweitzer
LIBRARY OF CONGRESS

account of the life of Jesus in the Gospels could be trusted. Since he couldn't see the kingdom that Jesus said He established, Schweitzer thought Jesus's promises had failed. Schweitzer was quite talented and even won a Nobel Peace Prize for his work with African hospitals, so his words were considered seriously.

Another German philosopher, Friedrich Nietzsche (1844–1900), went as far as declaring that "God is dead," meaning He "has become unbelievable." He opposed Christianity for teaching people to be meek and humble. He thought Christians were weak and that the world needed strong people.

Friedrich Nietzsche
LIBRARY OF CONGRESS

Karl Marx
LIBRARY OF CONGRESS

The German Karl Marx (1818–1883) wrote that "religion is the **opium** of the people," like a drug that keeps people sleepy and submissive to the government and the wealthy. He believed that no one would need religion in a world where everyone was equal. He thought Communism could create this type of world. Marx's ideas were popular in a world where many poor people suffered injustice and mistreatment without a chance to be heard.

These men didn't think they were giving bad news to the world. Strauss thought that all religions are based on ideas and not on facts, so even if Jesus was not God, we can still follow His good teachings. Schweitzer agreed. To him, what mattered was not whether Jesus was God or not but just "Jesus as spiritually arisen within" the heart.

Nietzsche was the most optimistic of all. To him, the "death" of God represented a "new dawn" when "every daring venture of new knowledge is again permitted." If people didn't have to believe the Bible, he thought, they could believe anything they wanted, and the sky was the limit. In fact, he thought that Christianity, with all its talk of submission and humility, had kept human beings down for too long, and it was time for the strong, for a "superman," to rise.

Great Questions of the Church

IS CHRISTIANITY BASED ON FACTS?

Faced with challenges from scientists and philosophers, many Christians began to believe, like Strauss and Schweitzer, that the facts of the Bible are not important. Instead of looking at the evidence that Jesus rose from the dead and was who He said He was, they chose to believe He could just be "spiritually arisen within" the heart.

> *Think about It*
>
> - Strauss believed that all religions are based on ideas and not on facts. This might be true of some religions. If Buddha or Confucius never existed, their followers could still make good use of their advice. But is this true of Christianity? What happens to Christianity if you take away the historical fact of Christ's resurrection? What did the apostle Paul mean when he said, "If Christ is not risen, your faith is futile [useless]; you are still in your sins!" (1 Corinthians 15:17)?
>
> - The Bible makes it clear that God is so much higher than our thoughts that we could never know Him apart from what He has chosen to reveal. And He has revealed Himself mostly through His works—the history of His actions to save His people from the consequences of sin. If you took out every page of the Bible that tells you what God has done, what would be left? Would this help us to know God? Or would it just be a list of good suggestions? Explain your answers.
>
> - When people look for a god they can understand, what is that god usually like? Think about the gods of the Canaanites and Philistines in the Old Testament and the Greek and Roman gods of mythology. What name does the Bible give to this type of man-made god?

A CHANGING WORLD • 151

Challenges to the Gospel

Throughout history, Protestant churches had to fight the tendency to forget the gospel that motivated the Reformation. This is understandable because the gospel—the announcement that Christ has done everything to pay the price for human sin and reconcile sinners to God—seems too good to be true.

In some cases, when the established church would not encourage the preaching of the pure gospel, faithful Christians were left with the difficult choice of leaving that church and starting a new denomination.

THE FIRST DUTCH SECESSION

This is what happened in the Netherlands in 1834, mainly through a man named Hendrik de Cock (1801–1842). At that time, the Dutch church had drifted so far from the teachings of the Reformation that de Cock had been a pastor for several years without ever reading the Reformed confessions. Even though all Dutch preachers had to officially pledge allegiance to those documents, few took the time to read them. De Cock heard about them only from preachers who thought they were outdated.

When he actually read them, he realized they were important not only to preserve the pure preaching of the gospel but also to help Christians not to be deceived by the many incorrect interpretations of the Bible that were taught in his day.

But when he encouraged others to make changes in their churches, bringing them back to the teachings of the Reformation, the leaders of the Dutch church suspended him from preaching.

He accepted this decision, but his congregation didn't. They refused to listen to the new pastor sent by the government and provided other places for de Cock to preach. The opposition continued, and de Cock had to spend three months in prison.

Finally, the congregation reinstated de Cock as their pastor and signed an Act of Secession from the Dutch church. Other churches did the same thing. Within two years, the new denomination, called the Christian Reformed Church (CRC), had 120 churches. They held a synod, where they decided to adopt the **church order** established at the Synod of Dort.

Since the Dutch church was supported by the government, the state continued to arrest and imprison pastors who preached outside of it. It also forbade meetings of more than twenty people. This persecution continued until 1841.

The church at Ulrum, Netherlands, where the 1834 secession started

HARMEN DE JONG

From the start, de Cock was encouraged by his wife, Frouwe Helenius Venema de Cock (ca. 1804–1889), and by a pastor named Dirk Hoksbergen (1800–1870), who wrote de Cock a fifty-one-page letter of support and traveled with him from church to church.

De Cock and Hoksbergen parted ways at the second CRC synod when a pastor suggested discarding the church order established at Dort in order to adopt a new one. De Cock and Hoksbergen, who opposed this suggestion, were a small minority. In the end, de Cock decided to accept the new decision for the sake of unity, while Hoksbergen continued to oppose it. This created a division between the two friends. Eventually, however, the CRC went back to Dort's church order, which is still used today.

> *May you, by His Spirit and power, preach not your own ideas or the world's, but Jesus Christ crucified. Only in His light can we see the light, and through His strength alone are we preserved against error and human preferences.*
> —HENDRIK DE COCK to another pastor, translated from the Dutch by Marvin Kamps

Hendrik de Cock
ART COLLECTION 3, ALAMY STOCK PHOTO

A SECOND DUTCH SECESSION

A half century later, a pastor named Abraham Kuyper (1837–1920) found himself in a similar situation as de Cock. By then, things in the Dutch church had become worse. The standards for church membership were low, and people were hardly taught the Bible. In 1886, when Kuyper and others protested, they were expelled from the church. By 1889 the protesters, who called themselves the *Doleantie* (meaning "grieving ones"), had become so numerous that they had over 200 congregations, 180,000 members, and about 80 ministers. In 1892, through the efforts of influential pastors such as Kuyper and theologian Herman Bavinck (1854–1921), the *Doleantie* united with the Christian Reformed Church to form the Reformed Churches in the Netherlands.

Being concerned about Dutch society, Kuyper left the ministry and was elected to Parliament, where he tried to make the changes he considered beneficial for the people. He also founded the Free University of Amsterdam, which was free from government control.

Abraham Kuyper
RIJKSMUSEUM, AMSTERDAM, NETHERLANDS

A CHANGING WORLD • 153

Great Questions of the Church

HOW CAN CHRISTIANS LIVE IN AN UNBELIEVING WORLD?

Abraham Kuyper thought much about this question. He concluded that Christians see the world differently from unbelievers. For example, those who don't believe in the Bible think that death is just a natural event—the circle of life. For Christians, death is unnatural. It came to the world because of Adam's sin and will end one day because Jesus has defeated it.

There are many other differences in the way Christians understand things, but, Kuyper said, they don't need to change their beliefs just because the rest of the world disagrees.

Christians should be willing to learn from others. Kuyper believed that God gives common grace to all, allowing both believers and unbelievers to contribute knowledge, beauty, and peace to the world. Christians should just take what is good from the world around them and reject what contradicts the Bible.

At the same time, as Herman Bavinck explained, Christians should remember that "all culture, whatever significance it may have, just as all education, civilization, development, is absolutely powerless to renew the inner man." Only the gospel can do that. That's why Bavinck said Christianity is "the truth of all religions." It has what every religion of the world ultimately wants to have but can only be achieved through and because of Christ.

Did You Know?

- In 1834 the Dutch government made it illegal to preach apart from the authorized Dutch church. But they didn't forbid Christians to pray. So the pastors of the Christian Reformed Church decided to pray their sermons. Some people say that's the reason why some prayers in the Dutch Reformed church are so long today.

- People in Dutch Reformed churches are well-known for their custom of passing out mints during the worship service. Parents started doing this to keep their children quiet during the long church services. The most famous Dutch mints are the Wilhelmina peppermint candies, so-called because they bear, since 1892, the image of twelve-year-old Princess Wilhelmina.

Think about It

- What do you think about Kuyper's idea that Christians can learn many things from nonbelievers? Name some books written by or forms of art composed by nonbelievers that have taught you something important.

- What do you think about Bavinck's idea that Christianity is the truth of all religions? Why can true justice, hope, love, peace, and truth be achieved only through and because of Christ?

Herman Bavinck
REFORMATION ART

The Scottish Disruption

Another division happened in Scotland where, like during the secession of 1733, the government claimed the right to assign preachers to churches and supervise other aspects of church life. Quite often, the government's priority was not the pure preaching of the gospel. The disagreements between those who wanted the church to be independent and those who were content with the way things were going continued for years.

In 1843 one-third of the ministers and half of the members of the Church of Scotland started a separate denomination called the Free Church. This secession became known as the Great **Disruption** because it was a much greater conflict than in any previous secessions. Like in the past, these pastors faced much hardship because they were no longer paid by the state, but they believed the freedom of the church was worth the sacrifice.

Thomas Chalmers (1780–1847), a moderator of the general assembly at that time, is considered the main leader of the Great Disruption. Like de Cock, Chalmers had discovered the gospel only after becoming a preacher and was saddened by preachers who wanted to teach people only to do good. They preached only God's law ("Do this and live") and not the gospel ("Christ has done it for you"). Chalmers, instead, was convinced that only the gospel could motivate people to do good.

Thomas Chalmers
WELLCOME COLLECTION GALLERY

THOMAS CHALMERS AND THE FIGHT AGAINST POVERTY

Chalmers saw the fruits of his emphasis on the gospel while he was pastor of a church in Glasgow. In that large city, he came face-to-face with the problems of what is known as the Industrial Revolution: the creation of factories that made the production of goods much faster but left without work many people who made those goods by hand. Those who crowded the cities seeking work in the newly built factories were often overworked and underpaid.

Distressed by the poverty he saw around him, Chalmers continued to believe that the preaching of the gospel could make a difference. The city of Glasgow decided to give him a chance and put him in charge of the funds for the relief of the poor. Soon Chalmers proved once again that when people understand what Christ has done for them, they become much more willing to help others.

Chalmers also believed that pastors should become involved in the lives of the people in their congregations instead of just preaching on Sundays. Besides running successful programs for the poor, he opened schools to bring free education to all and provided many opportunities for Christians to help their communities.

> *I am now most thoroughly of the opinion that on the system of "Do this and live" no peace can ever be found. It is: "Believe on the Lord Jesus Christ and thou shalt be saved."*
> —THOMAS CHALMERS

Back to Rome

In the nineteenth century, a group of Oxford professors protested some tendencies in the Church of England to compromise Christian teachings in order to accommodate modern philosophy. In fact, many Christians didn't even know these teachings because they had learned to give more importance to personal experience than to the Bible and the creeds and confessions that summarize it.

But these professors' answer was different from what other Protestants had given. In their desire to show people the authority of the church in its teachings and sacraments, they didn't go back to the Reformation, but to what the church was before the Reformation. They promoted candles, vestments, incense, kneeling, chants, holy water, images and statues, and the veneration of Mary and the saints.

The group became known as the Oxford Movement. A sermon preached by John Keble (1792–1866) in 1833 is considered its official start. Between 1833 and 1841, its leaders produced some pamphlets they called *Tracts for the Times*, which gave the members of the group the alternative name Tractarians.

When one of the movement's leaders, John Henry Newman (1801–1890), went as far as suggesting that the Thirty-Nine Articles of the church, which had been written during the Reformation, could be interpreted as promoting Roman Catholicism, the movement met the final disapproval of the Church of England. In 1845 Newman followed the logical consequence of his teachings and converted to Roman Catholicism. He became a priest, then a cardinal. In 2019 the Roman Catholic Church counted him among its saints.

Newman's actions caused some disunity in the Church of England, as some followed his example while others stayed in the Church of England as Anglo-Catholics. The Anglican bishop John Charles (J. C.) Ryle (1816–1900) said that one problem was

A statue of John Henry Newman as a Roman Catholic cardinal in front of Sacred Heart Hall, Newman University, Wichita, Kansas

JANELLMARIE, WIKIMEDIA COMMONS

J. C. Ryle

ART BY MARCOS RODRIGUES

that the Church of England didn't really explain to its members the teachings of the Reformation, so they were left with a mixed crowd that didn't really know what they believed. Ryle emphasized these teachings in his preaching and his tracts—about two hundred in all, which sold twelve million copies in his lifetime.

The Baptist Charles Haddon Spurgeon (1834–1892), who is considered the greatest British preacher of the nineteenth century, fiercely opposed the Oxford Movement. Like the Puritans, he thought the return to some practices and ceremonies of the Roman Catholic Church created a distraction from the preaching of the gospel. He also believed that the Tractarians, in their effort to rediscover the early church fathers, didn't go back far enough and neglected the pure teachings of the New Testament. Overall, he saw their movement as an attack on the gospel of salvation by grace alone, through faith alone, in Christ alone, relying on Scripture alone.

Charles Haddon Spurgeon
INTERNET BOOK ARCHIVES

Some Men of the Nineteenth-Century Church

OTHER PROTESTANT PREACHERS REAFFIRMING THE REFORMATION

Like Spurgeon and Ryle, other European preachers believed that many problems in the Protestant church were because people forgot the principles of the Reformation. Because of this, they devoted their lives to preaching the gospel.

When the Scot **ROBERT HALDANE** (1764–1842), one of the first members of the London Missionary Society, visited Geneva, Switzerland, he realized that the churches in that city had moved far from the teachings of early founders like John Calvin. At the same time, a few Christians were eager to rediscover them. When some of these people asked Haldane to stay as their teacher, he did. As a result, a revival, known as *Le Réveil*, began to take root in Switzerland and France.

Later, some of Haldane's students brought the gospel to other countries in Europe and beyond. The preaching of one of these students, **JEAN HENRI MERLE D'AUBIGNÉ** (1794–1872), inspired a revival in parts of Germany and the Netherlands. D'Aubigné also wrote a booklet about the Oxford Movement, showing how it attacked basic biblical teachings, such as **justification** by faith alone and the authority of the Bible above any human statement.

Another strong proclaimer of the gospel was **HORATIUS BONAR** (1808–1889), an important pastor in Scotland after the Disruption. Today he is best known for his hymns, such as "Not What My Hands Have Done" and "I Heard the Voice of Jesus Say." Many of his hymns talk about the return of Christ, which Bonar called the "blessed hope." Later in life, he went with other Scottish pastors on a mission to the Jews.

Horatius Bonar
ZU_09, ISTOCK

Even many Lutherans had forgotten much of what Martin Luther had taught. They mostly saw him as a fighter for the freedom of Germany from the pope. The German historian **KARL HOLL** (1866–1926) tried to remedy this problem by emphasizing Luther's teachings of justification by faith alone.

Great Questions of the Church

CAN A CHURCH HAVE NO CREED?

Many Christians in the nineteenth century were concerned about the decline of the church. Spurgeon called it a "downgrade," a dangerous walk down a slippery slope. Like many others, he believed the answer was a return to the gospel as it is proclaimed in the Bible and explained in the creeds and confessions of the Reformation. John Nelson Darby (1800–1882), an Irish minister, had different views. He believed the church was "in ruins," but instead of encouraging Christians to return to the Protestant confessions, he told them to go back to the early church when, he said, there were no denominations. Unlike the early church, his followers (called Brethren) met without written creeds and pastors.

John Nelson Darby
INTERNET BOOK ARCHIVES

C. I. Scofield
WIKIMEDIA COMMONS

Darby thought the church had been passing through different phases, which he called dispensations. He created a set of calculations that showed Jesus was going to return soon. Unlike most Christians of his day, who thought that Jesus will return in one event that "every eye will see" (Revelation 1:7), Darby suggested that Jesus will come first to take all believers out of this world to protect them from a series of hard punishments sent for unbelievers. Today, people who believe in this teaching call this the rapture of the church. Then, after three and a half years, He will return with the believers to judge the rest of the world.

Darby's ideas became popular. People were intrigued by his charts and calculations that seemed to predict the events of the last years of this earth. They often looked at current events to see if they could match some of the Bible's predictions.

Darby's ideas became even more popular in 1909 when the American C. I. Scofield (1843–1921) published a Bible full of notes that agreed with Darby's ideas. One problem with these notes was that many people followed them as though they were the official interpretation of the Bible. That's why Bible societies had avoided adding notes to their Bibles before this.

Darby's and Scofield's division into dispensations, with a separation between Old Testament law and New Testament grace, also disagreed with the prevalent teaching of the church that the Bible tells one unified story. These ideas continue to be popular today.

Think about It

- A creed is a statement of something a person or church believes. When Darby said he didn't believe Christians should have denominations or creeds, did he express a creed? Can his teaching on dispensations be called a creed? Explain why everyone has a creed, even if they say they do not.

- Some portions of the Bible have been interpreted in different ways. Even teachers who were later considered heretics thought they were following the Bible. Since this is a danger, is it safer for Christians to say they have no creed but the Bible or to compare their interpretations with the ones that have been accepted by many Christians before them? Explain your answer.

- Notes can be helpful in Bibles. They can tell a lot about dates, people, places, and the meaning of words in the original languages. But when they interpret a text, we should remember it could be just one person's opinion. It's always good to compare new interpretations with what the church has taught for centuries.

The area around Lake Keswick

IMAGE BY 3855198 FROM PIXABAY

ARE THERE TWO LEVELS OF CHRISTIANS?

Another group of Christians thought that the answer to the problems of the church lay in a greater commitment to be more than ordinary Christians. They met in Keswick, England, in 1875 to discuss their ideas. Because of this, their teachings became known as the Keswick Theology.

Like John Wesley, Keswick Theology taught that Christians received two blessings: one when they first believed in Jesus as their Savior, and another when they accepted Him as their Lord and master. This second stage, they said, happened when Christians emptied themselves and let God fill them. They called Christians who don't make much progress in their spiritual lives carnal Christians and those who show much fruit spiritual Christians.

In America, the Methodist Phoebe Palmer (1807–1874) taught something similar, saying that Christians must simply surrender their whole life to God, ask Him for holiness, and believe they have received it. The movement in which she was prominent became known as the Holiness Movement.

Today, if you meet someone who talks about "getting saved" at one point and "surrendering to Christ" at a later time or who tells you to "let go and let God," they are influenced by the Keswick Theology, whether they realize it or not.

Today's Keswick Ministries, based in England, are different. Most of the people who belong to this group don't talk about living a higher life but instead focus on teaching and preaching God's word in a way that is faithful to the Bible.

Think about It

- The Keswick Theology's division between carnal and spiritual Christians came from their interpretation of 1 Corinthians 2:14, which talks about "the natural man." Luther, instead, taught that Christians are sinful and righteous at the same time. Which interpretation seems closer to the overall message of the Bible? Why?

- Does the Bible talk about two separate blessings, the second one leading to a "higher life" of holiness, and that some Christians have only one blessing? Does 2 Corinthians 5:17 help you to answer this question? How?

- The Keswick Theology talked about letting God work in us or making it possible for Him to work. This has caused some confusion for Christians who worry about "being in God's way." Do you think God is waiting for our permission or for us to get out of His way before He can work in us? Why or why not?

A Difficult Union

Prussia, a large region in the eastern Germanic states, had been a refuge to European Protestants during the Thirty Years' War because the Prussian rulers allowed both Lutheran and Reformed churches.

In 1797 the crown passed to the Reformed prince Frederick William III (1770–1840), who was married to the Lutheran Louise of Mecklenburg-Strelitz (1776–1810). For the most part, Frederick and Louise shared a common faith, but when it came time to take the Lord's Supper, they parted ways and worshiped separately. In spite of their differences, Frederick and Louise loved each other very much.

Frederick thought his subjects could live in unity like he and his wife in spite of their different religious views. But how? He decided to unite both Lutherans and Reformed in one state religion. In 1817, seven years after Louise's death, he started a series of decrees to make that happen.

There were some obvious problems. For one thing, some ceremonies, such as the Lord's Supper, could be done only in a Lutheran or Reformed way. Mixing the two was impossible. Since Frederick was Reformed, he gave preference to Reformed practices, even though Prussia had about 7,000 Lutheran churches and only about 170 Reformed. Also, in order to unify the churches, they could no longer use the confessions reflecting their specific Lutheran or Reformed beliefs that had been written during the Reformation.

Most Lutherans conformed, but those who refused to obey were arrested. One of the toughest persecutions happened in 1834, when the government sent five hundred soldiers to attack a dissenting church. It was only when Frederick died and his son Frederick William IV (1795–1861) assumed the throne that these impositions were dropped.

A LUTHERAN EMIGRATION

The decrees of Frederick William III caused many Lutherans to rediscover the value of their confessions. It also caused some to look for religious freedom outside Europe—particularly in North America and Australia.

One of the first groups to leave was composed of 250 people led by Pastor August Ludwig Christian Kavel (1798–1860). Getting all the necessary permissions and funds to leave was not easy, but they finally landed in Australia in 1838. Another group of 274 people joined them in 1841 led by Pastor Gotthard Daniel Fritzsche (1797–1863). These new congregations based their beliefs on the Lutheran confessions that were written at the time of the Reformation.

But the Prussians were not the only Lutherans to leave Europe. In Saxony, another region of today's Germany, a group of eight hundred people led by Pastor Martin Stephan (1777–1846) left for America and settled in Missouri, where they divided into two parishes. The leadership soon passed to another pastor, Carl Ferdinand Wilhelm (C. F. W.) Walther (1811–1887). Like other emigrants, Walther was committed to bringing the Lutheran church back to the teachings of Martin Luther. To this purpose, he founded a college for the training of pastors that eventually became Concordia **Seminary** in St. Louis. In 1847 the Lutheran Church–Missouri Synod was founded, pledging allegiance to the Lutheran confessions.

Frederick William III
LIBRARY OF CONGRESS

Louise of Mecklenburg-Strelitz
NEMO 65, FLICKR

This Russian Orthodox Church on Unalaska Island, one of the Aleutian Islands of Alaska, was built in 1894.
SONIA, FLICKR

Missions to and from Russia

In 1812 Moscow went up in flames. This calamity came just after a disastrous loss against Napoleon's invading armies. It was enough to discourage any ruler. But Czar Alexander I (1777–1825) had a different reaction. "The judgment of God filled me with a warmth of faith I had never felt before," he said. Raised in a court where the ideas of the Enlightenment had taken priority over religion, he had begun to study the Scriptures and "learned to know God as He is revealed by the Bible…. It is only since Christianity has become the important object of my life, since faith in my Redeemer has manifested itself in me, that the peace of God—and I thank God for it—has entered my soul."

Inspired by this newfound faith, Alexander opened Russia to the work of foreign missionaries and approved and partially funded the founding of a Russian Bible Society. The official Russian Bible, translated by Orthodox scholars, was published in 1820. By the following year, the Bible was translated in most languages of the Russian Empire, and hundreds of thousands of copies were distributed.

This work was very important because few Russians in the nineteenth century attended church regularly, especially in the countryside, where churches were often far from the people's homes. For this reason, many priests preached only three or four times per year, during special holidays.

Around midcentury, there was also an increase of missionary efforts by the Russian Orthodox Church, going as far as Alaska (which was part of the Russian Empire until 1864) and Japan. Innocent Veniaminov (1797–1879), metropolitan of Moscow (the highest position in the Russian Orthodox Church) and previous missionary to Alaska, founded the Orthodox Missionary Society, which lasted until the Russian Revolution of 1917.

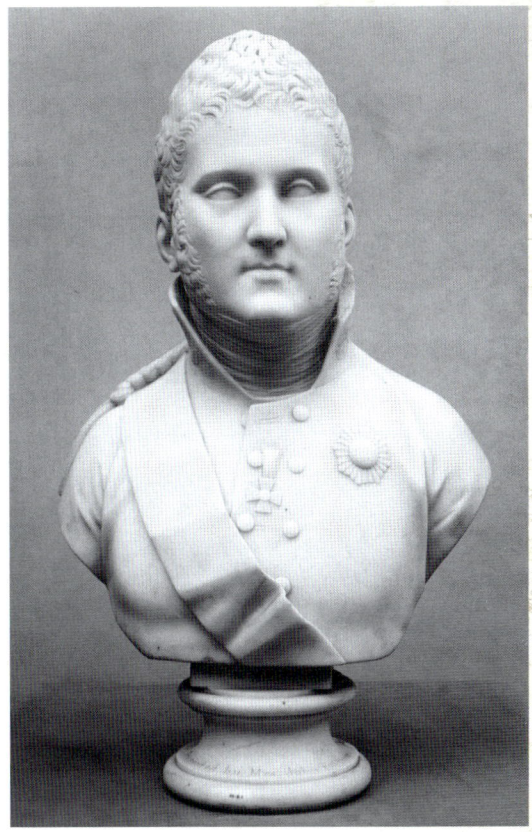

A marble bust of Alexander I of Russia
THE MET MUSEUM

THE CHURCH AND THE SERFS

While Czar Peter I abolished the practice of slavery, most of the peasants in Russia (known as serfs) were not allowed to own lands and had to work as servants of landowners, with few or no rights. The church had no authority to change this system but could tell the landowners to exercise justice. Bishop Tikhon of Zadonsk (1724–1783) wrote a manual teaching landowners to care for their serfs' spiritual and material needs. Metropolitan Filaret Drozdov (1782–1867) preached clearly, "A person is not a thing which one can use and toward which one bears no obligation." Filaret encouraged Czar Alexander II (1818–1881) to abolish the practice of keeping serfs, which the czar did in 1861.

NORTH AMERICA, 1789–1913

1791 — A first amendment is added to the US Constitution establishing a separation of church and state.

1797 — Isabella Graham starts the Society for the Relief of Poor Widows.

1801 — About ten thousand people gather at a religious camp meeting in Cane Ridge Church near Paris, Kentucky.

1806 — The Haystack Prayer Meeting of students at Williams College is considered the beginning of the American Protestant missions movement.

1820 — On the insistence of the native Opukahaia, the American Board of Commissioners for Foreign Missions sends their first group of missionaries to the Hawaiians.

1830 — Charles Finney preaches in Rochester, New York. The same year, Joseph Smith publishes *The Book of Mormon*.

1865 — Slavery is abolished in the United States.

1881 — A. A. Hodge and B. B. Warfield write an important article on the inspiration of the Bible, showing that the Bible is inerrant.

1895 — At a conference near Ontario, Canada, a group of Christians establish five basic teachings of the faith.

1906 — At a church meeting in Los Angeles, Christians surprise the world by speaking in unknown languages.

Los Angeles

Pacific Ocean

Francis Asbury, one of the first circuit riders, was ordained minister of the gospel in 1784. The ordination ceremony, as it is shown in this image, was typical of most churches at that time and is still performed in a similar way in some churches today. In some churches, ministers are also asked to sign a document, promising to be faithful to the teachings of the church.
LIBRARY OF CONGRESS

The Second American Awakening

CIRCUIT RIDERS AND CAMP MEETINGS

By the nineteenth century, settlers were spread throughout most of North America. They often lived far from each other and from any church building. That's why some preachers traveled from place to place to meet the settlers wherever they were.

One of the first preachers to do this was Francis Asbury (1745–1816), an English Methodist who had been appointed by John Wesley. He traveled about thirty thousand miles around America on horseback, crossing the Appalachian Mountains sixty times. Under his ministry, the Methodist church in America gained over two hundred thousand members.

He also trained new men to do what he did. By 1776 he was assisted by 24 of these men. The number grew to 695 in 1816 and to 4,479 in 1844. These traveling preachers became known as circuit riders.

Most circuit riders asked the settlers to meet in some convenient place, where they preached in the open air or under large tents. Not knowing when they could be back, sometimes they preached for several

The Circuit Rider is a statue erected in Salem, Oregon, in honor of "the labors and achievements of the ministers of the Gospel, who as circuit riders became the friends, counselors and evangels to the pioneers on every American frontier."
WIKIMEDIA COMMONS

days. Many of them attracted large crowds and caused great emotional responses, which led them to believe God's Spirit was moving in an extraordinary way. This time in American history is often described as the Second Great Awakening.

This awakening lasted from about 1795 to 1835, and it's usually divided into three phases. The first phase was characterized by camp meetings that took place especially in Kentucky and Tennessee.

The largest camp meeting included about ten thousand people. It was held in 1801 at Cane Ridge Church near Paris, Kentucky, and was set up by Barton W. Stone (1772–1844). Stone, and other preachers like him, believed that there shouldn't be any denominations and that all believers should just call themselves Christians. They also rejected any type of creeds or confessions because they believed the only creed that was necessary was the Bible. They called themselves the Christian Church.

In the end, similar churches sprang up, so many that by 1860 there were over two thousand of them in America. Sharing the common belief (or creed) that there should be no creed or denomination, they could be considered in many ways a denomination too.

In many cases the lines between denominations were already blurred as different groups worked together to bring the gospel to other parts of America. As people continued to migrate west, preachers and pastors of all denominations would follow.

THE AWAKENING IN COLLEGES AND CHURCHES

The second phase of the Awakening had to do with an attempt to arouse more enthusiasm for religion in colleges and churches, especially in the Northeast, where many people had become either tired or skeptical. Two of the main representatives of this phase were Timothy Dwight (1752–1817), a grandson of Jonathan Edwards and president of Yale College (now Yale University, New Haven, Connecticut), and Lyman Beecher (1775–1863), a pastor who became president of Lane Theological Seminary in Walnut Hills, Ohio (today a neighborhood of Cincinnati).

SOME EFFECTS OF THE SECOND AWAKENING

As it was with the First Awakening, most of the preachers of the Second Awakening reached out to people of all races and promoted the abolition of slavery. Harriet Beecher Stowe (1811–1896), daughter of Lyman Beecher, wrote a book that helped to change many attitudes toward slavery: *Uncle Tom's Cabin*. The book sold about three hundred thousand copies in America and many more in Britain. Today some people criticize this book for the stereotypes it created about Black people. At that time, however, it was an important tool in the fight against slavery. Some say it helped to lay the groundwork for the American Civil War (1861–1865), which split up the country and its churches on the issue of slavery.

Another important result of the Awakening was a renewed interest in missions. A prayer meeting for the people of Asia, held in 1806 by five students in a field by Williams College, Williamstown, Massachusetts, is considered the beginning of the American Protestant missions movement. This is remembered as the Haystack Prayer Meeting. Within four years of that meeting, some of the students founded the American Board of Commissioners for Foreign Missions (ABCFM), which sent missionaries all over the world, starting with China and Ceylon. Timothy Dwight was one of its members.

Two later preachers who were influenced by the awakening were Dwight L. Moody (1837–1899) and Billy Sunday (1862–1935), who attracted large crowds wherever they went.

A Methodist camp meeting
LIBRARY OF CONGRESS

Native American Missions

From the time of the early colonies, many Christians had been concerned about Native American people and wanted to bring the gospel to them. Unfortunately, many European traders took advantage of the Native Americans. The American government also felt entitled to take over lands that belonged to the Native Americans, removing the people to other parts of the country.

In spite of this, many Native Americans came to know the gospel of Christ, which has nothing to do with politics. Catharine Brown (ca. 1800–1823) and her brother, David (ca. 1806–1829), for example, became zealous missionaries to their own people, the Cherokees.

Catherine first discovered the gospel in 1817 when she attended the Brainerd School, established by missionary Cyrus Kingsbury (1786–1870), near Chickamauga, Tennessee. She was about seventeen at that time. Initially, she simply saw going to school as an opportunity to learn English, a language that had become essential for Native Americans. But when she understood what Christ has truly done for men and women of all nationalities and colors, she became determined to share that message with her people.

In 1820 she became a teacher in Creek-Path School, near her village. She continued for three years, until she died of tuberculosis. David continued her mission after studying to become a pastor. He also translated the New Testament into Cherokee. He died just before the Indian Removal Act of 1830, when the American government forced native tribes to move to reservation lands. On that sad occasion, the Cherokees had to walk 1,250 miles in what is now known as the Trail of Tears.

In the course of time, several Native Americans became preachers, missionaries, and translators.

Early Mission to the Hawaiians

In 1807 a young man named Opukahaia (ca. 1792–1818) found a way to embark on an American ship as a way to leave his island, where his family had been killed by an enemy tribe. On the ship he learned to speak English and was given the name Henry. Through the help of some friends, he was able to enroll in a school while working in the home of Yale's president, Timothy Dwight. Opukahaia became a Christian in 1811. He and other young men from Hawaii (then known as the Sandwich Islands) inspired the American Board of Commissioners for Foreign Missions to open the Foreign Mission School for the training of young men who intended to bring the gospel to their own lands. Opukahaia died of typhoid fever in 1818, but his insistence on sending missionaries to the Hawaiians inspired others to take on the work he could not do in person. In 1820, when a first group of twelve missionaries arrived in Hawaii with the message of the gospel, they were able to use the dictionary, grammar, and spelling book Opukahaia had prepared and his translation of the book of Genesis into Hawaiian.

Christianity was well received in Hawaii not only by the people but also by the rulers, who had already discouraged many practices of the traditional religions, such as human sacrifices.

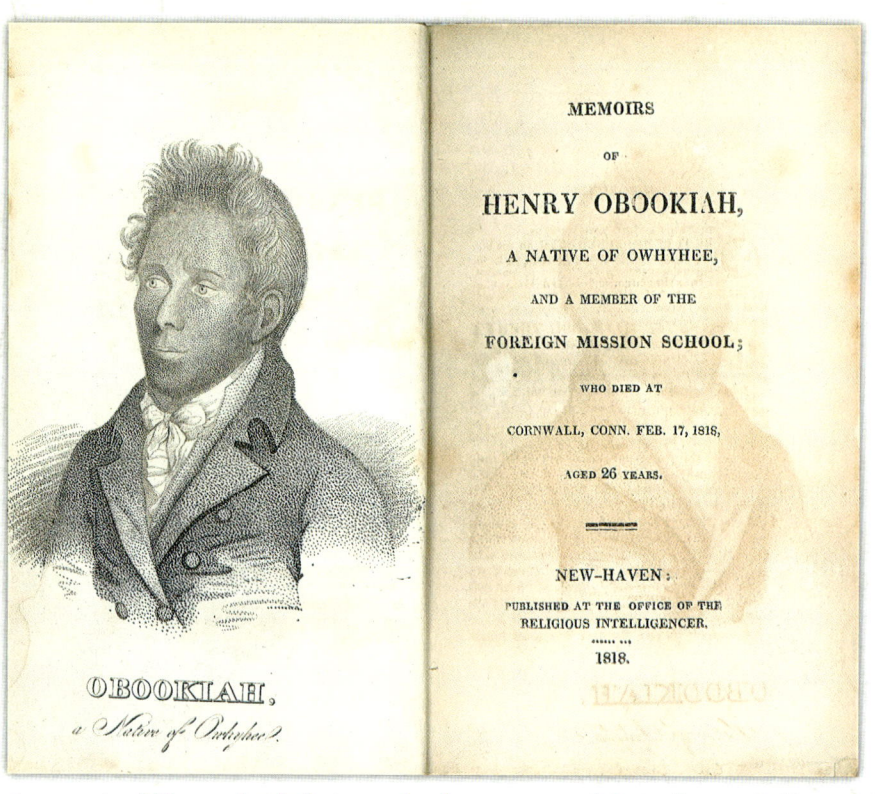

A portrait of Henry Opukahaia on the frontispiece of the collection of letters and memoirs compiled by Timothy Dwight's son, Edwin

WIKIMEDIA COMMONS

Turning Preaching into a Science

While Christians agreed on the importance of helping people understand the exciting story of God's grace for sinners, not everyone agreed on how to do it. Some were so eager to see a revival that they focused on creating the right atmosphere and saying the right words in order to provoke religious excitement. Others thought they should just preach the gospel and let God do the rest.

The most famous preacher of the first kind was Charles Grandison Finney (1792–1875), a former law clerk who went as far as writing manuals on how to generate a revival. He thought preaching could be treated like a science, where the right methods produce the right results. Finney's activities represented the third and final phase of the Awakening, which started in small towns in western New York and spread to the largest cities in the United States and Britain.

One of Finney's most questionable methods was called the anxious bench. It was a bench on which people who were not yet converted could sit while the whole church prayed for them. Many people did not approve of this new technique. John Williamson Nevin (1803–1886) pointed out that it focused on people's emotions, which come and go, instead of teaching people the Bible and catechisms to help them understand what being a Christian really means.

One of Finney's main opponents was Asahel Nettleton (1783–1844). Nettleton traveled around the country too, but instead of moving quickly from place to place, he stayed in each community for weeks or months, often filling a pulpit when the pastor was absent. In this way, he encouraged people to establish and attend local churches instead of attending occasional revival meetings.

Finney agreed that excitement can't last long, but he believed that Christ would come within a few years and that Christians could keep up their excitement until then. Around the end of his life, however, he realized that keeping up religious enthusiasm is not always easy. For example, some regions of New York State where he had preached became known as the "burnt-over district," where excitement gave way to disillusionment.

Since he didn't believe in most basic Christian teachings, such as that through Adam all human beings are born in sin and that Jesus took on Himself the sins of His people, Finney's message led preachers to trust in their methods and abilities rather than in the gospel and the supernatural work of God's Spirit.

A PHILOSOPHER OF FEELINGS

While most Enlightenment philosophers stressed the importance of reason, the German Friedrich Schleiermacher (1768–1834) stressed the importance of feelings. To him, the experiences and religious feelings of Christians were more important than the facts described in the Bible. What really mattered, he said, was not a set of creeds and confessions or a moral choice, as Kant had taught, but "a feeling of utter dependence from God." His views influenced the church so much that he is often called the father of modern **liberalism**.

Friedrick Schleiermacher
UNIVERSITÄTSBIBLIOTHEK LEIPZIG

A CHANGING WORLD • 167

New Religious Movements

Since America never had a single religion that was protected and supported by the government, it was easy for new religious groups to take root and prosper. Independent religious groups that reject some basic Christian doctrines or add new revelations to the Bible are called **cults**.

A cult that started in the nineteenth century is the Church of Jesus Christ of the Latter-day Saints, whose members are today known as Mormons. It was founded by a man named Joseph Smith (1805–1844). Smith claimed that God told him in a series of visions not to join any of the existing churches because they were all far from true Christianity and to start his own group instead. He said he had received a separate revelation, called *The Book of Mormon*, written on golden tablets in a language only he could translate.

Smith said he saw God and Jesus as separate beings and not one God. He also taught that it was permissible for a man to have more than one wife. This practice caused his followers some trouble because it was illegal. Eventually, Mormons went back to allowing only one wife.

Mary Baker Eddy (1821–1910) was the founder of Christian Science. She taught that Jesus came to save the world not from sin, but from incorrect thoughts. In fact, everything physical, including illnesses, is just an illusion created by these thoughts. Those who free themselves of these illusions through faith and prayer can live a life without sickness, sin, pain, and death.

Mary Baker Eddy
LIBRARY OF CONGRESS

William Miller (1782–1849) believed he had discovered the date of Christ's return, even though the Bible says that no one can know it (Matthew 24:36). He set a date in 1843, then changed it to October 1844. His followers sold all their property and traveled to a hill where Jesus was supposed to come. When nothing happened, this event became known as the Great Disappointment.

Some people refused to believe that Miller was mistaken. One of these people, Ellen G. White (1827–1915), said that Jesus had returned invisible and in glory. She was one of the cofounders of a group that became known as Seventh Day Adventism. Seventh Day Adventists believe that Saturday, not Sunday, is the day that Christians must keep holy.

Charles Taze Russell (1852–1916) was cofounder of the Zion's Watch Tower Tract Society. The members of one of the society's branches became known as Jehovah's Witnesses. Jehovah's Witnesses don't believe in the Trinity. They believe that Jesus is not God but was created directly by God. They have their own translation of the Bible and claim they are the only true church.

This 1901 cartoon shows the followers of William Miller waiting on roofs in a humorous light. In reality, this was a sad occasion because many people lost their properties and became terribly discouraged.

KEPPLER & SCHWARZMANN, LIBRARY OF CONGRESS

Princeton Seminary and the Authority of God's Word

By the beginning of the nineteenth century, it was obvious that Christians had to be better prepared to face the doubts and questions raised by philosophy and science. That's why in 1809 Ashbel Green (1762–1848), a professor at the College of New Jersey (now Princeton University), persuaded his denomination to establish a new seminary for this task. The school, called Princeton Theological Seminary, started in 1812 with three students and one professor, Archibald Alexander (1772–1851). Another professor, Samuel Miller (1769–1850), joined him the next year, and a third one, Charles Hodge (1797–1878), joined in 1822.

Ashbel Green
PRINCETON UNIVERSITY ART MUSEUM

All the professors were committed to teaching the Bible as it had been carefully interpreted in the historical Reformed confessions. Hodge liked to say that in the whole time he had been at Princeton, there had never been a new idea. New ideas are good in art or technology, but Christians should not try to change the teachings of the Bible. The idea that Christians can modify biblical teachings in order to adapt to their culture is called liberalism or **modernism**.

One professor at Princeton, Benjamin Breckenridge (often referred to as B. B. Warfield (1851–1921), became one of the greatest defenders of the Bible and of the historical Reformed confessions that explain its meaning. He is remembered for his studies and writings that prove the Bible can still be trusted. An article he wrote in 1881 with his friend and colleague A. A. Hodge (1823–1886) helped Christians understand how God inspired the Bible and how the Bible is without error.

The men who wrote the Bible, Warfield and Hodge said, weren't inspired the way you may be inspired to read this book or to put it away. Nor did God dictate the Bible to them. Instead, He gave them the right words to say without changing the way they normally expressed themselves.

That's why sometimes we can find in the Bible some expressions that are commonly used, even if they are not absolutely scientific. For example, we say the sun rises even though it's the earth that turns. This is what Bible authors did. Warfield believed that the Bible was not meant to teach science, history, or geography in a technical manner, but it is absolutely accurate even in these subjects when they are understood in the way the writers intended.

B. B. Warfield
REFORMATION ART

THE PRINCETONIANS AND DARWINISM

Charles Hodge thought that Darwinism was **atheism** because the idea of natural selection removes God from creation. And without God, creation has no purpose or design.

B. B. Warfield agreed with Hodge. He thought that some form of evolution after creation could be possible, but God would still be the author because He works in both creating and sustaining the world. What mostly concerned Warfield was that Darwin's theory had provided an excuse for those who rejected any idea of God's supernatural creation. Also, by making human beings the result of a long evolution, Darwin denied their unique dignity as creatures with distinct souls made in the image of God.

Great Questions of the Church

MAY WE QUESTION WHAT THE BIBLE SAYS?

For centuries scholars had been studying ancient texts to see if they were the original versions and to determine their authors and the place where they were written. For example, in the fifteenth century, Lorenzo Valla had been able to prove that a document the Roman Catholic Church claimed to be a letter from Constantine I was instead written at least two hundred years after the emperor's death (see p. 46). This method was often used to determine when and how the books of the Bible had been written.

Some Christians disliked this treatment of the Bible. They thought the Bible should be believed without asking questions.

This letter (known as the Gallio Inscription) from Emperor Claudius (10 BC–AD 54) to Proconsul Gallio is a main key in establishing the dates for the apostle Paul's letters and ministry. Archaeological findings like this have repeatedly confirmed the truth of the New Testament.

ANDY MONTGOMERY, FLICKR

Many others welcomed it. After all, they thought, if the Bible is God's word, it should be able to stand up to any examination. Besides, knowing about the intentions of the biblical authors and the culture of their time can help readers to understand the Bible better.

According to B. B. Warfield, examining the Bible carefully is a Christian duty. Since Christians base all their hope of eternal life on the words of the Bible, he said, they should make sure these words are telling facts. He also did his own investigations and determined that even some of the most frequently doubted New Testament texts were the same texts that early Christians read.

But Warfield disagreed with those who looked for contradictions in the Bible, to prove that it's not God's word, and who wouldn't even consider the Bible's teachings that Christ is God.

Think about It

- Name some examples in the Bible where God uses means to accomplish His purposes, even though these means are imperfect.

- Have you ever found some passages in the Bible that seemed to contradict each other or that appeared too difficult to believe? Is it a good idea for you to ignore your questions, or should you ask your parents or pastor about it? Explain why.

- Do you think Christians should ignore doubts and questions raised by unbelievers? Why or why not?

- During Warfield's time some critics accused Christians of being intolerant of other ideas because the Christians, after taking time to examine their critics' conclusions, expressed their disagreement. "Is the critic only to be free and the Church bound?" Warfield asked. Give an example of how Christians can respect other people's ideas without denying their own.

Helping the Poor and Oppressed in North America

Nineteenth-century North America was a land of extremes, as there were people who had great fortunes on one hand and those who suffered dreadful poverty on the other. The famines and wars that struck the European Continent (especially the Great Irish Potato Famine in 1845) caused many people to move to the other side of the Atlantic in order to survive. Between 1870 and 1900, the population of North America grew from thirty-eight million to seventy-four million. Often poverty gave way to disease, violence, drunkenness, and crime. Like Christians in Europe, many American Christians took on the challenge, both as a personal effort and by raising societies.

An early pioneer of this type of society in America was the Scottish Isabella Graham (1742–1814), who established the Society for the Relief of Poor Widows in 1797. This was one of the first women's societies to successfully raise funds from petitions. Besides providing basic assistance, Isabella offered the women education, friendship, encouragement, and help in finding jobs. She bought flax and spinning wheels so they could make clothes and found customers who would buy them.

She also founded the Orphan Asylum Society and the Society for Promoting Industry among the Poor and started the first Sunday school in New York for adults who could not read or write.

During the Civil War, many Christian women devoted their lives to the care of the wounded, both in their cities and on the battlefields. Many, like Margaret Elizabeth Breckinridge (1832–1864), saw it as a mission to help men wounded in both body and spirit.

After the war there was a lot to do to rebuild what had been destroyed, to help families who had lost their men in the war, and to encourage peace and reconciliation. The African American community also needed a lot of assistance because the Thirteenth Amendment that abolished slavery (1865) didn't put an end to poverty, hatred, and violence.

Margaret Elizabeth Breckinridge devoted her time to help those who were wounded in the Civil War.
INTERNET BOOK ARCHIVE

Many Christians, both Black and White, worked toward that end. The Presbyterian minister Francis James Grimké (1850–1937) became particularly influential. In 1909 he helped to found the National Association for the Advancement of Colored People (NAACP) in order to help those who were rejected, mistreated, and killed by violent mobs just because of the color of their skin. It was around this time that a group of resentful White men from the South formed a secret racist society that grew into what is now known as the Ku Klux Klan. Grimké also wrote letters to President Woodrow Wilson (1856–1924) to protest his decision to divide Blacks and Whites in society (a practice known as segregation) and to close many government positions to Blacks.

Francis James Grimké
WIKIMEDIA COMMONS

While fighting for basic human rights, Grimké didn't forget to point his hearers to Christ. In 1918, when the nation was just recovering from the Spanish flu that killed over 675,000 Americans, he could rejoice that in spite of deadly illness and persistent racism, the greatest comfort for Christians had always been "to feel that we were in the hands of a loving Father who was looking out for us, who had given us the great assurance that all things should work together for our good. And, therefore, that come what would—whether we were smitten or perished, we knew it would be well with us, that there was no reason to be alarmed."

Great Questions of the Church

WHAT IS THE GOSPEL?

While many Christians like Graham, Breckinridge, and Grimké were able to work toward a better society while pointing others to Christ, His word, and His church, others focused all their efforts on the need for action. One of these was Walter Rauschenbusch (1861–1918), a pastor in an area of New York that was so full of poverty and crime that it was nicknamed Hell's Kitchen.

Rauschenbusch believed that Christians should devote their lives to bringing God's kingdom on earth through social work. There were others who shared this idea, but he became well known because of a book he wrote on the subject. This idea became known as the social gospel.

Rauschenbusch's idea sounded good, but many Christians worried that he and others like him were forgetting the true gospel, which is the announcement of the good news of what Christ has done for sinners, who, without Him, would be left with the greatest problem any human being can have: how to be reconciled to God.

An artist's view of Five Points, one of the poorest areas of nineteenth-century New York. In 1858 the *New York Herald* called it a "nest of drunkenness, roguery, debauchery, vice, and pestilence."

BEQUEST OF MRS. SCREVEN LORILLARD (ALICE WHITNEY), FROM THE COLLECTION OF MRS. J. INSLEY BLAIR, 2016, THE MET MUSEUM

Think about It

- The idea of devoting one's life to improving the lives of others sounds good, but in the end many churches focused on this *instead* of thinking and speaking about Christ, His word, and His work for sinners. Because of this, they became just like any other social movement, and the Jesus they presented to others was just another social reformer. Is this why Jesus came to earth—to make sure poor people could have food, clothing, and a good education? Why or why not?

- Is it a message of good news that Jesus came just to save people from poverty and that He needs us to carry on His work? Why or why not?

- Rauschenbusch believed that Christians should devote their lives to bringing God's kingdom on earth through social work. According to the Bible, who is the author of God's kingdom, and when will it come in full?

- If the gospel is an announcement of what God has done for us in Christ and His kingdom is a reality He is bringing on earth, does that mean we should be indifferent to the needs of other human beings? Why not? Find some verses in the Bible that tell us to love justice and to care for others and their needs.

Pentecostal Beginnings

On April 18, 1906, a religious event made the headlines of the *Los Angeles Daily Times*. It was a meeting in an old, abandoned African Methodist Episcopal Church on an alley, 312 Azusa Street. There, William Seymour (1870–1922), the son of former slaves, preached a rousing message.

Like other preachers from the Holiness Movement, he spoke of a second blessing from God. But he also believed in a third blessing, when God gave the believer power to witness about Christ. As Seymour preached these views, some of his hearers claimed that they were given the gift of speaking in foreign languages.

This refers to an event in the life of the apostles when they were all together in one room and received the Holy Spirit (Acts 2:1–4). At that time, the apostles could speak in foreign languages they had never spoken before and that visitors to Jerusalem could understand (Acts 2:5–13). It was a miracle, like many miracles God allowed the apostles to perform.

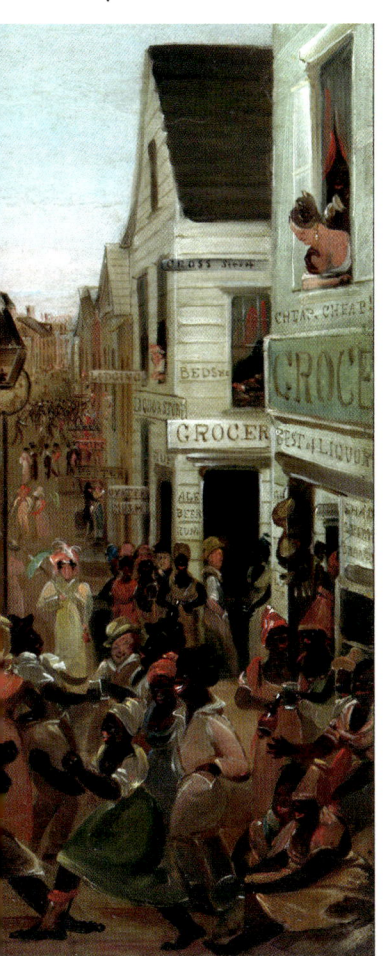

But the languages the people on Azusa Street used were mostly languages no one had ever heard, which the newspaper called a "weird Babel of tongues." The word *tongues* means "languages" in older English, and Babel was a biblical place where people started to speak in languages that others could not understand (Genesis 11:1–9). The difference was that at Babel, God was punishing the people because of their pride by confusing their language. And the people on Azusa Street thought they could miraculously interpret what was being said.

The event made news all over the world, and more people wanted to receive the Holy Spirit in the same way. A new movement started that is now known as the Pentecostal movement. (Pentecost was the name of the biblical feast the apostles were attending when they received the Holy Spirit.) Since then, the movement continued to grow, so much that today there are about a half billion **Pentecostals** in the world.

To more traditional Protestants, Pentecostals seemed to reject the Reformation teaching of *sola Scriptura* by saying that Christians need to receive new revelations from the Spirit. Pentecostals, instead, thought that traditional Protestants were limiting God's Spirit.

BASIC CHRISTIAN BELIEFS

Fearing that many Christians were drifting far from biblical Christianity, a group of Christians met at Niagara-on-the-Lake, Ontario, Canada, at the end of the nineteenth century to define essential teachings all Christians must believe. They made a list of five: the Bible is free of errors, Jesus is God, Jesus was born of a virgin (Mary), Jesus died to take the punishment for the sins of those who believe in Him, and Jesus rose after death. These five statements later became known as the fundamentals (or basics) of the Christian faith.

This sign on Azusa Street reminds viewers of the event that took place there.

CALLSIGNPINK, WIKIMEDIA COMMONS

A CHANGING WORLD • 173

LATIN AMERICA, 1789–1913

1837 — The Argentinian constitution allows for freedom of religion, even though Roman Catholicism is the favored religion of the day and the president is to be a Roman Catholic.

1840 — The British claim the Falkland Islands as a colony, opening the door to Protestant missionaries.

1857 — A new constitution restricts the rights of the Roman Catholic Church in Mexico, provoking a civil war.

Changes in Latin America

By the nineteenth century, much of Latin America was Roman Catholic. In fact, the constitution of some states declared that the Roman Catholic Church was the only acceptable church. Protestants were often persecuted and deprived of some legal rights. In Argentina, until 1837, children of Protestants could not receive birth certificates and had no legal rights at all (as if they were never born). When Protestants died, they had to be buried outside the city.

Much of this began to change as more Protestant missionaries arrived. Also, as the Latin American nations gained their independence from Spain and Portugal, they began to restrict the rights and privileges of the Roman Catholic Church and to allow for freedom of religion.

Protestant Missions

Until the nineteenth century, much of the missionary work in Latin America had been done by Roman Catholics. In most cases, conquest and religion went hand in hand. For example, when Spain conquered a country, its people had to become Roman Catholic.

Protestant missionaries were few, and they were mostly in the larger cities. Some settled in the Falkland Islands, which the British claimed as a colony in 1840. Among the first to come was Allen Francis Gardiner (1794–1851), a former British Royal Navy officer who also served as a missionary in Chile and Bolivia.

Gardiner tried hard to raise funds and encourage more missionaries to serve in the Falkland Islands, but few people responded. Together with other missionaries, he died of starvation after they were surrounded by aggressive local tribes. The British ship that had been sent to help them arrived too late. But Gardiner's diary, later published in England, did what he couldn't do in life—move more missionaries to follow in his footsteps.

A new group of missionaries was led in 1869 by George Pakenham Despard (1813–1881), who left the islands after he was attacked by locals. His adoptive son Thomas Bridges (ca. 1842–1898), only seventeen years old, took over leadership. He learned the local language (Yámana) well enough to create a dictionary and grammar book. His six children grew up speaking English, Spanish, and Yámana.

Protestant Challenges in Roman Catholic Countries

Local tribes were not the only threat to Protestant missions. Many Protestants suffered persecution from Roman Catholics. One of these Protestants was the Brazilian José Manouel da Conceição (1822–1873), a former Catholic priest who heard the gospel from the American Ashbel Green Simonton (1833–1867), the first missionary to plant a Protestant church in Brazil. Conceição joined the Presbyterian Church. In 1865 he became the first Protestant pastor in Brazil. His ordination was December 17, 1865. After serving for some time in Sao Paulo, Brazil, he decided to travel from village to village to take the gospel to people who lived outside the cities. He also visited his old parishes to explain his decision to leave the Roman Catholic Church and to apologize for some of his earlier teachings that he now considered wrong. But many Roman Catholics considered him a heretic, and he was often insulted and beaten. Once, he was stoned and left for dead.

Allen Francis Gardiner
WIKIMEDIA COMMONS

In 1873 the church elders decided that Conceição should stop traveling and come back to Rio de Janeiro to take care of his health. While he traveled there by train, he was arrested by a policeman who thought he was homeless. By the time he was released, Conceição had no money to take another train and had to walk many miles to the city. He finally died of exhaustion. His life inspired other missionaries to take the gospel to the countryside. A seminary in Sao Paulo is named after him.

A Baptist pastor who fought for religious freedom was the Swiss Pablo Besson (1848–1932), who served in Argentina for forty-five years. His newspaper articles and his persistence with the Argentinian authorities brought legal changes. He also organized the first Spanish-speaking Argentine Baptist church and produced an important translation of the New Testament from Greek into Spanish.

The Mexican Revolt

In 1857 Ignacio Comonfort (1812–1863), president of Mexico, proclaimed a new constitution stating that the Roman Catholic Church would no longer be the only acceptable church in the country or have control over education. It also limited the amount of land the church could own.

The Roman Catholic Church excommunicated Comonfort and those who supported the new constitution. Then it started a rebellion that turned into a civil war. In the end, the clergy and those who supported them were defeated and the Roman Catholic Church lost even more rights.

Jamaica

In the nineteenth century, so many people in Jamaica became Christian and attended church that other countries began to take notice. One of the first missionaries to Jamaica was the Baptist George Liele (ca. 1750–1828), a former slave from Virginia who had been serving as a pastor in Georgia. In Jamaica, where slavery had not been abolished, he received much persecution from slave owners, but he continued to be polite and respected their reasonable requests. Other pastors followed his example. By the 1830s, about fifty thousand people had become Christian through the preaching of Baptist pastors.

Pentecostal Churches in Latin America

The Pentecostal movement grew rapidly in Latin America. One reason is that its emphasis on the gifts of the Holy Spirit gave the impression that anyone who had faith could receive messages from God, financial supplies, and healing. In fact, those who suffered from leprosy, a serious disease that can cause painful damage to the skin and nerves, were among the first people to turn to Pentecostal churches in Brazil.

Also, Pentecostal preachers spoke simply, like the majority of the people who came to their churches, and used popular rhythms for their music. Today, tens of millions of people in Latin America attend Pentecostal churches.

An abandoned nineteenth-century ship off the coast of the Falkland Islands
AMANDA, FLICKR

> Let us all place ourselves at the feet of the great Savior Jesus Christ. Let us all be at his service until he comes, until we say: "Blessed is he who comes in the name of the Lord." May God be with you, until the great day of the reunion of the children of God, saved by the blood of Jesus Christ, our Redeemer.
> —PABLO BESSON

Like in other parts of the world, until the nineteenth century, Asia had learned about Christianity mainly from Roman Catholic missionaries, especially Jesuits, and a few Moravians. Most countries were closed to foreigners, and missionaries were often persecuted. In the nineteenth century, however, as Asian countries began to open up their borders, they saw a growth in missions.

EAST ASIA AND OCEANIA, 1789–1913

1792 — The founding of the British Missionary Society and the preparation of their first team to India marks an important moment in the history of missions.

1793 — William Carey, known as "the Father of Missions," goes to India.

1798 — A three-year persecution of Christians begins in Vietnam.

1807 — Robert Morrison is the first Protestant missionary to China.

1815 — Joseph Kam, a Dutch Reformed minister, revitalizes missions in Indonesia.

1839 — The Welsh missionary John Williams is killed by cannibals in the Pacific Island of Erromango.

1882 — A Korean treaty with the United States allows American missionaries to enter Korea.

1883 — Seo Sang-ryun starts the first Presbyterian church in Korea.

1899–1901 — Many Christians are killed in the Boxer Rebellion in China.

1907 — After a great revival, the Korean Presbyterian Church becomes self-supporting under Korean elders and deacons.

1910 — Korea becomes a Japanese territory, and the church suffers persecution.

A CHANGING WORLD

Missionary Societies

The nineteenth century has been called the golden century of Protestant missions, as the interest in taking the gospel to other nations increased. This was largely through the missionary societies that sprang up all over Europe and North America. The goals of these societies included raising funds, training missionaries, spreading information, and inspiring others to serve in mission fields.

The first Protestant society founded specifically to send and supervise overseas missions was the Baptist Missionary Society (BMS), begun in 1792 by twelve Baptist leaders. At a time when many Protestants thought they could just pray for the conversion of people in other lands and wait for God to produce it, BMS reminded them that God works through means, sending Christians to take His gospel to others. The same year, William Carey (1761–1834), a BMS member, wrote an influential book on this subject.

The first BMS missionary to India was the medical doctor John Thomas (1757–1801), who knew one of the local languages, Bengali. Carey volunteered to go with him. Today, Carey is known as the father of modern missions because his pleas and example inspired hundreds of missionaries to follow in his footsteps. He moved to India in 1793 and stayed there until his death. His motto was "Expect great things, and attempt great things."

Carey did most of his missionary work in Serampore, near Calcutta, together with William Ward (1769–1823), Joshua Marshman (1768–1837), and their wives. Now known as the "Serampore trio," Carey, Ward, and Marshman wrote an important document, the Serampore Covenant, promising to devote themselves to the people of India, taking the gospel to them, caring for them, avoiding any English habit that might offend them, and preparing them to become missionaries to others.

The trio's first Indian convert was Krishna Pal (1764–1822), who had already heard the gospel from Moravian missionaries. Pal went on to become a preacher and wrote some hymns in Bengali, including one that is translated into English, "O Thou My Soul, Forget No More."

Reports from BMS's missionaries soon inspired other societies. The London Missionary Society (LMS) started in 1795 largely through the efforts of David Bogue (1750–1825), who insisted on the importance of giving missionaries an excellent education. The Church Mission Society (CMS) was founded in London in 1799. Many more followed in both Europe and North America. Later on, some denominations began to send and supervise their own missionaries without working through missionary societies.

William Carey studying with Brahmin Pandit. Brahmins were men who belonged to a special social class devoted to the duties and ceremonies of the Hindu religion.

WIKIMEDIA COMMONS

Christianity in India

By the time William Carey arrived in India, there were already some growing Christian communities, particularly in Tamil Nadu (see p. 131). In 1799, for example, whole villages became Christian after hearing the gospel from David Sundaranandam, a disciple of Satyanathan Pillai. These mass conversions worried the owners of those lands, who began to persecute Christians, torturing and killing some of them and burning their books and chapels. Sundaranandam disappeared and was never found. Outside that region, Christians started some villages of refuge to care for those who escaped the persecution, which continued until 1806.

In other parts of India, missionary work proceeded at a slower pace. Some blame goes to the East India Company, which was responsible for part of the administration of India as a British colony and for trade between India and Britain. The company was mostly concerned with keeping a peaceful trade and was afraid that missionaries would hinder it by offending the Hindu and Muslim communities.

Some major changes happened when the Scot Charles Grant (1746–1823) took charge of the company. Grant had first arrived in India with the goal of getting rich. But in 1776, when two of his young daughters died of smallpox within nine days of each other, he remembered the gospel he had heard from his parents and began to devote his life to Christ.

He used his position to bring to an end some policies of the East India Company, such as the support of local temples (through raising taxes for pilgrims), and some local practices he considered cruel, such as the custom of burning widows alive next to the bodies of their husbands.

Missionary Methods

Alexander Duff (1806–1878) was the first missionary sent to India by the Church of Scotland. He focused on education. His school in Calcutta, India, attracted many young people who were disappointed with their traditional religion. He also organized and led New College in Edinburgh, Scotland, a school to prepare missionaries to face the new questions raised by people in different cultures. This school taught the history, geography, languages, literature, and beliefs of different countries. It was the first school of this kind in the world.

Alexander Duff
ZU-09, ISTOCK

American minister Rufus Anderson (1796–1880) also believed in education, with the goal of preparing the locals to present the gospel in a way their own people would understand and to plant and lead their own churches. He thought foreign missionaries should stay in a place only long enough to help to organize these churches.

Anderson's concept was that local churches had to be self-propagating, self-governing, and self-supporting. In other words, they were supposed to take care of themselves without depending on foreign churches. This concept was created by either Anderson or by Henry Venn (1796–1873), who acted as honorary secretary of the Church Missionary Society for thirty-two years.

John Livingston Nevius (1829–1893), also from America, took Anderson's method a step forward by encouraging the local Christians to raise their own support from the start so that people wouldn't become Christians just to get foreign money. Foreign missionary societies should develop only programs that the local churches could support. He and his wife, Helen Coan Nevius (1833–1910), were missionaries in China and Korea, where they put his method into effect. After John's death, Helen published an account of their missionary experience.

A CHANGING WORLD • 181

Closed and Open Doors

Many Asian emperors believed that Europeans and Americans were a negative influence on their countries and that Christianity angered their gods, so they closed the doors to any interactions with the West. They also banned the spreading of any religion other than their own. Still, a few missionaries managed to enter their countries.

CHINA

When Robert Morrison (1782–1834) arrived in Macao in 1807, encouraging someone to embrace a religion other than Buddhism or **Confucianism** was a crime punishable by death. So was teaching Chinese to foreigners. But Morrison, who is considered the first Protestant missionary to China, managed to learn Chinese and found employment through the East India Company, which allowed him to stay in the country. This opened the door for other missionaries after him.

After 1860, when China began to open its borders to foreign merchants, foreign missionaries took advantage of the opportunity to bring the gospel to this large region where few people had heard of Christ.

But this open door came as a result of two painful wars between Britain and China. The first of these started in 1840 after the Chinese rulers had tried unsuccessfully to stop Britain from bringing into their country opium, a dangerous and addictive drug that destroyed lives and brought poverty to many families.

Most Christian missionaries tried to stop this trade. Some, however, became involved in it or in the wars that came from it. Karl Gützlaff (1803–1851), one of the first Protestant missionaries to Thailand and Korea and the first Lutheran missionary to China, served as an interpreter and administrator on British ships smuggling opium to China. In any case, the wars that resulted from this trade hurt missionary work because many Chinese people associated foreign missionaries with the trading companies that shipped this dangerous drug into their country.

> The owner of the boat that took Robert Morrison to China: *And so, Mr. Morrison, you really expect to make an impression on the idolatry of the great Chinese Empire?*
>
> Robert Morrison: *No, sir, but I expect God will.*

A Korean Christian who was brought to Christ through the American Bible Society

LIBRARY OF CONGRESS

KOREA

In the meantime, while Korea was still closed to foreigners, the gospel entered the country through a local merchant, Seo Sang-ryun (1848–1926). Seo Sang-ryun fell seriously ill while he was in Manchuria and received medical and spiritual care from the Scottish missionaries John Ross (1842–1915) and John MacIntyre (1837–1905). He helped them to translate the Bible into Korean, then brought it back into his country. He and his brother Seo Sang-u set up the first Presbyterian church in the Korean village of Seorae, near Seoul.

Some foreign missionaries were able to enter closed countries by offering their services as medical doctors. This was the case of medical doctor Horace Allen (1858–1932), a Presbyterian missionary who moved to Seoul, Korea, in 1884 as a physician for the small foreign community. That December, during a banquet in the royal court, some rebels wounded Prince Min Yong-ik (1860–1914), nephew of Empress Myung-Sung (1851–1895). In that climate of violence, all foreigners fled the city except Allen and his wife, who were bound to their duty to help the wounded. Summoned to the palace, Allen performed emergency surgery on the prince and saved his life. After this, Emperor Gojong (1852–1919), who had been suspicious of foreigners, authorized Allen to build and direct a government hospital and allowed more missionaries into Korea.

After 1882, when the Korean government made a treaty with the United States, the missionary work in Korea grew quickly.

A KOREAN REVIVAL

In 1910, after a war between Japan and Russia, Korea became a territory of Japan. By that time Christianity had made great progress in Korea, and Christian leaders were known and respected. Since Japan was strongly anti-Christian, it was only natural for Koreans to hope that the church would help them put an end to its rule.

An American missionary, William N. Blair (1876–1970), could foresee the results. If the church had supported a fight against Japan, "thousands would have welcomed her leadership and flocked to her banner." But is that what Korean Christians wanted?

From the time Jesus began to preach and do miracles, there had always been a temptation to see Him as a savior against an earthly oppressor. But the leaders of the Korean church knew that it was not what He had come to be. It took courage for them to preach love, patience, and forgiveness instead of anger and rebellion.

By then, the Korean church had already established a tradition of taking a week out of the year when everyone would put aside their work and devote their time to prayer and the study of God's Word. In the winter of 1906–1907, these meetings moved Christians to cry out to God in prayer, asking for forgiveness for their sins, including their hatred for the Japanese and their lack of trust in God.

This time of prayer and repentance prepared the Korean Christians for the creation of churches led by Korean elders. It also prepared them for the persecution the Japanese government was going to inflict on them.

Emperor Gojong of Korea
WIKIMEDIA COMMONS

> *When men get terribly confused in their minds, when they get deadly hatred in their hearts toward those whom they regard as oppressors, when they grow cold toward their leaders and find the message of love and forgiveness unwelcome, then a condition of things is brought about that the devil knows well how to use.*
> —WILLIAM BLAIR

Some Challenges and Persecutions

Foreign missionaries were not always welcome in Asian countries. Some rulers feared that these missionaries and the local people who followed them might be foreign spies. In other cases, it was the people who resented foreign missionaries because of the powerful and greedy nations they represented.

THE BOXER REBELLION

One of the worst nineteenth-century persecutions of Christians in China happened during the Boxer Rebellion of 1899–1901. The Boxers were a Chinese resistance group, mostly from the countryside, who called themselves the Society of Righteous and Harmonious Fists and fought according to the rules of the ancient Chinese **martial arts**.

Frustrated by increasing poverty, the Boxers placed much of the blame on the Western powers who had gained much control of China. Because of this, they fought against the foreigners who had come into their country, including Christians.

In 1900 the Boxers besieged the foreign embassies in Peking, the capital of China. The Empress Dowager Cixi (1834–1908) took their side. At the same time, marines from eight nations came to protect the foreigners. The Chinese imperial family fled the city. After fifty-five days of siege, the European troops won, but hundreds of foreigners and thousands of Chinese had already been killed.

A Chinese Christian who suffered during the Boxer Rebellion was Ding Limei (1871–1936), who had been trained and ordained as a pastor by the American Presbyterian Mission. Ding was thrown in prison for forty days, where he was whipped about two hundred times. After his release he accepted a call as a Presbyterian minister and traveled around the country to bring the gospel to others. Later in life, he taught at the North China Theological Seminary while continuing to serve as a pastor.

Chinese Christians fleeing during the Boxer Rebellion
LIBRARY OF CONGRESS

184 • A CHANGING WORLD

A Chinese Christian pastor and family in Canton, China. Pastors and their families were especially hated by the Boxers.
LIBRARY OF CONGRESS

THE MARTYRS OF VIETNAM

Another bloody persecution of Christians started in Vietnam in 1798, when Emperor Cảnh Thịnh (1783–1802) declared that Christianity was dangerous to the country as a means to promote foreign power. He then ordered the destruction of all churches and seminaries in Vietnam, which at that time were Roman Catholic. The persecution continued for sixty-three years with the next three kings of the Nguyen dynasty. European priests were thrown into rivers or into the ocean, and Vietnamese priests were cut in half. In the end, over one hundred thousand Vietnamese Catholics were killed.

BIBLE WOMEN

Some Asian traditions banned men from speaking to women outside their family. This rule was so strict that some churches placed a thick curtain between the section for men and the section for women. Chŏn Sam-dŏk, the first baptized Korean woman, had to stick her head through a hole in that curtain to receive the water.

For this reason, the task of bringing the gospel to Asian women fell mostly on missionary wives and single female missionaries. While they learned the Asian languages and culture, these missionaries often enlisted the help of local women, who became known as Bible women. Because most Asian women were not taught how to read, the missionaries opened schools specifically for them.

One of the customs learned by these foreign missionaries was that of hosting groups of women in someone's living room. When Rosetta Sherwood Hall (1865–1951), an American doctor and missionary to Korea, had a baby, at least fifteen hundred women and children came to visit her. These were good opportunities to share the gospel.

Often, Bible women visited the sick and brought help to communities in remote areas. Some worked as translators for other missionaries, and some worked alone under the supervision of their missions. In some cases they even started Bible study groups that later grew into churches. Both men and women found Christ through the witness of Bible women.

A CHANGING WORLD • 185

Some Men and Women of the Nineteenth-Century Church

PROTESTANT MISSIONARIES TO ASIA

The Dutch **JOSEPH KAM** (1769–1833) revitalized the churches in the Maluku Islands, Eastern Indonesia, which had been planted by Dutch missionaries but were left without an ordained pastor. Along with preaching and teaching, he directed the construction of the church building, baptized about seventy-five hundred people, examined those who were already baptized, brought back the regular administration of the Lord's Supper, and oversaw a translation of the Bible and the catechisms. Later, he helped other missionaries to organize their churches along the same lines.

The front page of the oldest New Testament translation into Malay, which is at the foundation of today's languages of Malaysia and Indonesia. It was translated in 1612 by Albert Cornelius Ruyl, a Protestant trader with the Dutch East India Company.

BLEE19, WIKIMEDIA COMMONS

WILLIAM MILNE (1785–1822), the second Protestant missionary to China, worked with Robert Morrison and **LIANG FA** (1789–1855) to translate the Bible into Chinese. Under his guidance, Liang became the first ordained Chinese evangelist, influencing more people than Morrison and Milne ever could. Liang kept preaching in spite of harsh persecution. He believed that Buddhism and Confucianism encouraged people to be selfish and didn't provide any peace to those who were battling against persistent sins.

BEHARI LAL SINGH (d. 1873) learned about Christianity in the school started by Alexander Duff. Impressed by what the Bible says and the example of his teachers, he and his brother became Christians. After studying some time in Scotland, Singh gave up his government job to become a missionary. As the only Indian at the 1860 Liverpool Conference on missions, he gave the representatives much valued advice. He said that missionaries should give more responsibilities to local Christians, ask for their help to produce better translations, and give them a better education so they could confidently explain Christianity to learned Hindus and Muslims.

ADONIRAM JUDSON (1788–1850) was an American Baptist missionary to Burma. During the First Burmese War with Britain, when the government suspected all foreigners of being spies, he spent nineteen months in terrible conditions in two different prisons. His wife, **ANN HASSELTINE JUDSON** (1789–1826), known as Nancy, kept petitioning for his freedom and gave presents to the jailers to get their permission to bring her husband food. She also gave Adoniram a pillow with his Burmese translation of the Bible hidden inside. A student of languages, she translated the books of Daniel and Jonah into Burmese and a catechism and the Gospel of Matthew into Thai. Adoniram remarried twice after Ann's death. **SARAH BOARDMAN JUDSON** (1803–1845) and **EMILY CHUBBUCK JUDSON** (1817–1854) continued Ann's work of translation and mission.

Adoniram Judson
INTERNET BOOK ARCHIVE

HUDSON TAYLOR (1832–1905) is considered one of the most influential missionaries to China. Unhappy with the policy of most missionary societies to keep missionaries in major ports, he founded the Chinese Inland Mission, encouraging missionaries to reach the millions of Chinese who lived inland. He believed that missionaries must live like the locals. At the same time, he condemned many Chinese traditions, such as the worship of ancestors. Besides preaching the gospel, Taylor helped the victims of a famine and fought against the British trade of opium to China.

CHARLOTTE DIGGES "LOTTIE" MOON (1840–1912) was an American Southern Baptist missionary who spent thirty-nine years in China, sharing the gospel with women and opening schools. She adopted Chinese dress and customs and learned the local language. At first people were afraid to talk to her, but the smell of freshly baked cookies in her doorway attracted the local children. Through them, she met their mothers. The letters she sent home, begging other Christians to either come to China or send support, greatly helped the growth of missionary work in China.

The Canadian **GEORGE LESLIE MACKAY** (1844–1901), the first Presbyterian missionary to Taiwan, is considered one of the greatest evangelists ever born. Simply through preaching and without much help from Canada, he pastored a church that grew to include over twenty-four hundred baptized members. He also oversaw the founding of sixty churches led by local pastors. He started a hospital and a number of schools, including a college to train pastors. In the course of time, the people of Taiwan built several statues of Mackay. On the anniversary of his death, the Taiwanese government issued a stamp in his honor. Children still read comic books about his life, and young people wear T-shirts displaying his portrait and his motto: "It is better to burn out than rust out."

Wang Laiquan
(also known as Wang Lae-Djun)

FROM *THE STORY OF THE CHINA INLAND MISSION* BY GERALDINE GUINNESS (1893)

HORACE GRANT UNDERWOOD (1859–1916) was one of the most important missionaries to Korea. Within twenty-three years of missionary work, about one hundred thousand people converted to Christianity. He built a home and school for orphan boys with a vision of establishing future leaders in society. He also founded the Korean Tract Society and a few schools and colleges, including some that are still operating.

A statue commemorating Horace Grant Underwood at Yonsei University in Seoul, Korea
RICKINASIA, WIKIMEDIA COMMONS

WANG LAIQUAN (1835–1901) helped Taylor run the hospital and went with him to England when Taylor had some medical problems. Wang helped translate the New Testament into his local language. After returning to China, he became a pastor.

AMY CARMICHAEL (1867–1951) is probably the most famous Protestant missionary to India. She left her native Ireland in 1895 and lived in Dohnavur, in southern India, until the end of her life. Along with announcing the gospel, she fought to free girls who, from a young age, were made to be properties of the local temples and treated as objects. Her efforts were rewarded in 1947, when the Madras state Parliament made it illegal to dedicate young girls to temple service. In 1919 she was awarded the kaisar-i-Hind medal for services to the people of India. During her life, Carmichael published thirty-eight books, mostly about her missionary service.

A CHANGING WORLD • 187

Taking the Gospel to Australia

Until the middle of the nineteenth century, few missionaries went to Australia intending to preach to the native populations. By the time more missionaries arrived, some of the settlers who had occupied the land had done much damage, robbing the natives of their lands and rights, mistreating them, and teaching them bad habits, such as getting drunk.

This bad example made it hard for the natives to trust foreign missionaries. Besides, some missionaries still needed to learn important lessons in understanding and respecting other cultures. But many missionaries spoke out the loudest against injustice, declaring the truth of Acts 17:26: "[God] has made from one blood every nation of men to dwell on all the face of the earth."

In spite of this slow start, the gospel continued to spread and the Bible was gradually translated into native languages. The first New Testament in an Australian language (Dieri) was published in 1897. In 1965 the Lutheran church performed the first ordination of native Australian pastors, Conrad Raberaba and Peter Bulla.

> *I preached about what God was like and His creation of the first man in this world. I spoke about Jehovah, who created the first man; the sinning of that man and the death of mankind because of that sin; also about God's great love in giving His Son to absolve that sin so that all men should live.*
>
> —TA'UNGA

This cross commemorates Samuel Marsden's first sermon on Oihi Bay, New Zealand. The land was gifted to the mission by Rutara, a native chief who interpreted the sermon for his people and continued to help the missionaries until his death.

NICK THOMPSON

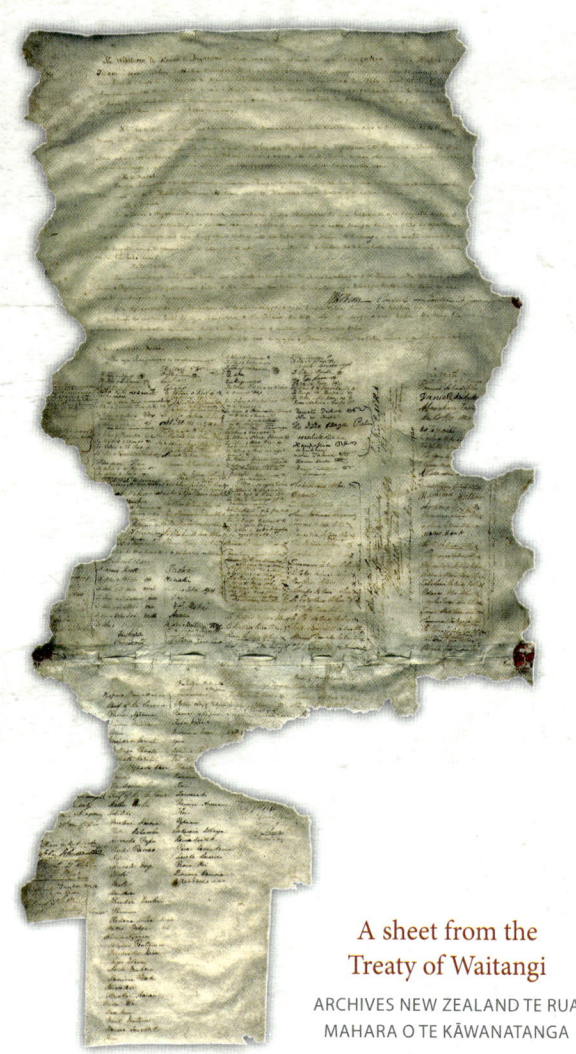

A sheet from the Treaty of Waitangi

ARCHIVES NEW ZEALAND TE RUA MAHARA O TE KĀWANATANGA

Taking the Gospel to the Pacific Islands

In New Zealand the gospel spread even faster. By 1845, about thirty years after the English missionary Samuel Marsden (1765–1838) preached his first sermon on Oihi Bay, about two-thirds of the native population, known as Māori, attended church. Some missionaries were surprised to find, in areas without any foreigners, hundreds of Māori who met to pray and sing hymns learned from other Māori.

As it was in Australia, many settlers took advantage of the Māori, but the missionaries played an important role in defending the Māoris' rights. In fact, they promoted and translated the Treaty of Waitangi, a document signed in 1840 by Māori chiefs and representatives of the British government as a promise of peace, cooperation, and protection from abuse.

Some historians also agree that the Christian teachings on peace and forgiveness played an important role in ending the terrible Musket Wars fought among Māori between 1807 and 1837. There had always been battles between Māori tribes, but the bloodshed caused when guns arrived on the island made them realize their need for Christ.

Both in New Zealand and in other Pacific Islands, most missionaries tried to convert the rulers of the tribes or at least get their permission to spread the gospel. For example, after the Tahitian Chief Pomare II (1803–1824) became Christian, the island began to keep Sunday as a holy day, people went to church, and hundreds were baptized. The missionaries then put the Tahitian language into writing, translated the Bible and the catechisms, and taught the natives how to read and write.

Here too, the gospel was often brought from island to island by natives. One of these, known as Ta'unga (ca. 1818–1898), a native of the Cook Islands, helped with the work of translation and provided a description of his experience as a missionary in New Caledonia. He was the first to put the language of New Caledonia into writing.

Because of the constant wars between tribes, some missionaries lost their lives while preaching the gospel. Some were killed and eaten by cannibals, including the Welsh John Williams (1796–1839). In a ceremony in December 2009, the descendants of the cannibals who killed Williams offered their apology to his descendants.

John Coleridge Patteson (1827–1871) was an Anglican bishop who fought fiercely against the slave traders who traveled to the Pacific Islands to capture slaves. He was killed by someone who mistook him for a trader. The natives gave him an honorary funeral. He later became a symbol for the fight against slavery.

> *In the sight of the Creator, their souls I believe to be of infinite importance…. If we therefore now hasten their destruction or neglect to promote their salvation, shall we be innocent or without blame?*
> —ROBERT CARTWRIGHT (1771–1856), Anglican chaplain in Australia, writing about the natives

A London Missionary Society's steamer *John Williams*, built in 1893. The original *John Williams*, built in 1845 in memory of the missionary who had been killed, was used to transport missionaries across the ocean. The cost of this ship (17,055 British pounds) was raised through contributions by English schoolchildren.

NATIONAL LIBRARY NZ

Other Nineteenth-Century Protestant Missionaries to Oceania

The Englishman **WILLIAM WILLIAMS** (1800–1878) had a great ability to learn languages. He supervised the translation of the New Testament and the Book of Common Prayer in the Māori language.

WILLIAM RIDLEY (1819–1878), an English missionary to Australia, wrote some important books to help others appreciate the native Australians and their culture. The natives loved him much in return.

CARL FRIEDRICH THEODOR STREHLOW (1871–1922) helped to translate the New Testament into Dieri and translated the whole Bible into Aranda. He was assisted in this translation work by **MOSES TJALKABOTA** (ca. 1869–1954), a native of South Australia, who insisted on studying at the missionary school in spite of his parents' fears—his mother thought his head would implode. In 1905 Tjalkabota became blind as a result of a heat stroke but continued to serve the mission as teacher and preacher.

Africa and the Middle East, 1789–1913

1792 — A group of freed slaves from Nova Scotia, Canada, move to Sierra Leone and establish Freetown.

1799 — Johannes Theodore van der Kemp starts his missionary work in the Cape of Good Hope, a British colony in today's South Africa.

1855 — David Livingstone maps the Victoria Falls.

1864 — Samuel Ajayi Crowther becomes the first African bishop of the Anglican Church.

1908 — William Henry Sheppard reports the abuses against the people of the Congo.

Conflicts and the Gospel in Africa

Few people know that Africa was once a land of rich and powerful kingdoms. Some of these, particularly impressive during the Middle Ages, continued until the nineteenth century. As it often happens with human kingdoms throughout history, these great African kingdoms, one by one, eventually declined and gradually disappeared.

Some Europeans were ready to take advantage of the situation with superior weapons and little regard for the humanity of their subjects. At the same time, many sincere missionaries risked their lives to work in this difficult environment in order to bring the gospel of Christ to people who had never heard it. Many fought to put an end to the slave trade and to defend the African populations who had been abused.

A CHANGING WORLD • 191

North Africa and the Middle East

In the nineteenth century, most of the nations in North Africa and the Middle East were still largely Muslim, with some Eastern Orthodox Christians. The churches in Egypt, Armenia, Syria, and Ethiopia belonged to a group of Orthodox churches that traditionally had some disagreements with the Council of Chalcedon. Some traditions in these churches are similar to those in other Orthodox churches, but some are unique in each country. The Orthodox Church in Egypt is usually known as Coptic, from the name of the ancient language that is still used in worship.

Many missionaries thought that Muslims would never receive the gospel, but Samuel Marinus Zwemer (1867–1952) was convinced of the opposite. He spent many years in Bahrain and Egypt, traveled around other Muslim countries, and taught other missionaries. In Bahrain, he and his wife, Amy Elizabeth Wilkes Zwemer (1865–1937), a nurse, worked in a hospital, earning the trust of both the people and the rulers.

> *Thou, O Christ, art all I want and Thou, O Christ, art all they want.*
> —SAMUEL M. ZWEMER

West Africa

Starting in 1792, a large number of formerly enslaved Africans were transported from North America to Freetown, Sierra Leone, as a way to give them a new start in the land of their ancestors. Since many of them were now Christian, they brought their own pastors. From Freetown, many of them brought the gospel to other parts of West Africa. In 1816 another African region, Liberia, began as a settlement for African Americans.

Samuel Ajayi Crowther
WIKIMEDIA COMMONS

An important missionary raised in Freetown was Samuel Ajayi Crowther (ca. 1809–1891). Kidnapped at age twelve by African traders, he was freed by the British and housed in Freetown by a family from the Anglican Church Missionary Society. Noticing his talents, the society sent him to study in England so that he could return to preach the gospel in his homeland. In 1864 he became the first African bishop of the Anglican Church. He supervised the translation of the Bible in Yoruba, a local language. During one of his travels in Nigeria, he was surprised to find his mother still alive and led her to Christ. Around the end of Crowther's life, some young missionaries criticized his methods as being too slow. They also doubted that Africans could properly hold important responsibilities in the church. But when they tried to replace Crowther and his youngest son (who was an archdeacon), his churches rebelled. All these problems weakened Crowther, who was now in his eighties, and might have been partially responsible for the stroke that afflicted him in 1891, five months before his death.

North Africa and the Middle East were not the only regions where missionaries had to learn to communicate with Muslims. By the nineteenth century, Islam had spread to much of Africa. Crowther had many conversations with Muslim leaders. As always, he listened carefully, tried to find common ground, and used the Bible to answer their questions, "After many years of experience, I have found that the Bible, the sword of the Spirit, must fight its own battle, by the guidance of the Holy Spirit," he said.

> **Did You Know?**
>
> Many missionaries to Africa were Africans who had been enslaved in other countries and wanted to return to share the gospel with their people. Some, like the group that landed in Sierra Leone in 1792, came from North America. A large number also came from Jamaica.

The Congo

In 1884, when many European leaders met in Berlin, Germany, to discuss their rule over African states, King Leopold II (1835–1909) of Belgium convinced the others to assign to him a large region in Central Africa known as the Congo Free State. He told the rulers that his motives were noble and that he wanted to improve the lives of the people in that area. In reality, he began to abuse his subjects, allowing his forces to torture, murder, and cut off the hands of those who didn't produce as much rubber as he wanted. No one was spared, not even children.

Around that time, an African American missionary, William Henry Sheppard (1865–1927), was preaching the gospel to the Kuba people, a tribe he described as exceptionally intelligent and creative. Faced with Leopold's abuses, Sheppard and other missionaries sent a report with photos to newspapers in Europe. Furious, the rubber company sued Sheppard and another missionary, William Morrison (1867–1918), for slander. But more people spoke out against the abuses and in the end were proved right. In 1908 the Belgian Parliament took control of the Congo away from the king.

East Africa

East Africa had its own settlement for freed slaves: Frere Town, near Mombasa, Kenya, established by the Anglican Church Missionary Society. The first Kenyan pastors were ordained there in 1855. Other missionaries, both local and foreign, had been working in the region. In 1901 the Uganda Railway, which connected Mombasa with the eastern portion of Lake Victoria, allowed missionaries to travel more freely.

Other roads were opened by missionaries such as James Hannington (1847–1885), first Anglican bishop of East Africa who was killed by men sent by Mwanga II (1868–1903), king of Buganda (a kingdom in today's Uganda), while he was exploring a new route from Mombasa. Hannington was the first of Mwanga's victims. The following year, the king ordered the death of at least twenty-two young Christians who were at his court. In spite of this, Christianity spread fast throughout Buganda. In 1888, when Mwanga was dethroned by Muslims, about five hundred Christians helped him regain power. After that, he gave Christians important government positions, making Buganda, to a large extent, a Christian kingdom.

But Christianity had arrived in East Africa much earlier. Ethiopia had been a Christian country since the fourth century. It survived repeated attacks by its neighbors, including a destructive Muslim invasion in the sixteenth century, when thousands of Christians were killed and hundreds of churches burned. Through it all, it was never conquered and was able to maintain its religious traditions. Many of these traditions are unique because Ethiopia has been isolated from other Christian countries.

The majority of Christians in the country belong to the Ethiopian Orthodox Church, which has traditions that are similar to those in other Orthodox churches. To these, however, the Ethiopian Orthodox Church adds some Jewish laws, such as mandatory days of fasting and strict food restrictions.

Carved in the shape of a cross, the Church of Saint George is one of twelve churches that were carved from rock in Lalibela, in northern Ethiopia, between the seventh and the thirteenth centuries. Lalibela was planned by King Gebre Mesqel Lalibela (ca. 1162–1221) as a representation of Jerusalem. Its churches are among the most extraordinary works of architecture in the world.

ROD WADDINGTON, WIKIMEDIA COMMONS

BIBLE TRANSLATIONS IN EAST AFRICA

Until the nineteenth century, the Bible used by the priests in the Ethiopian Orthodox Church was in Ge'ez, the ancient language of Ethiopia, which the people could no longer understand. The first translation of the Bible into Amharic, the national language, was done at the turn of the century by Abu Rumi (ca. 1750–1819), who worked as a translator for a Scots explorer.

Still, there were in Ethiopia some groups of people who didn't speak Amharic. The Oromo, a large population who had been conquered by the Ethiopians, had their own language. Concerned that they had no way to read the Bible, Pauline Johannes Fathme (ca. 1830–1855), a young lady from the Oromo tribe, encouraged some German missionaries, such as Johann Ludwig Krapf (1810–1881), to travel to Ethiopia. Fathme had become a Christian in Germany after spending many years as a slave in Egypt.

After spending some time in Ethiopia and Kenya, Krapf returned to Germany for health reasons and started to work with another former slave, Christian Paulus Ludwig Rufo (ca. 1848–1871), on a partial translation of the Bible into the Oromo language. Both Fathme and Rufo died of lung disease before they could fulfill their dream of serving as missionaries to the Oromo.

The Bible was completely translated into Oromo by Onesimos Nesib (ca. 1856–1931) and Aster Ganno (ca. 1872–1964), who were also former slaves. The complete Oromo Bible was printed in 1888. Later, Nesib; his wife, Lidia Dimbo (ca. 1872–1933); and Ganno moved to a region of west Ethiopia, where they founded schools and worked as teachers. Today, they are included in the list of saints of the Lutheran church.

A page from an Ethiopian gospel compiled in the sixteenth century. It was written in Ge'ez, the traditional language of the Ethiopian Orthodox Church, which most of the population could not read.

WALTERS ART MUSEUM, BALTIMORE

Did You Know?

The Ethiopian Orthodox Church in Aksum claims to have the original ark of the covenant described in the Book of Exodus. According to tradition, the ark was brought to Ethiopia in the tenth century by men of King Menelik I, who believed he was a direct descendant of King Solomon. The ark is locked up and no one can see it but the guard of the ark. Other Ethiopian Orthodox churches keep copies of the ark.

On January 19, Ethiopians celebrate Timkat, a commemoration of Jesus's baptism that falls just two weeks after the Ethiopian Christmas. The ceremony, the greatest of the year, includes a blessing of the river and a procession in which the priest carries a model of the ark of the covenant on his head. Some people participate by immersing themselves in the water, remembering their own baptism. The celebrations continue with dances, military parades, games, and more.

ROBERT WILSON, FLICKR

Madagascar

The first Protestant missionaries arrived on the island of Madagascar in 1818 but had to leave in 1836, when Queen Ranavalona I (1778–1861) launched a period of persecution. Aware of the benefits Christian missionaries had brought to her country, she allowed them to stay on condition that they didn't try to persuade her people to change their religion. If they did, they would be put to death, together with the people who had become Christian.

A view of Antsahatsiroa (today known as Antananarivo), the capital of Madagascar, in a photo by William Ellis (1794–1872), a member of the London Missionary Society. Ellis had also been a missionary to Hawaii and Tahiti. His photographs of Madagascar are some of the earliest in existence.
THE MET MUSEUM

Those condemned to die were usually given poison together with three pieces of chicken skin. If they vomited the pieces and lived, their lives would be spared. Since the queen's mandate didn't mention printing, the missionaries continued to print and distribute Bibles. They went back to preaching in 1862 after the queen's death.

Southern Africa

Dutch settlers first arrived in the southern part of Africa in 1652. In time their small settlement developed into a colony. Like most European settlers, they had pastors who ministered to them but rarely communicated with the natives.

Some things began to change with the arrival in 1799 of Johannes Theodore van der Kemp (1747–1811). A son of a Reformed pastor, he was a medical doctor and the founder of the Dutch Missionary Society. Van der Kemp respected and adopted the local culture, learning the local language and training men from the local population to be teachers and missionaries to their own people.

When the British took over South Africa in 1806, some of the Dutch settlers became upset when the British abolished slavery the following year. They thought slavery was a normal part of life, and their economy depended on it. Van der Kemp, instead, rejoiced when slavery was abolished and composed a hymn to mark the event as a day of public thanksgiving.

In 1836 about ten thousand Dutch settlers (known as Boers) moved, together with about five thousand indentured servants, to a region of South Africa where they declared their independence from Britain. This led to the foundation of new states, such as Transvaal (or South African Republic), the Natalia Republic, and the Orange Free State. The migration forced some native tribes to move from their lands. When the official Dutch Reformed Church in South Africa refused to approve of this migration, the Boers started new denominations.

The abuses and desire for control shown by some Europeans worried King Moshoeshoe I (ca. 1786–1870) of Basutoland (in today's Lesotho). Wanting the advice of trustworthy Europeans, he invited the French missionary Eugène Casalis (1812–1891) to be his counselor. Casalis stayed in Basutoland until 1855, when he returned to France to train other missionaries.

King Moshoeshoe I on a banknote from Lesotho
ISTOCK

Casalis was followed by his student François Coillard (1834–1904), who led an expedition to nearby regions, and the Swiss Adolphe Mabille (1836–1894), who oversaw the translation of the Bible in the local language, Sotho, and installed the first Sotho minister, Esaia Leeti.

François Coillard and his missionary team
BRITISH LIBRARY

More Men and Women of the Nineteenth-Century Church

OTHER MISSIONARIES TO AFRICA

ROBERT MOFFAT (1795–1883) was a Scottish missionary with the London Missionary Society. He lived for forty-nine years southeast of the Kalahari Desert, planting one of the largest Protestant churches in Africa at that time. He also translated the Bible into the language of the Tswana. He believed that one way to stop the slave trade was to present Africans with a better source of income, so he worked to improve their methods of farming.

DAVID LIVINGSTONE (1813–1873), son-in-law of Robert Moffat, is famous for discovering routes and creating maps that became helpful to both spreading the gospel and improving the African economy. He was the first to locate Victoria Falls on a map at a time when most people didn't know the waterfall existed. He also sent important reports about the slave trade, helping to put an end to it and challenged the Church of England to send more missionaries to Africa. The best-known result of his missionary activities was the conversion of King Khama III (ca. 1837–1923), who adopted Christianity as the religion of his Bangwato tribe.

When David Livingstone shot a lion that was terrorizing the villagers, the lion struck back, biting his arm. The lion was killed, but Livingstone's arm, bandaged without proper medical care, never healed completely, and he could never raise it above his head. This bronze statue is kept at the David Livingstone Centre, Blantyre, Scotland.

DEFACTO, WIKIMEDIA COMMONS

TIYO SOGA (1829–1871) was a South African missionary, translator, and author. Raised a Christian by his mother, he was invited by the principal of the missionary school to receive a higher education in Scotland. There, he was ordained as a Presbyterian minister. When he returned home, the Xhosa people were starving after losing most of their cattle first to tuberculosis, then because they obeyed the false prophecy of a girl who told them to kill the rest. Soga believed that education would help his people rise from poverty. He helped to revise a translation of the Xhosa Bible, translated John Bunyan's *Pilgrim's Progress* into Xhosa, and wrote hymns in that language. In his Christian ministry, he stressed the importance of keeping Sundays free for worship and rest. When Christians in England became lazy with this practice, he said, their faith began to decline.

JOHN MACKENZIE (1835–1899), also Scottish, defended the rights of the native Africans at a time when Cecil John Rhodes (1853–1902), prime minister of the British Cape Colony (today's South Africa), believed that Europeans were a superior race with a right to rule Africa.

JOHN KNOX BOKWE (1855–1922) was a South African journalist who became a Presbyterian minister, wrote many well-known hymns, and helped to compose a singable version of the Psalms in Xhosa.

ENOCH MANKAYI SONTONGA (ca. 1873–1905), a Methodist composer, is famous for writing the first two stanzas of the song "Nkosi Sikelel' iAfrika" (God bless Africa), which has become South Africa's national anthem.

Another famous missionary in West Africa was the Scottish Presbyterian **MARY SLESSOR** (1848–1915), who brought the gospel to the Efik people of Calabar, Nigeria. She helped stop some harmful cultural practices of the Efik, such as leaving twin babies to die and giving poison to people who were suspected of crimes. (The local people believed that those who were innocent would live even after taking poison.) She adopted every abandoned child she found.

A TERRIBLE MISREADING

Some Christians supported slavery because they misread Genesis 9:25, where Noah cursed his grandson Canaan for a shameful sin committed by Canaan's father, Ham. Since the Bible refers to Egypt as "the land of Ham," these people connected Africa with Ham and with slavery.

In reality, Noah's curse was directed only at Canaan—not at Ham or at Canaan's three brothers. The Bible tells us that the descendants of Canaan were in fact enslaved, first by a league of eastern kings (Genesis 14) and then by the Israelites (Joshua 9:27), but this had nothing to do with Africa or with race.

Mary Slessor and her four adopted children
WORLD HISTORY ARCHIVE - ALAMY STOCK PHOTO

> *Christ never was in a hurry. There was no rushing forward, no anticipating, no fretting over what might be. Each day's duties were done as each day brought them, and the rest was left with God.*
>
> —MARY SLESSOR

Think about It

What can we learn from this terrible misreading? How should we study the Bible? How can we make sure we don't try to make the Bible agree with our own ideas?

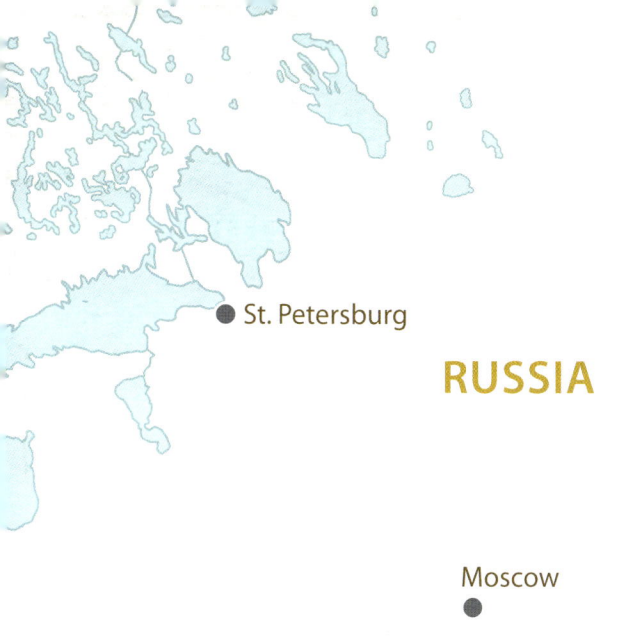

A Preserved Church

God's story in the twentieth century brings us close to our own day. Your parents and grandparents might remember living through some of the events described in this section. Looking back, they can tell you that Christ has kept His church even when many people tried their best to destroy it. In fact, the church has grown where you would least expect. And Christ has preserved His message, the gospel, in spite of those who have tried to change it, confuse it, limit it, or use it for their purposes. As He has always done, God has provided true shepherds to stand up for the true gospel, and Jesus's sheep have continued to hear His voice.

EUROPE, 1914–2000

- **1914–1918** — World War I causes great destruction and loss of life in Europe.
- **1917** — The Russian Revolution marks the beginning of a persecution of people of all religions.
- **1925** — Benito Mussolini becomes dictator of Italy.
- **1929** — The Lateran Treaty puts an end to most disagreements between the Roman Catholic Church and the Italian government. It establishes the Vatican State and makes Roman Catholicism the official religion of Italy.
- **1933** — Adolf Hitler is appointed chancellor of Germany, where he takes absolute power.
- **1934** — About two thousand German pastors sign the Barmen Confession.
- **1935** — The Italian government bans Pentecostal worship in Italy.
- **1936–1939** — Over six thousand Roman Catholics are killed in the Spanish Civil War.
- **1937** — The pope officially condemns racism and nationalism.
- **1955** — Francis and Edith Schaeffer found a community, L'Abri, where people could discuss their religious questions.
- **1962** — The Second Vatican Council accepts Protestants as "separated brethren." It also encourages translating and reading the Bible and holding services in the language of the people and cancels the excommunication of the Eastern Orthodox Church.
- **1974** — The Lausanne Convention gathers nearly 2,500 representatives of churches from over 150 countries to unite all evangelicals in the task of evangelizing the world.
- **1989** — The fall of the Berlin Wall marks the beginning of the fall of Communism in Eastern Europe.
- **1997** — Pope John Paul II apologizes for the Roman Catholic Church's silence during the Holocaust.
- **1999** — Lutherans and Roman Catholics sign a declaration in an effort to resolve their differences about salvation.

The Great War and Its Consequences

World War I (1914–1918) is called the Great War because it shook Europe more than any other war before it. It brought four empires to an end, created new nations, caused a stunning loss of human lives, and triggered events that continued to change the Continent and the world, including **genocides**, revolutions, conflicts in the Middle East, the rise of Nazism, and World War II. It is called a *world* war because it involved nations outside Europe, especially the United States.

But the war did more than change governments and nations. It marked the end of the wave of optimism that had accompanied the Enlightenment and the scientific and technological discoveries of the last few centuries and moved dictators to put into practice the extreme views of philosophers like Marx and Nietzsche. When these views showed their ugly side, most people became discouraged about the future and uncertain about the purpose of life. Once again, the gospel proved to have the answers people needed in Europe and around the globe.

The Russian Revolution

In 1917 Russia was losing World War I. This caused much unrest in a country where the poor were already treated like slaves. In February, after protests against food shortages and strikes in the capital, Petrograd, the ruler of Russia, Czar Nicholas II (1868–1918), lost control of the army and gave power to leaders from his Parliament.

The war and the food shortages dragged on. In October Vladimir Ilyich Ulyanov—better known as Vladimir Lenin (1870–1924)—seized power with a small group of violent revolutionaries. He promised a distribution of riches so that everyone would be the same—there would be no rich and no poor. Like Marx, he claimed that this would bring peace and happiness.

Lenin established the Russian Soviet Republic with a one-party system. This means that there was only one political party, and no one was allowed to argue with its decisions. In 1922, after taking over neighboring lands, the new nation became known as the Soviet Union, or USSR (Union of Soviet Socialist Republics).

The government taught its citizens to see Lenin as a national hero. Preschool children sang songs about him. Once children went to school, they had to join organizations that praised Lenin and the new government he had started.

In reality, Lenin was brutal with anyone who expressed disagreement and ended up killing many of the people he had promised to help. He also discouraged Russians from practicing any type of religion. In 1922 his government took all valuables from Russian churches.

Joseph Stalin (1878–1953), who took over the government after Lenin, was even tougher and found many ways to convince the people that God was just a human invention. For example, his government issued posters, booklets, and films that denied the existence of God and turned hundreds of churches into museums that promoted atheism. In 1931 the same government blew up the Cathedral of Christ the Savior in Moscow as a display to the world. Of the fifty thousand churches that existed in 1917 in the Russian Empire, less than one thousand were still standing twenty years later, and few people attended their services.

Lenin
PAVEL SEMYONOVICH ZHUKOV, WIKIMEDIA COMMONS

For those few churches, catechism classes, religious schools, study groups, Sunday schools, and religious publications were illegal. Many Christians were imprisoned under terrible conditions. They were often tortured and killed, particularly those with a higher level of education who could most influence others. At least one hundred thousand Christians were executed just during the so-called Great Purge of 1936–1938.

In spite of this, many people continued to believe in God. In a 1983 speech, Russian author Aleksandr Isayevich Solzhenitsyn (1918–2008), who was imprisoned for many years, said the Soviet government had never imagined that, "beneath this Communist steamroller the Christian tradition would survive in Russia."

Finally, in 1988 Mikhail Gorbachev (b. 1931), the last leader of the Soviet Union, recognized the value of religion in society and allowed freedom of worship. In 1989 the wall that for twenty-eight years had separated the western side of Berlin, Germany, from the Communist-ruled eastern side was suddenly torn down. This marked the beginning of the fall of Communism in eastern Europe, an event that few had predicted. The church still has a lot to do to erase the wrong ideas about Christianity that Communism has spread in much of Eastern Europe.

The Russian Orthodox Saint Isaac's Cathedral in St. Petersburg was converted in 1931 into the Museum of the History of Religion and Atheism.

DENNIS JARVIS, FLICKR

> *It is here that we see the dawn of hope: for no matter how formidably Communism bristles with tanks and rockets, no matter what successes it attains in seizing the planet, it is doomed never to vanquish Christianity.*
> —ALEKSANDR ISAYEVICH SOLZHENITSYN

Some Men of the Modern Church

CHRISTIANS UNDER THE SOVIET REGIME

Many Christians suffered under the Soviet regime, both in Russia and in other occupied countries. The first Russian Orthodox bishop to be executed under Lenin for speaking out against Communism was **VASILY NIKIFOROVICH BOGOYAVLENSKY** (1848–1918). Among Protestants, a strong voice came from Baptist pastor **GENNADI KRYUCHKOV** (1926–2007), who cofounded a council of churches promoting religious liberty and a separation of church and state. Because of this, he had to live in hiding for most of his life.

In Slovakia, the Lutheran pastor **PAVEL UHORSKAI** (1919–2010) had a similar story, which included imprisonment, torture, and forced labor as a woodcutter in the Slovakian forests. In his memoirs, he explains how the intention of the Communist regime was to eliminate Christianity altogether. In 1990, after he was freed, he was elected the first non-Communist bishop of the Slovak Lutheran Church. He was a peacemaker at a time when those who had resisted Communist oppression had a hard time working with those who had cooperated.

When news of the suffering of Christians reached Western Europe, many people found ways to help. The Dutchman Anne van der Bijl (known in English-speaking countries as **BROTHER ANDREW** (b. 1928) brought Bibles across the so-called Iron Curtain, the borders that divided the Communist countries from the rest of the world. Someone called him God's smuggler.

Brother Andrew was so confident of God's protection that sometimes he left Bibles in plain view. When Czechoslovakia was occupied by Soviet troops, he even gave Bibles to the Soviet soldiers. He also brought Bibles to other Communist countries outside Europe, such as China and Cuba. After the fall of Communism, he devoted his time to the Middle East.

THE MODERN WORLD • 201

Nazism and the Church

In the treaty signed at Versailles, France, ending World War I, Germany was condemned as the main aggressor and was forbidden to manufacture weapons. Some Germans thought it was unfair. Feelings of **nationalism** grew strong, giving birth to the National Socialist German Working Party, abbreviated in English as Nazi.

Starting in 1921, the party was led by Adolf Hitler, who became chancellor in 1933. Hitler used his power to turn Germany into a dictatorship. The German people referred to him as *Führer*, meaning "guide." To strengthen his power in Europe, Hitler made an alliance with like-minded leaders: Benito Mussolini (1883–1945) in Italy and Francisco Franco (1892–1975) in Spain.

Initially, Hitler proclaimed his movement to be Christian, but his attitude soon changed. Like Nietzsche, he thought Christianity made people weak. He allowed churches but wanted them to be ruled by the government. Many of his officials wanted to eliminate Christianity altogether. Heinrich Himmler (1900–1945), head of the *Schutzstaffel* (SS), the top guards of the Nazi regime, called Christianity the "greatest of plagues that could have happened to us in our history, which has weakened us in every conflict."

Most churches were attracted by Hitler's strong personality and his vision to rid the world of Communism, which looked like a frightening threat. Some even included Nazi symbols in their churches. They didn't understand that his plan was equally threatening.

Soon Hitler convinced the people that Germans were a superior people and needed to get rid of all "impurities," including Jews and people with disabilities. In fact, he thought that Jews were secretly trying to take over the country. Because of this, he stripped them of their civil rights. After a while, he began to send Jews away from their homes. He said he was sending them to places where they could live together. In reality he sent them to camps where they were horribly abused and killed. This persecution and massacre of Jews is known as the **Holocaust**.

Not all Christians went along with Hitler's plan. In 1934 about two thousand German pastors signed a document known as the Barmen Confession, where they stated, "Jesus Christ, as he is attested for us in Holy Scripture, is the one Word of God which we have to hear and which we have to trust and obey in life and in death."

More pastors signed the document later. Those who signed described themselves as the Confessing Church because they confessed that their loyalty belonged first to Christ, whose authority was greater than that of any government. In the end, many of them were dismissed, punished, or exiled.

Adolf Hitler
LIBRARY OF CONGRESS

HOW THE NAZIS TRIED TO STEAL CHRISTMAS

After trying to turn the German population against the Jews, some Nazi authorities thought it was strange to celebrate year after year the birth of a Jew—Jesus of Nazareth. Because of this, they encouraged Germans to go back to the religion of their pagan ancestors (for example, replacing Christmas with pagan winter solstice celebrations). Some even rewrote hymns, taking out references to Bethlehem and to Jesus. The government supported the singing of a new carol, "Exalted Night," which told how the world will be saved through faith in the Nazi system—not in Jesus.

In 1937 Pope Pius XI (1857–1939) condemned racism and nationalism. He said, "Whoever exalts race, or the people, or the State, or a particular form of State, or the depositories of power, or any other fundamental value of the human community—however necessary and honorable be their function in worldly things—whoever raises these notions above their standard value and divinizes them to an idolatrous level, distorts and perverts an order of the world planned and created by God; he is far from the true faith in God and from the concept of life which that faith upholds."

Pius's main concern, however, was to defend the rights of Roman Catholics to worship in Germany. His successor, Pius XII (1876–1958), didn't attack specifically the mass killing of Jews but told Roman Catholics to protect them as much as they could. Sixty years later, Pope John Paul II (1920–2005) apologized to the world for the silence of the Roman Catholic Church, which should have protested more during the Holocaust.

Pius XI
LIBRARY OF CONGRESS

CALLING MURDER BY ITS NAME

From 1939 to 1941, the Nazi government ordered the death of seventy thousand people with physical and mental disabilities. They called it "mercy death" because they assumed that these people could not live a full and satisfying life. In reality, they were simply putting into practice the principles of eugenics (see p. 159) they had understood from Darwin's theories. They wanted to create a pure master race, free of weakness and disabilities. Often they informed relatives after they had killed their loved ones.

Judge Lothar Kreyssig (1898–1986), who was also a member of the Confessing Church, protested against this practice and charged one of the Nazi leaders with murder. He was asked to retire. He is still remembered as the only judge who took such a stand.

New voices rose in protest. But when Reinhold Sautter, councillor of the Württemberg State Church, called these "mercy killings" murder, the government replied, "The fifth commandment, Thou shalt not kill, is no commandment of God but a Jewish invention."

The strongest voice against these killings was that of Clemens von Galen (1878-1946), the Roman Catholic bishop of Munster, who denounced them as murder in a series of sermons he preached and published. He also explained that by following this law, the government could kill anyone because some disabilities can show up later in life. What about the soldiers who were serving the country? Would they be killed when they became disabled?

Hitler was furious, but von Galen was too popular to be killed. Hitler then drew back the law, but many doctors continued the killings with the backing of the government. The last person to die this way was a four-year-old boy in 1945. Some estimate that over 750,000 people were killed altogether.

A 1996 German stamp commemorating Bishop Clemens August Graf von Galen.
MIRT ALEXANDER, SHUTTERSTOCK

More Men and Women of the Modern Church

SOME LEADERS OF THE CONFESSING CHURCH WHO OPPOSED HITLER

KARL BARTH (1886–1968) opposed Hitler and became one of the founders of the Confessing Church. Because of this, he had to give up his teaching position at the University of Bonn, Germany, and return to Switzerland, the country of his birth. Barth had already raised his voice during World War I when people claimed that God was on the side of Germany. He reminded them that in our Christian age, God is not allied with any human nations. He is simply bringing all nations to Christ.

Today, Barth is famous for his writings against religious liberalism—for example, against the tendency to understand God by human reasoning. While appreciating his efforts to bring Christians back to the wonders of God as He is revealed in Christ, some think his ideas are still too far from the confessions of the Protestant Reformation. For example, he seemed to deny that the Bible is without error and that there is a hell.

MARTIN NIEMÖLLER (1892–1984) was a pastor and cofounder of the Confessing Church. He was sent to a **concentration camp** in 1937 and stayed there until 1945, when the American troops freed the prisoners. In a famous poem, he regretted he had not done more when the government had started to persecute different groups of people. Those who fail to stand up for others may not have anyone to stand up for them later, he said.

DIETRICH BONHOEFFER (1906–1945) did more than speak out. He worked with groups who organized a resistance against Hitler. Sometimes he brought messages from one group to the other. In the course of this work, he was informed of a plot to kill Hitler. When the plot was discovered, Bonhoeffer had already been in prison for eighteen months. He was transferred to a high security prison, then to a concentration camp where he was executed just two weeks before American soldiers came to bring freedom. In some of his writings, he insisted that Christians must be willing to sacrifice and suffer for their faith.

The German Lutheran **ERNST LOHMEYER** (1890–1946) suffered under two dictatorial governments. When he spoke out in defense of the persecuted Jews, he lost his job at the University of Breslau and was sent to fight in Russia. After the war, as president of the University of Greifswald in East Germany, he was arrested and killed by the occupying Soviets for promoting freedom of speech. Through his careful studies of the New Testament and his knowledge of poetry, Lohmeyer found that some New Testament authors (particularly Paul in Philippians 2:5–11) were quoting ancient Christian hymns. If he is correct, Christians had been singing of Christ's divinity before Paul's writings—proving wrong those who said the early church didn't believe that Jesus was God.

Postage stamp printed in Germany in 1986 commemorating the Swiss theologian Karl Barth

WANTANDDO, SHUTTERSTOCK

Postage stamp printed in Germany in 1992 commemorating the pastor and anti-Nazi hero Martin Niemöller

OLGA POPOVA, SHUTTERSTOCK

Postage stamp printed in Germany in 1995 commemorating the German theologian and resistance fighter Dietrich Bonhoeffer

ROOK76, SHUTTERSTOCK

ACTS OF MERCY

EDITH CAVELL (1865–1915) was a British nurse who was imprisoned and executed for helping wounded Allied soldiers escape from German-occupied Belgium. Many nations protested her treatment, especially because Belgium had been neutral and Germany had no right to occupy it. "Ask Father Gahan to tell my loved ones later on that my soul, as I believe, is safe, and that I am glad to die for my country," she told a friend before her execution.

Edith Cavell
LIBRARY OF CONGRESS

BO GIERTZ (1905–1998) was a Lutheran bishop who opened his home to Danish people who were hunted by the Nazis. He had a true pastor's heart and worked hard to bring the teachings of the Reformation to a part of Europe that had largely forgotten them. He became famous for his novel *The Hammer of God*, in which three discouraged pastors learn to accept God's promises in their lives and to trust that God would work in the hearts of those who heard the gospel.

IRENA STANISŁAWA SENDLER (1910–2008) was a Polish Roman Catholic who protected twenty-five hundred Jewish children and found a place of refuge for them.

CORRIE TEN BOOM (1892–1983) and her family hid many Jews who were escaping from the Nazis in their home in the Netherlands. The family was caught, and she was sent to the Ravensbrück concentration camp. Her most famous book, *The Hiding Place*, explains how she found hope in God and how she learned to love and forgive her enemies.

DIET EMAN (1920–2019) and her fiancé, **HEIN SIETSMA** (1919–1945), helped many Jews in the Netherlands by finding places of refuge and providing false ID cards. Hein was arrested in 1944 and deported to the concentration camp in Dachau, where he died. After the war, Diet moved to the United States and wrote an autobiography, *Things We Couldn't Say*, for those who wouldn't believe in the Holocaust.

The French pastor **ANDRÉ TROCMÉ** (1901–1971) and his wife, **MAGDA** (1901–1996), inspired the people in their village, Le Chambon-sur-Lignon, to protect and assist persecuted Jews. André was captured but was released after four weeks. His nephew **DANIEL TROCMÉ** (1910–1944), who was caught together with some Jewish children, refused to let the children go and was taken to a concentration camp, where he died. The people of Le Chambon-sur-Lignon rescued about five thousand refugees, including about thirty-five hundred Jews.

The Protestant church at Le Chambon-sur-Lignon as it looks now and as it looked in 1900
JEANNE, FLICKR

Italian Fascism and the Church

In Italy Benito Mussolini rose slowly to power, becoming the leader of the Italian Fascist Party. Like Hitler, he encouraged feelings of nationalism. In 1922 he became president of the council (the highest position after the king) and gradually turned Italy into a one-party nation with himself at its head. Like Hitler, he asked the people to refer to him as their guide by using the Latin word *duce*.

He also adopted many of Hitler's policies and ideas, including (starting in 1938) the discrimination of Jews as "dangerous to the Italian people." For example, Jews were not allowed to go to public schools or to own factories, banks, and newspapers. Later, many Jews were arrested and sent to concentration camps in Germany.

Mussolini thought it was good to have Pope Pius XI as an ally. But since 1861, popes had considered themselves as political prisoners (see p. 156), and many priests and Catholic organizations felt free to speak against the Italian government.

Instead of banning the church from speaking out, Mussolini proposed an agreement. In 1929 he invited the pope to a meeting where they signed a document called the Lateran Treaty. By this treaty, the area of Rome where the pope lived became an independent state called the Vatican State with the pope at its head, and the Roman Catholic Church was free from the duty of paying taxes to the Italian government. In exchange, the pope agreed to discourage priests and Catholic organizations from being involved in politics.

The pope took advantage of this treaty to ask for the government's help in controlling the activities of evangelicals in Italy. Many evangelicals suffered from the same restrictions that were imposed on the Jews. In 1935 the Italian government passed a law forbidding Pentecostals from holding their religious services because the excitement many of them expressed during those services seemed dangerous to people's minds, "especially to women and children." Many churches were closed, and numerous Pentecostals were arrested. As it often happens, however, the persecution only caused the number of Pentecostals to grow.

Benito Mussolini speaking to a crowd
LIBRARY OF CONGRESS

New Roman Catholic Teachings

In 1950 Pius XII introduced a new teaching in the Roman Catholic Church: the Assumption of Mary. For Roman Catholics, this means that Mary, mother of Jesus, went up to heaven in body and soul when she died. There is no mention of this in the Bible, but, like many other teachings of the Roman Catholic Church, it was based on traditions that were passed on from generation to generation. In addition, Pius also said that Mary was "free from all sin, original or personal." The Bible speaks of only Jesus as free from all sin (Hebrews 4:15). But since the Roman Catholic Church has declared that popes are infallible, these teachings confirmed by Pius are now part of its official doctrines, and all Roman Catholics are required to believe them.

Eastern Orthodox Christians have a similar tradition. Many believe that Mary went to heaven in body and soul after her death. But for them, it's not something you have to believe to be part of their church.

The Spanish Civil War

When in 1931 the majority of the people of Spain voted to change the country from a monarchy to a republic, the population was split into two groups: the Nationalists, the Roman Catholic Church, and all those who wanted to keep things as they were on one side; and the Republicans, who included Socialists, Communists, and the people of some regions who wanted to become independent from Spain on the other.

The alliance of the Roman Catholic Church with the Nationalists is understandable because the Republican government, in an effort to give the country a new start, passed many laws against the practice of religion. It banned priests from teaching in schools, even though the church owned or managed most of the schools in the country, and outlawed processions, religious festivals, and even church bells, claiming that they might offend the ears of nonbelievers. These restrictions created huge problems because the church in Spain had been influential for centuries and most people counted on it as an essential part of their daily life.

The rebellions that followed escalated into a bloody war that saw, in the space of just three years (1936–1939), the murder or execution of hundreds of thousands of people, including over six thousand members of the clergy.

The civil war gave Francisco Franco, general in the Spanish army, the opportunity to rise to power. In order to win the war, he enlisted the help of Mussolini and Hitler, turning the Spanish Civil War into an international conflict.

This memorial to Francisco Franco in Plaza Mayor in Salamanca, Spain, was removed in 2017.

BASILIO, WIKIMEDIA COMMONS

Did You Know?

Franco made Roman Catholicism the state religion. Although the 1945 Spanish Bill of Rights granted freedom of private worship, Protestants could not open their services to the public and could not have non-Catholic translations of the Bible. Protestant schools were also closed, and Protestants were not allowed to become teachers or officers in the government or armed forces.

Only in the early 1960s were Protestant churches able to hold public services, and a shipment of Protestant Bibles was allowed to enter the country for the first time in December 1963.

In contrast to his treatment of Protestants, Franco was generous to the seventy thousand Moroccan mercenaries he recruited during the Spanish Civil War, some of whom he kept as his personal bodyguards. He built a mosque in Córdoba in their honor. This mosque, known as Al Morabito, is considered Spain's first modern mosque.

A Different Council

In 1962 Pope John XXIII (1881–1963) surprised the Roman Catholic world by calling a council, the Second Vatican Council. There, he surprised people with his suggestions. He said the Roman Catholic Church should accept Protestants as "separated brethren." He canceled the excommunication of the patriarch of the Eastern Orthodox Church (see p. 55). He also encouraged translations of the Bible in other languages and said that the Mass should be celebrated in the language of the people who attended instead of in Latin, which had been used until that time.

Some Protestants wondered how the pope could call them brethren without canceling the statements of the Council of Trent that still condemn them as cursed. Some Roman Catholics also objected to the tone of the council, which seemed to suggest that the world is a place that can be improved with love and goodwill and not a place that is lost without Christ. Other Roman Catholics were nostalgic for the Latin Mass, which they considered more appealing and reverent than its translation. But many Roman Catholics were happy with the changes.

A statue of Pope John XXIII in front of St. Anthony of Padua Church, Istanbul, Turkey
VOLKANKOVANCISOY, ISTOCK

A procession marking the Second Vatican Council
MANHAI, FLICKR

Lutherans and Catholics Together

In 1999, after many years of discussion, the Roman Catholic Church and the World Lutheran Federation signed a declaration that was supposed to bring agreement on their teachings about justification (how we can solve the problem of sin and its just punishment). To do so, the Roman Catholic Church agreed that justification is through faith alone, but "such a faith is active in love and thus the Christian cannot and should not remain without works."

Some Christians saw it as an encouraging sign of unity. After all, Lutherans could agree that Christians who are saved by faith alone will always do good works because it is God who causes them "both to will and to do for His good pleasure" (Philippians 2:13). But that's not what Roman Catholics meant.

The Roman Catholic Church made it clear that it still holds to the Council of Trent (see p. 94), which cursed anyone who believed they were saved by grace alone through faith alone. In fact, the declaration openly condemned the teaching that "justification can take place without human cooperation."

In the end, the declaration forced the Lutherans to compromise their beliefs, while Roman Catholics kept theirs. Also, it gave the false impression that the disagreements between the two groups are not important, when they are based on completely different views of salvation and the authority of the church (see "A Summary of Reformation Teachings," p. 95). For this reason, many Lutheran churches refused to recognize this declaration.

Disappointment and Hope

The Russian Revolution, the rise of Fascism and Nazism, the Holocaust, and the horrors of two world wars left the people of Europe exhausted, shocked, and confused. The churches that had supported the Fascists and the Nazis had some serious apologies to make. In an official statement known as the Declaration of Guilt, the Evangelical Church in Germany accepted the blame "for not witnessing more courageously, for not praying more faithfully, for not believing more joyously, and for not loving more ardently."

Many people realized it was time to repent and return to God. Looking back at the horrors of the Soviet regime—in fact, at all the horrors of the twentieth century—Aleksandr Solzhenitsyn could only agree with what some elderly people had told him at the beginning of the Russian Revolution: "Men have forgotten God; that's why all this has happened."

One pastor who tried to point people to Christ during World War II was Martyn Lloyd-Jones (1899–1981), a medical doctor who left his career in order to become a pastor. In 1939 he preached a series of sermons to prepare the people of London for the upcoming war. It was a scary time. Once during the pastoral prayer, a bomb fell so close to the church that some plaster from the roof fell on the heads of the congregation. Everyone stood in fright. Lloyd-Jones paused for a moment, then went on to finish praying "as one who believes that a Christian has a right to be at peace in every situation," knowing that God is in control of everything.

Martyn Lloyd-Jones
ART BY MARCOS RODRIGUES

TALES OF HOPE

During the first half of the twentieth century, many writers expressed the discouragement of the people around them. Some of them feared to give answers or a ray of hope because they had been disappointed too many times. In this dark climate, two authors wrote books particularly full of hope.

J. R. R. Tolkien (1892–1973) became particularly famous for his trilogy *The Lord of the Rings*, inspiring his readers to believe in a better world where the choices of common people are vital and evil will eventually be defeated. A devout Roman Catholic, he didn't believe that stories should try to convince people to embrace a particular religion. Readers should just enter into the story and draw their own lessons. He was largely responsible for helping his friend C. S. Lewis (1898–1963) to become a Christian.

Lewis had been raised in an Anglican family. As a teenager, he began questioning his faith. This caused conflicting emotions. He didn't think God existed, and at the same time he was "very angry at God for not existing." He was also angry at God for creating a world that seemed to go wrong in so many ways. He returned to the Anglican Church after a discussion with J. R. R. Tolkien and after reading some books. His Chronicles of Narnia series also talks about a better world and draws some parallels with the story of Christ.

> "I wish it need not have happened in my time," said Frodo.
>
> "So do I," said Gandalf, "and so do all who live to see such times. But that is not for them to decide. All we have to decide is what to do with the time that is given us."
>
> —J. R. R. TOLKIEN, *The Fellowship of the Ring*

Explaining Christianity to a Confused Generation

Although he is famous for writing works of fiction, C. S. Lewis is also well known for his explanations of what it means to be a Christian. He could speak to people from many different backgrounds, young and old, because he took the time to listen and to learn to speak in a way that they could understand. He was convinced that children could understand much more than most people realize as long as things were explained clearly.

To Lewis, people shouldn't believe in the gospel hoping to feel better or become better people. They should believe because it's true. Many of his writings are meant to show how the gospel is true and how it makes perfect sense.

On the contrary, he said, talking about Jesus simply as a good moral teacher or role model makes no sense at all. Jesus said He was God. If that's not true, He would have been a liar or would have had some condition that caused His mind to believe something that is not real. In either one of these cases, it wouldn't be wise to follow Him. But He was not just a good moral teacher. "He did not leave us that option," Lewis said. "He did not intend to."

Another important apologist of the twentieth century was Francis Schaeffer (1912–1984). In 1955 he and his wife, Edith (1914–2013), founded a community in the small village of Huémoz-sur-Ollon at the foothills of the Swiss Alps. He called it L'Abri (French for "shelter"). It was a place where people could stay and discuss their questions. At a time when young people were especially confused, L'Abri received so many visitors that more centers opened in other countries.

Schaeffer and his staff treated each person as an individual and spent a lot of time listening. He didn't like to use formulas or methods because each person is unique. Living in community with others helped him to be closer to them and to try to be an example of Christian living.

Schaeffer was also one of the first modern Protestants to seriously study how art and music are influenced by the way each generation thinks about life. He criticized Christians who had been living like ostriches with their heads in the sand—happy with their Christian books, music, and way of speaking and unaware of the life and thoughts of those around them.

Both Lewis and Schaeffer went through a period when they doubted their faith and could understand others who had the same experience. Many have claimed to have found faith in Christ after reading books by either Lewis or Schaeffer.

> *Reality, in fact, is usually something you could not have guessed. That is one of the reasons I believe Christianity. It is a religion you could not have guessed. If it offered us just the kind of universe we had always expected, I should feel we were making it up. But, in fact, it is not the sort of thing anyone would have made up.*
>
> —C. S. LEWIS, *Mere Christianity*

C. S. Lewis
ART BY MARCOS RODRIGUES

A road leading to L'Abri
ALLAN KROEKER PHOTOGRAPHY

Francis Schaeffer

ALLAN KROEKER PHOTOGRAPHY

More Men of the Modern Church

OTHER IMPORTANT CHRISTIANS OF TWENTIETH-CENTURY EUROPE

JOHN STOTT (1921–2011) encouraged Christians to study the Bible carefully so they could both understand it and take its message to others. To do so, he wrote many helpful books on specific books of the Bible and on Christianity in general. With the money he made from the sale of his books he founded the Langham Trust to pay for the education of needy preachers all over the world. He also cofounded the London Institute of Contemporary Christianity to encourage people to take Christ to others in their daily lives by obeying Christ's commandment to be "salt and light" to the world (see Matthew 5:13–16). His sermons and books made such an impression on people that in 2005 *Time* magazine named him among the one hundred most influential people of the year.

John Stott

PHOTO BY KIERAN DODDS, USED WITH KIND PERMISSION OF LANGHAM PARTNERSHIP

THE LAUSANNE CONVENTION

In 1974 the first International Congress of World Evangelization met in Lausanne, Switzerland "to unite all evangelicals in the common task of total evangelization of the world." There had been some smaller conferences before, but this one included about 2,500 representatives from over 150 countries of the world who presented their needs and the lessons they had learned while preaching the gospel in different cultures. At a time when there was some confusion on the role of missionaries, the convention defined *evangelism* as "the proclamation of the historical, biblical Christ as Savior and Lord, with a view to persuading people to come to him personally and so be reconciled to God."

JAMES I. PACKER (1926–2020) was born in England but spent half of his life in Canada. He had the ability to explain important truths in a way that everyone could understand. His book *Knowing God* sold over a million copies, helping people to realize the importance and the joy of knowing God as He has revealed Himself in the Bible. Packer also wrote books about the Puritans, reminding people of the great treasures that can be found in their writings.

NORTH AMERICA, 1914–2000

- **1923** — J. Gresham Machen publishes *Christianity and Liberalism*, defining the meaning of the word *Christian*.
- **1925** — The Scopes trial ("Monkey Trial") draws attention to the teaching of evolution.
- **1929–1941** — A period of great economic crisis in America becomes known as the Great Depression.
- **1934** — J. Gresham Machen founds the Independent Board of Foreign Missions.
- **1942** — Cam Townsend starts the Wycliffe Bible Translators.
- **1946–1991** — The Cold War, a period of tension between the United States and the Soviet Union, creates much anxiety in America.
- **1954** — President Eisenhower adds the words "under God" to the American Pledge of Allegiance.

Poverty and Rumors of War

The twentieth century brought many new challenges to America, from the poverty of the Great Depression of the 1930s to the fear of destruction during the Cold War against Russia. In an effort to encourage people through these challenges, the American churches offered different answers—some more biblical than others.

Crowds and Excitement

In the twentieth century, many preachers used the methods promoted by Charles Finney to create excitement and inspire repentance. Some, such as Aimee Semple McPherson (1890–1944), commonly known as Sister Aimee, staged dramatic shows to attract people.

McPherson first started preaching in 1914, often from the back of her convertible car while speaking through a megaphone. Within a few years, she had become a national celebrity. She was the first woman to preach on radio. Eventually, she built a large denomination called the International Church of the Foursquare Gospel, with a huge church in Los Angeles, California: the Angelus Temple. There, she staged elaborate productions, hiring the best actors and professionals to act out biblical stories. She even brought animals—such as horses, camels, monkeys, and eagles—as sermon illustrations. She became one of the most popular women in America.

But McPherson lost many followers when she led everyone to believe that she had drowned in the ocean. When she suddenly reappeared, she said she had been kidnapped. Her story had flaws, and many people doubted it and thought it was another publicity stunt.

Billy Graham (1918–2018) is probably the most famous evangelist of the twentieth century. He gave his messages through radio, books, and especially large meetings, often called crusades, throughout the world.

Aimee Semple McPherson in 1927
LIBRARY OF CONGRESS

He had natural speaking talent and attracted many people. He adopted some of Charles Finney's methods.

Unlike Finney, Graham believed that human beings are born in sin and have a tendency to sin and that on the cross Jesus took on Himself the punishment for all human sin. Also, unlike Finney, he collected the names of those who came forward at his meetings and gave those names to local churches where they could continue to hear the gospel. He provided spiritual counsel to every American president from Harry S. Truman (1884–1972) to Barack Obama (b. 1961).

Graham traveled to many regions and countries of the world, including Eastern Europe, Brazil, and Korea. He also played an important role in organizing the Lausanne Convention (see p. 221). His wife, Ruth Bell Graham (1920–2007), was born in China to a missionary family and encouraged him to take trips there. Ruth wrote many books and was recognized with her husband in 1996 when they were both awarded a Congressional Gold Medal by the US Congress.

The Grahams kept alive the excitement of past revivals and were publicly recognized. This made some American Protestants more confident and prouder of their country. Many pastors started to model their churches after Graham's example, trying to attract large crowds and gaining the approval of famous people.

The Angelus Temple as it looks today
BRUCE BOEHNER, WIKIMEDIA COMMONS

Billy Graham
ORIGINAL ART BY MARCOS RODRIGUES

A Religion of Positive Thinking

Some American preachers took inspiration from earlier movements that promised a "higher life," such as the Holiness Movement, to teach what they called the "power of faith."

One evangelist, Essek William (E. W.) Kenyon (1867–1948), taught that "dominating faith" could bring not only victory over sin but unlock a treasure of blessings from God. To unlock the treasure, Christians should repeat formulas such as "I am a child of the living God." He called this "positive confession" and encouraged Christians to "claim" God's promises as their right. In quoting Jesus as saying, "If you ask anything in My name, I will do it" (John 14:14), Kenyon replaced the word "ask" with "demand."

Kenyon's books inspired many so-called faith healers who traveled around America with a similar message, promising immediate healing to all those who believed. If someone was not healed, they said, it was for lack of faith.

Fred Francis Bosworth (1877–1958) was one of the first to broadcast on the radio a message of "dominating faith." He called it "appropriating faith" and "victorious faith." This message was appealing to Americans during the Great Depression, the worst economic crisis that had hit the Western world, lasting from 1929 to 1941. One preacher, Major Jealous Divine (ca. 1876–1965), known as Father Divine, told his followers that the Great Depression was a result of negative thinking and could be overcome by positive thinking. The power of positive thinking was also preached in the 1950s by Norman Vincent Peale (1898–1993), who became a popular author, and by Robert Harold Schuller (1926–2015), who built the enormous Crystal Cathedral. Schuller taught that what people inherited from Adam is not sin but fear, so the answer is not Christ's obedience and death in our place but self-esteem.

The Crystal Cathedral
WATTEWYK, WIKIMEDIA COMMONS

The 1980s saw a large number of preachers who promised health and riches through faith. This type of preaching became popular in other countries too. Some forms of it are known as the prosperity gospel. While some of these preachers were sincere in their beliefs, others took advantage of the situation and promised health and riches to those who would give them money.

Think about It

- Did Jesus ever promise health and riches in this life? What did He promise?
- If poverty and poor health are a sign of a lack of faith, what should we think of the many Christians (including the apostles, especially Paul) who have suffered much throughout church history?

Great Questions of the Church

WHO CAN BE CALLED A CHRISTIAN?

Concerned that many people still had confused ideas about Christianity, between 1910 and 1915 two oil millionaires, the brothers Lyman (1840–1923) and Milton (1838–1923) Steward, financed the publication of a series of essays on teachings that were essential for everyone who bore the name of Christian. These included the five basic teachings listed at the 1895 Niagara Conference.

The essays, written by some of the best scholars of the time, were collected into twelve volumes and sent to pastors, theology professors and students, Sunday school teachers, and missionaries for a total of about three million copies. These teachings became known as fundamentals. In time, the people who supported them were called **fundamentalists**.

Not everyone agreed with these essays. Some people, commonly known as liberals or modernists, thought that some of those teachings had to be brought up to date. For example, most liberals didn't believe in miracles and tried to explain those described in the Bible as misunderstandings of natural events.

People wondered which of these two groups better represented Christianity. Are Christians supposed to stick faithfully to a set of beliefs, or are they supposed to adapt them to a changing world? In 1923 a professor at Princeton Seminary, J. Gresham Machen (1881–1937), wrote a book called *Christianity and Liberalism*, in which he suggested that liberalism should not be considered another version of Christianity. It's a completely different religion because liberals don't believe that the Bible is the word of God. By definition, a Christian must believe in the words of Christ and the words about Christ as they are recorded in the Bible.

J. Gresham Machen
REFORMATION ART

> ### Think about It
>
> - If you don't believe in what the Bible says about Christ, can you really call yourself Christian, or would it be more honest to say that you have created a new religion or are imagining a different Christ? Explain your answer.

If Jesus was only what the liberal historians suppose that He was, then trust in Him would be out of place: our attitude toward Him could be that of pupils to a Master and nothing more. But if He was what the New Testament represents Him as being, then we can safely commit to Him the eternal destinies of our souls.
—J. GRESHAM MACHEN

A New Denomination

Liberalism is particularly dangerous, Machen said, because it presents a different religion while sounding Christian. Machen's book was a warning that the greatest threat to the church comes from inside. Over the centuries, the church has been persecuted and scorned by unbelievers, but that only made it stronger. The true danger comes when people who claim to be Christian start spreading teachings that are opposite to what the Bible says.

At the same time, Machen said, being a Christian doesn't necessarily mean being a fundamentalist. By then, most fundamentalists had started to add other teachings to their list of fundamentals. For example, they thought all Christians should avoid drinking alcoholic drinks. Most of them also thought that Christians should agree with the writings of John Nelson Darby or C. I. Scofield. Others believed Christians should be very involved in politics.

Machen explained that the Bible doesn't teach any of these things. Although he agreed with fundamentalists more than with liberals, he didn't want to be classified as a fundamentalist. He said the word *fundamentalism* sounded like a new religion. He was just a Christian.

Machen tried to bring his denomination and Princeton Seminary back to the tried and proven Reformed confessions. But his denomination was not ready for a change, and his insistence on this point caused him to be banned from preaching. He ended up founding a new denomination, the Orthodox Presbyterian Church, and a new seminary, Westminster Theological Seminary, in Philadelphia, Pennsylvania.

> *The early church didn't say, "Look what the world is coming to!" They said, "Look what has come into the world!"*
> —CARL HENRY

Salt and Light

The journalist and theologian Carl F. H. Henry (1913–2003) believed in the basic teachings of the Bible but disagreed with the fundamentalists' tendency to separate themselves from the world around them. He believed that Christians should be part of the world and provide the salt and light the world can get only in Christ (see Matthew 5:13–16). He was a cofounder of Fuller Theological Seminary in Pasadena, California, and started a Christian magazine, *Christianity Today*.

Henry was also moved by poverty and suffering. Besides telling people about the gospel, he spent time taking care of their needs whenever he could. Some students remembered seeing him come to class tired and untidy because he had spent all night talking to homeless people. He believed that taking care of others is a Christian's duty. He believed the church has no authority to support laws or political parties in the name of Christ. But the church has a responsibility to proclaim God's word, which speaks about God's love for justice, His care for the poor, and His hatred for oppression.

Carl Henry
COURTESY OF THE HENRY CENTER FOR THEOLOGICAL UNDERSTANDING

THE MODERN WORLD • 217

Great Questions of the Church

ARE ALL RELIGIONS THE SAME?

In 1932 the Presbyterian Board of Foreign Missions published a report called "Re-Thinking Missions." Instead of taking the good news of the gospel to those who had never heard it, the report said, missionaries should just focus on helping people with their problems, recognizing that other religions have much truth in them.

The document, financed by the millionaire John D. Rockefeller Jr. (1874–1960), was approved by an author who was considered one of the most famous missionaries to China, Pearl S. Buck (1892–1973).

Pearl S. Buck
LIBRARY OF CONGRESS

Shocked by this new idea of missions, J. Gresham Machen wrote a response called "The Responsibility of the Church in Our New Age." The church should still take the gospel, he said, not just "as one way of salvation, but as the only way." The reason was simple: "All are lost in sin. None may be saved except by the way set forth in the gospel."

The leaders of Machen's denomination rejected his report without giving him a chance to discuss it. Because of this, he and others created a new missionary organization, the Independent Board for Presbyterian Foreign Missions (IBPFM), to send out missionaries who were committed to preaching the gospel. This board sent out almost 150 missionaries in its first twenty years.

Think about It

- Machen was a strong advocate of religious freedom. He believed that governments should not impose any religion, not even in schools. At the same time, Christian missionaries had to repeat what Jesus said: "I am the way, the truth, and the life. No one comes to the Father except through Me" (John 14:6). Can missionaries who contradict Jesus's words call themselves Christians? Why or why not?

- "Re-Thinking Missions" was based on the assumption that all religions are basically good and teach the same thing. It's true that most religions teach some good things. But Christianity is not about that. The main message of Christianity is that human beings have rebelled against God and are now "dead in trespasses and sins" (Ephesians 2:1). Without a Savior, they are helpless and doomed. But God has provided a Savior in the person of His Son, Jesus. This is a very different message. Do you think the message needs to be told, or is it something that people can figure out by themselves?

Always the gospel would have been received with favor by the world if it had been presented merely as one way of salvation; the offense came because it was presented as the only way, and because it made relentless war upon all other ways.
—J. GRESHAM MACHEN

The property at 153 Maplewood Avenue, Philadelphia, where IBPFM met starting in 1939. Before then they met at the Drake Hotel.
COURTESY OF IBPFM ARCHIVES

WYCLIFFE BIBLE TRANSLATORS

When the American missionary William Cameron (Cam) Townsend (1896–1982) went to Guatemala to sell Spanish Bibles, he was surprised to see how many people didn't speak Spanish. They spoke Cakchiquel, and there was no Bible in that language. Realizing how many other people all over the world were in the same situation, in 1942 he founded Wycliffe Bible Translators, an organization devoted to the translation of the Bible in minority languages.

The Monkey Trial

In May 1925 the American Civil Liberties Union (ACLU) challenged the state of Tennessee regarding a law that banned the teaching of evolution in public schools. The ACLU thought that teachers in public schools should be free to teach different views, including evolution.

They looked for a teacher who was willing to challenge the law. John T. Scopes (1900–1970), a high school teacher in Dayton, Tennessee, agreed to help them. He then taught evolution in his classroom and was accused of breaking the law. This allowed the ACLU to take the case to court, providing Scopes with one of the best lawyers in the country, Clarence Seward Darrow (1857–1938). William Jennings Bryan (1860–1925), a politician with strong Christian convictions, volunteered to defend the state laws.

William Jennings Bryan
LIBRARY OF CONGRESS

Bryan was not well prepared to answer Darrow's scientific questions, and the newspapers made fun of him for this reason. They nicknamed the trial "Monkey Trial" because the discussion shifted from whether Scopes had broken the law to the question of whether he had taught that man descended from other species, including monkeys.

Clarence Seward Darrow, the lawyer defending John T. Scopes
LIBRARY OF CONGRESS

The court condemned Scopes for breaking the law, but changed the verdict two years later because he had been fined too heavily. Still, questions about evolution continued throughout America. The fundamentalists, who most vigorously opposed teaching evolution in schools, ended up being accused of going against science. Since Bryan had mostly been on the defensive, newspapers began to describe fundamentalists as ignorant people who are afraid of anything that might shake their beliefs. This also caused many fundamentalists to retreat to their communities, creating their own Christian culture.

Today, some Christians believe that teaching evolution in public schools is not a threat to their faith as long as it is presented as a theory and is taught together with the views of creation. Others prefer to keep their children away from these teachings by homeschooling them or enrolling them in Christian schools..

At one point, the Scopes trial had to move outside because of the heat.
LIBRARY OF CONGRESS

God and Politics

The Cold War, a period of tension between the United States and the Soviet Union (the only superpowers left after World War II), created much anxiety. It started in 1946 and ended in 1991 with the fall of the Soviet Union. Even though the United States and the Soviet Union didn't fight each other directly, they backed opposing sides in other wars around the world. Many Americans feared that the Soviet Union might attack the United States. During this frightening time, many people found comfort in religion. Since the Soviet Union was officially atheist, Americans thought that God was on their side.

With this in mind, President Dwight David Eisenhower (1890–1969) encouraged people to practice their religion. "And I don't care which one," he said. In 1954 the US Congress voted to add the words "under God" to the American Pledge of Allegiance, making it what it is now.

Other American politicians mentioned God in their speeches to convince Americans that their causes were not only right but were blessed by God. In some cases, two opposing parties claimed that they were doing God's will.

Seeing how easy it was for some groups or politicians to use the Bible to support their programs, many Christians became convinced that politicians should not appeal to religion, and churches should not support political parties. Instead, churches should teach how to properly read the Bible, and each Christian should make political choices according to his or her conscience.

The Jesus People

During the 1960s, many young people began a widespread movement of protest against the Vietnam War, America's emphasis on material goods, and rules they considered unnecessary. Some people called them hippies.

Many of these hippies found a new interest in Jesus, but their unusual appearance, with long hair and colorful clothes, made them stand out in traditional churches, where they often felt out of place. A few pastors decided to change their style of preaching and make their churches more informal so that these young people would feel more welcome. One of these was Chuck Smith (1927–2013), who founded a denomination called Calvary Chapel. Smith had a lot of success reaching hippies with the gospel.

The Jesus People Movement inspired hundreds of young people to find a new interest in the Bible and to share their enthusiasm with everyone they met, even stopping strangers in the streets. In some churches, it gave way to a new type of songs, often accompanied by guitars, and to an informal atmosphere. In spite of its general lack of supervision, which opened the door to some false teachings, the movement inspired some Christians to bring the gospel to more people outside their churches.

A group of young people sitting on top of a van during the Jesus People march in 1969

PHOTO MADE AVAILABLE BY FULLER THEOLOGICAL SEMINARY, WWW.FULLER.EDU

Think about It

- As enthusiastic as the Jesus People were about the Bible, not every one of them was prepared to answer challenging questions. A young man who approached people by asking, "Are you saved?" was stumped when the Reformed pastor R. C. Sproul (1939–2017) replied with a question: "Saved from what?"
  What do you think? Was there something missing in the young man's question? How would you have answered R. C. Sproul?

- What can we learn from the Jesus People?

Back to the Basics

Around the end of the twentieth century, many Christians agreed that the emphasis on big churches, prosperity, and excitement was moving away from the teachings of the Bible. These things could attract crowds but didn't help people understand the gospel and the true meaning of being a Christian. In fact, twentieth-century American Christians knew less about the Bible than the generations before them.

Because of this, some pastors began to steer Christians back to the basics of the Reformation, reminding them of the importance of belonging to faithful churches where they could hear the gospel, receive the sacraments, and find biblical guidance and encouragement.

R. C. Sproul
ART BY MARCOS RODRIGUES

One of these pastors was R. C. Sproul, who founded Ligonier Ministries "to awaken as many people as possible to the holiness of God." He was also one of the main planners of the International Council on Biblical Inerrancy (ICBI), a group of theologians and pastors convinced that the Bible in its original form is inerrant—that is, free of mistakes.

This doesn't mean that everything every Bible character says is free of mistakes. Some people in the Bible told lies, and the Scriptures report these lies truthfully. It also doesn't mean that everything in the Bible must be taken literally (there are some figures of speech, and there may be some numbers that have been rounded).

The chair of ICBI, James Montgomery Boice (1938–2000), pointed out another problem in the way Christians viewed the Scriptures. Many Christians, he said, don't believe that the gospel can really work in people's hearts, so they come up with other methods to attract and influence people. Boice cofounded the Alliance of Confessing Evangelicals, an organization that has the purpose of reviving a passion "for the truth of the Gospel."

James Montgomery Boice
COURTESY OF THE ALLIANCE OF CONFESSING EVANGELICALS AND OF MRS. LINDA BOICE.

Boice was also a gifted hymn writer. At a time when many hymns had become repetitive and shallow, focusing on personal efforts and experience instead of the Scriptures, he helped Christians sing about Christ and His treasures. Boice's hymns, some people noticed, are like sermons, where each stanza corresponds to the preacher's points.

Among the Lutherans, hymn writer Jaroslav Vajda (1919–2008) did something similar. His songs express both the questions that are in people's hearts and the wonder of God's love and revelation.

Still, some churches prefer to sing the biblical psalms because they are what God has provided as songs for His people.

THE MODERN WORLD • 221

LATIN AMERICA, 1914–2000

- **1919** — The government of Uruguay renames all religious holidays, discouraging people from connecting them with the Bible.
- **1926–1929** — Mexican peasants launch the Cristero War to protest the increasing government restrictions on the Roman Catholic Church.
- **1948–1958** — Protestants are persecuted in Columbia
- **1956** — Five American missionaries are killed by the Waorani people of Ecuador's rain forest.
- **1968** — Some Roman Catholic bishops challenge the church to oppose unjust governments and fight for the good of the people. This became known as liberation theology.
- **1984** — The Vatican condemns liberation theology for mixing religion and politics.
- **1992** — Pope John Paul II calls the Protestants in Latin America "rapacious wolves."

New Missions and New Challenges

Around the middle of the twentieth century, many missionary organizations that had until then worked in the main cities began to send teams to remote regions to bring the gospel to indigenous people. Some missionaries gave their lives for this cause.

Many missionaries had to learn new languages because most indigenous people, unlike the people who lived in the Latin American cities, didn't speak Spanish or Portuguese. With the help of the natives, many of these missionaries translated the Bible into local languages.

The political unrest in Latin America has also provided many challenges, making it difficult for missionaries to travel. A different challenge has been faced in Uruguay, where the government has tried to minimize the influence of religion. In 1919, for example, it officially renamed all religious holidays (Christmas is "Family Day" and Easter week is "Tourism Week"). In other countries, Protestants have had their rights restricted. The worst situation has been in Columbia, where Protestants have been mistreated and some of their churches attacked and burned from 1948 to 1958.

In spite of these challenges, the number of Protestants continues to grow. In fact, some Protestant churches in Latin America are now sending missionaries to other parts of the world. For example, Brazilian missionaries have gone to Portugal and Angola.

THE MODERN WORLD

The Mexican Revolution

From 1910 to 1920, Mexico became the theater of one of the major revolutions of the twentieth century. The former government was overthrown, and a constitution was signed in 1917. While generally fair, the constitution restricted the rights of Roman Catholics more than it had before. Many church buildings and lands became the property of the state. Some were burned or painted red. Most Roman Catholic festivals and processions were forbidden; nuns, priests, monks, and friars were forbidden from teaching, even in private schools; and the government claimed the right to decide how many priests could serve in each area.

In 1926 the Mexican government became stricter in enforcing these portions of the constitution, prompting a great number of protests. While most protests were peaceful, some Mexican peasants armed themselves and started a rebellion that became known as the Cristero War. Their battle cry was "Viva Cristo Rey!" (Long live Christ the King). Over the course of three years, ninety thousand people died in the Cristero War.

Some soldiers in the Mexican Revolution
LIBRARY OF CONGRESS

In the end, the church and the Mexican government came to a compromise, allowing worship to resume in Mexico and giving back to the church the right to use its properties.

Liberation Theology

At a time of great poverty, oppression, and violence, some Roman Catholics challenged the church, which had traditionally supported unjust governments, to fight for the good of the people. This challenge was officially expressed in 1968 during a conference of Latin American bishops. The belief that the church should do anything to help the poor, including being involved in politics, became known as liberation theology.

Initially, the pope remained quiet. But when some priests and bishops openly supported political parties and revolutions, even taking on positions of political power, the pope spoke out against it. In 1984 the Vatican officially condemned liberation theology for understanding the Bible as a political book that sounded more like Marx than the Scriptures.

Cardinal Joseph Ratzinger, later Pope Benedict XVI (b. 1927), who wrote the document, called liberation theology "a fundamental threat" to the church. Christians should always be ready to help people in need, but when that becomes the main focus of the church, it ends up limiting the message of the Bible. It leads Christians to misunderstand, above all, Ratzinger said, "the person of our Lord Jesus Christ, true God and true man" and to forget that the salvation He gave us "is above all liberation from sin, which is the source of all evils." In spite of this, the ideas of liberation theology continued in Latin America and in other parts of the world.

> **RECOVERING THE REFORMATION**
>
> In much of Latin America, like in other countries, many Christians have grown tired of the empty promises of both liberation theology and the prosperity gospel and have returned to the historical churches that stay faithful to the teachings of the Protestant Reformation. In Brazil alone, about a million Christians are now members of these types of churches, and many more have shown a great interest in what these churches have to teach.
>
> For these reasons, some Christians have organized new publishing companies to provide Latin America with good books about the Bible and historical Christian teachings. They have also established seminaries to train new pastors.

The Mission to the Waorani

Many Christians were killed in South America—some by oppressive governments and some by revolutionaries who fought against the governments. A few were killed by local people who didn't understand their mission.

This is what happened to five American missionaries—Jim Elliot (1927–1956), Nate Saint (1923–1956), Ed McCully (1927–1956), Peter Fleming (1928–1956), and Roger Youderian (1924–1956)—who traveled to the rain forest of Ecuador to take the gospel to the Waorani, an isolated population that was known for their violence.

Waorani huts in the Amazon forest
DEPOSITPHOTOS

At first the missionaries flew over the Waorani villages, dropping gifts from their plane. On January 3, 1956, they set up a camp along the Curaray River and waited to make contact. They were hopeful. Instead, a group of Waorani warriors attacked them and killed them with their spears. The news of their deaths was broadcast around the world.

Two years later, the widow of Jim Elliot, Elisabeth (1926–2015), and the sister of Nate Saint, Rachel (1914–1994), returned to Ecuador as missionaries to live among the Waorani. Unlike the five men, these two women, together with Elisabeth's young daughter, were not considered a threat and were welcomed.

Through these missionaries' work, many Waorani became Christians, including some of those who had killed the men. Years later Steve Saint, son of Nate Saint, met Mincaye (d. 2020), the man who threw the spear at his father that killed him. Mincaye became a preacher and elder and considered Steve his adopted son. When Steve and his sister, Kathy, as teenagers, decided to get baptized, they asked Mincaye to perform the ceremony in the same waters where the five missionaries had been killed.

Some documentaries have been made about the five missionaries. Elisabeth also wrote a story of her experience and many other books that inspired Christians everywhere to live a life of love and forgiveness.

The work with the Waorani is probably the most famous Protestant mission in South America. But there were many others in which the natives were welcoming from the start. The Paumarì, for example, who live in the Amazon region of Brazil, told the first missionaries that they had heard about Jesus on the radio and had been expecting God to send someone to tell them about Him. Today, many South Americans have heard the gospel and can read the Bible in their own language, but there are still more people groups waiting.

> *He is no fool who gives what he cannot keep to gain that which he cannot lose.*
> —JIM ELLIOT

Jim Elliot
ALPHA HISTORICA / ALAMY STOCK PHOTO

EAST ASIA, 1914–2000

1919 — Koreans declare their independence from Japan. Since many of the people who sign the declaration are Christians, the Japanese government increases its persecution against Christians.

1945 — Korea divides into North Korea and South Korea. The rulers of North Korea ban Christianity since they consider it a Western religion.

1949 — Mao Tse-Tung begins the People's Republic of China. His government allows only state-approved churches.

1966–1978 — Chinese churches are forced to close during the Cultural Revolution. Chinese Christians are persecuted by the Red Guards.

Persecuted, but Not Forsaken

At the start of the twentieth century, Christians in Asia faced two major challenges: persecution by some rulers and pressure to compromise their beliefs. In some cases, these happened at the same time, and people who compromised were able to escape persecution. Many Christians were imprisoned, tortured, and killed. In spite of this, Christianity has grown in Asia more than ever before.

Persecution in Korea

Like many other rulers, the emperors of Japan saw Christians as a threat, both because Christianity had come through foreign missionaries and because it was growing. Loyal citizens were expected to follow the local Shinto religion, which worships different spirits and considers emperors to be gods. Christians were allowed to practice their religion only if they bowed to the emperor and to shrines and let the government regulate their worship and actions.

Under pressure, some Christians made compromises. They submitted to the government's inspections and agreed to bow before the emperor and shrines. In their eyes, it was like saluting a flag, not an act of worship. Other Christians resisted and were severely punished, often by being tortured and killed.

This also happened in the Japanese territories in Asia, including Korea. Korean Christians were particularly persecuted after 1919, when some of them joined an effort to declare independence from Japan. The persecution ended in 1945 with the defeat of Japan in World War II. At that point, pastors had to work hard to comfort those who had been suffering. They also had to clarify that Christians could not worship Christ and idols at the same time.

In Korea, however, troubles were not over. Three days before the Japanese left the country, the Soviet Union invaded from the north. When the Americans, who entered Korea from the south, established a line the Soviets were not supposed to cross, the country divided into North Korea and South Korea. The dictatorial leader of North Korea, Kim Il-sung (1912–1994), banned Christianity as a Western religion, forcing many Christians to worship in secret or flee the country. Those who stayed and proclaimed their faith were imprisoned and often killed.

In spite of all these challenges, the church in South Korea has continued to grow faster than in any Western nation. Even during Japanese rule, the Korean church was able to send eighty Korean pastors to minister to Koreans in other countries, including the United States and Mexico. Their mission in China was particularly fruitful until 1957, when the Chinese government forced it to close.

Overall, the number of Christians in Korea had grown from 600,000 in 1950 to 7.2 million in 1980. In 2015 there were more than 26,000 Korean missionaries ministering in over 170 countries. In North Korea, still under a dictatorial government, Christians continue to suffer from harsh persecution.

Four Korean preachers at the start of the twentieth century. Rev. Choi Pyung-Hun, second from the left, was imprisoned for his faith. Through his witness, all eighteen of his cellmates became Christian. At his right, Rev. Son Chun Do, was the first missionary sent by the Korean church to Manchuria. He was banished and persecuted almost to death.

UNIVERSITY OF SOUTHERN CALIFORNIA DIGITAL LIBRARY

More Men and Women of the Modern Church

MEN AND WOMEN OF THE TWENTIETH-CENTURY KOREAN CHURCH

KYUNG-CHIK HAN (1902–2000) was born in North Korea to Confucian parents and became a Christian at age seven through the witness of a cousin. He was able to study at Princeton Seminary in America. When he returned to Korea, he was imprisoned by the Japanese for refusing to worship Emperor Hirohito (1901–1989). In 1945, when North Korea became Communist, he escaped to South Korea. There, he started a prayer group with twenty-seven members, which grew into the largest church in the world, with sixty thousand members, which was divided into six Sunday services. He also started a university, a seminary, an orphanage, a library, and a home for senior citizens. He is mostly remembered for the help he gave to other refugees from North Korea.

JOON GON KIM (1925–2009) was the pastor of one of the largest churches in South Korea and founder of Korea's Campus Crusade for Christ. During the Korean War (1950–1953), he and his family were attacked by a group of Communist soldiers who beat him almost to death and killed his wife and father. After praying, Kim took his daughter, who had survived the attack, and went to visit the leader of the soldiers to tell him that he forgave and loved him in Christ. The leader knelt in prayer and became a Christian. Soon other members of the group did the same, and Kim helped to build a church for them and other new Christians.

SOHN YANG-WON (1902–1950) was in North Korea when the Soviets took over. Two of his sons were killed by Soviet supporters. When one of the murderers, a young man named Chai-sun, was captured, Sohn asked the court to allow him to adopt him rather than send him to prison. Chai-sun became a Christian and later a pastor. Years later, Sohn was arrested, charged that he was pro-American and anti-Communist. He spoke about Jesus even to the guard who was beating him. In the end, he was shot to death.

ESTHER AHN KIM (1908–1997) was arrested for refusing to bow to the Japanese sun goddess. She managed to escape and hide but knew that she could easily be caught again. To prepare for prison, she memorized more than one hundred Bible chapters and many hymns. She was imprisoned from 1939 to 1945, when Japan was defeated in World War II. She then moved to the United States, where she died in 1997. She wrote a book about her experience titled *If I Perish*.

BRUCE F. HUNT (1903–1992) was born in Korea to an American missionary family. During the Japanese occupation, he was imprisoned for helping Korean Christians. He thoroughly believed that the only way for the Korean Presbyterian Church to survive was by preserving its historical faith against the challenge of liberal theology.

CHU KI-CHOL (1897–1944) was a Korean Presbyterian minister who refused to worship at the Japanese shrines. In 1938 he was arrested and imprisoned a few times. Altogether, he spent more than five years in prison. Weak from the beatings and torture he received, he died in a prison hospital. The South Korean government awarded him many honors, including the South Korean Independence Medal. In his sermons, he insisted that he was simply trying to obey God's word.

Rev. F. Herron Smith holding a Sunday school class with some of the many Japanese who moved to Korea at the start of the twentieth century

UNIVERSITY OF SOUTHERN CALIFORNIA DIGITAL LIBRARY

Persecution in China

For centuries, the ability of foreign missionaries to stay in China depended on the attitude of the local rulers. Knowing they could be expelled at any time, these missionaries did as much as they could to train local pastors. Most of them were sent away in 1949, when Mao Tse-tung (1893–1976) proclaimed the birth of the People's Republic of China—a Communist regime. Along with expelling foreign missionaries, the Chinese Communist Party started a strict oversight of local churches, forcing them to sign up with patriotic movements and to cut ties with foreign churches. For example, Roman Catholics couldn't receive any instructions from the pope, not even about the appointment of bishops.

Protestants had to join the Three-Self Patriotic Movement (TSPM)—a name inspired by John Livingston Nevius's idea of a church that can run, grow, and raise funds by itself. The idea went along with the government's efforts to cut ties with the West.

But even the churches that accepted these guidelines were forced to close from 1966 to 1978 during the so-called Cultural Revolution. During this time, young Red Guards under Mao's direction sacked many churches, mistreating Christians and burning their Bibles.

Churches were allowed to reopen at the end of 1978 under the supervision of the government. Christians had to pledge loyalty to the Communist party, avoid listening to Christian programs from outside China, and avoid engaging in missionary activities.

The Episcopal bishop Ding Guangxun, also known as K. H. Ting (1915–2012), head of TSPM, is credited for keeping the Chinese church alive through these difficult times. But he is also accused of making dangerous compromises. Preaching that God is love, he used this love as a way to minimize basic Christian teachings and to present Christianity as a good match for Communist beliefs. He thought this would also bring unity among Chinese Christians because "they believed in the same Father and the same Bible."

But many Chinese Christians disagreed. A pastor, Wang Mingdao (1900–1991), insisted that God the Father can be known only through the Son as He is revealed in the Bible. "The modernists who explain away the fundamental doctrines about Christ and say they are not essential to faith, are they not dishonoring, despising, and denying the Son?" he asked. And if they are, "how can we acknowledge that they abide with us in the same Father?"

A group of children at the kindergarten of the Presbyterian Mission at Nanjing, China, in 1926

LIBRARY OF CONGRESS

Wang was only defending Christianity, not opposing the government. Still, he and his wife, Liu Jingwen (1909–1992), were arrested for being unpatriotic and sent to prison. Ting was one of the people responsible for their capture.

After a little more than a year of suffering and torture, Wang confessed to crimes he had not committed and promised to join the government's church. He and Liu were released, but his conscience kept bothering him for what he had done. He then continued to preach Christ and was arrested again. Liu was condemned to prison for fifteen years and Wang to prison and hard labor for life.

Liu was released in 1973, blind in one eye. Wang was released in 1979 after many protests from human rights organizations. By that time, he was toothless and nearly blind and deaf. In spite of this, he continued to uphold the biblical gospel of Christ and the historical Protestant doctrines. His books and the example set by him and his wife have inspired many Christians.

Since most Christians who opposed the government's ideas of Christianity worshiped in secret in someone's house, their movement became known as the House Church Movement. Because they preached that salvation comes only through faith in Christ, they were also known as the Sola Fide Movement. By the time of Mao's death in 1976, this movement counted about six million people. It kept its name even after the worship moved to larger church buildings. Today, China is home to more believers than any other nation in the world.

A portrait of Mao Tse-tung in Tiananmen Gate, Beijing, China
LIBRARY OF CONGRESS

Today,
We will raise our banners high!
Let them wave,
Let them fly,
Let them face the sun,
Let them welcome the bright and shining King!

Yes,
Let the tempest quickly come!
Because,
When the world looms ever more dark, difficult, and dreary
We yet firmly believe, in the distance
The dawn is visible!
The dawn is visible!

—A portion of a poem by Bian Yunbo (1925–2018), a Chinese evangelist who was arrested with Wang Mingdao. Even after his release, he and his family continued to suffer persecution. The poem is titled "To the Unknown Evangelist, My Brother" and is dedicated to all Christians who are preaching the gospel.

Wang Mingdao
UTCON COLLECTION, ALAMY STOCK PHOTO

More Men and Women of the Modern Church

OTHER CHRISTIANS OF THE TWENTIETH-CENTURY CHINESE CHURCH

TSAI SU JUAN (1890–1984) also known as Christiana Tsai, became a Christian when she heard the gospel preached by the Presbyterian American missionary Charles Leaman. She studied at the Presbyterian school, then joined Leaman's daughter Mary (1879–1972) in taking the gospel to remote areas. Through her testimony of Christ, fifty-five members of her family became Christian—including her mother, who was also delivered from opium **addiction** and joined Christiana on some of her travels. In 1931 Christiana suffered from a serious case of malaria that affected her hearing and eyesight so much that she had to spend most of her time in a darkened room. While she couldn't go out, thousands of people went to see her. "My bed is not a prison," she said, "but a training school; the Holy Spirit is my mentor, and my visitors are my homework." Her books have inspired many people.

JEANETTE LI (1899–1968) first learned about Christ from a doctor at a missionary hospital. She and her mother, who had also become a Christian, were persecuted by their family, who saw them as a disgrace. When foreign missionaries were expelled from China, Jeanette took over their orphanage and continued to spread the gospel as long as she could. She was arrested in 1952 and kept in prison for seventeen months in terrible conditions simply because she had been in a church in Hong Kong when a missionary said a prayer for Taiwan's ruler Chiang Kai-shek (1887–1975), who had become a Christian and was opposed to the People's Republic of China. The prison guards didn't believe that Jeanette was just following the Bible's instructions to pray for political leaders. She was eventually released and served as a missionary in Canton and Hong Kong. She moved to the United States in 1962, where she wrote her autobiography, *A Girl Born Facing Outside*.

Like Korea, Indonesia has seen a large increase in the number of Christians, especially after 1965, when General Haji Mohammad Suharto (1921–2008) defeated the Communist party that tried to take over the country. Messiah Cathedral in Jakarta is one of the largest church buildings in the country and can hold about eight thousand people. Its members are committed to the creeds and confessions of the Protestant Reformation.

RUKUMAN, WIKIMEDIA COMMONS

GI PUNG YI (1868-1942) was the first Korean Protestant missionary and the first Korean martyr, often remembered as the father of the Korean Protestant church. It all began when he, still an unbeliever, threw a rock at the American missionary **SAMUEL A. MOFFETT** (1864–1939). Bothered by his conscience, he asked the missionary to forgive him and became a Christian and later a pastor. He died soon after being arrested and tortured by the Korean authorities who thought he was an American spy.

WATCHMAN NEE (1903–1972), or Ni Tuosheng, is the most famous Chinese Christian outside of China. His church meetings in 1922 are considered the start of the House Church Movement. He spent over twenty years in prison.

HISTORIC COLLECTION / ALAMY STOCK PHOTO

The Scot **ERIC LIDDELL** (1902–1945) is famous as the subject of the popular movie *Chariots of Fire*. The movie tells the story of how Liddell's faith prevented him from running in one of the most crucial 1924 Olympic races for Scotland because it was held on a Sunday. He eventually won a gold medal for Scotland in a different race, but his example surprised the world and helped Christians examine their priorities and convictions. Few people remember that he was a missionary to China from 1925 to 1943 and that he was kept in an internment camp when the Japanese took over China.

ALLEN YUAN XIANGCHEN (1914–2005) was imprisoned for more than twenty-one years for refusing to be a part of the government's church. After his release, he preached in one of the largest house churches of his time.

Eric Liddell
ART BY MARCOS RODRIGUES

A list of foreigners who were imprisoned in the Weixian Internment Camp in China during World War II. The missionary Eric Liddell was also imprisoned there.

ROLFMUELLER, WIKIMEDIA COMMONS

THE MODERN WORLD • 233

AFRICA AND THE MIDDLE EAST, 1914–2000

- **1915–1918** — The Ottoman Empire kills about 1.5 million Armenian and about 150,000 Assyrian Christians.
- **ca. 1930** — The East African Revival begins.
- **1960** — Seventeen African nations declare independence from Europe.
- **1974** — Mengistu Haile Mariam dethrones Emperor Haile Selassie and establishes a Communist regime in Ethiopia.
- **1977** — Anglican archbishop Janani Luwum is killed by Idi Amin's government for speaking out against the dictator's abuses.
- **1979** — The Ethiopian pastor Gudina Tumsa is kidnapped and executed by the government.
- **1994** — South Africa puts an end to apartheid, the practice of dividing people according to races, which gave preference to Whites.

Changes and Problems

During the second half of the twentieth century, many African nations declared their independence from the European countries that had ruled them. In 1960 alone, the so-called Year of Africa, seventeen African nations became independent. Their churches also became more independent of European help. But political independence didn't always mean peace. In some countries, it opened the door to rebellions and wars by people who wanted to gain power. In these cases, many churches provided stability and hope. As it was in Asia, in spite of these changes and problems, the number of Christians has grown more than ever—from about 9 million in 1900 to about 335 million in 2000 (45 percent of the total population of Africa). In fact many Africans today are serving as missionaries in Europe and North America.

THE MODERN WORLD • 235

Genocides in the Ottoman Empire

Armenia—the first nation to become officially Christian in 301—was conquered by the Ottoman Empire during the fifteenth century. In spite of being Muslim, the Ottoman government tolerated the Christian Armenian population, at least by law. In reality, Armenians had fewer rights and were often mistreated. Many were even killed. Their worst troubles started at the beginning of the twentieth century, when a small group of men in power believed the empire would be stronger with just one religion, Islam.

In 1913 this group took over the government by force. Two years later, they moved the Armenian men away from their communities. Initially, it was just to enlist them for war. Later, however, they placed them in camps where they were mistreated and deprived of food. In the meantime, they forced the rest of the Armenians—women, children, and the elderly—to march for weeks or months to some places where they would be relocated. In reality, many of those who survived the marches were killed. Only a few people were left to tell the story. This event, known as the Armenian genocide, resulted in the death of over one million Armenians.

The Armenians were not the only people to suffer under the Ottoman Empire. At least 275,000 Assyrians and 350,000 Pontic Greeks (traditionally from the regions of Pontus and Anatolia) were killed at that time. In these cases, the persecutions were not ordered by the government but were carried out by local rulers or Kurdish tribes.

A monument commemorating the flight of the Armenian refugees in the Armenian Genocide Memorial Complex built on a hill in Yerevan, Armenia

YOUNG SHANAHAN, FLICKR

A monument to the victims of the Assyrian genocide in the Peace Park at Locarno, Switzerland

PAKEHA, WIKIMEDIA COMMONS

Clarence Douglas Ussher
FROM *IN THE LAND OF ARARAT*, BY JOHN OTIS BARROW (NEW YORK: FLEMING H. REVELL, 1916)

Elizabeth Barrows Ussher
FROM *IN THE LAND OF ARARAT*, BY JOHN OTIS BARROW (NEW YORK: FLEMING H. REVELL, 1916)

William Ambrose Shedd
WIKIMEDIA COMMONS

MISSIONARIES TO GENOCIDE AREAS

The Armenian genocide was reported by missionaries who worked in the area, including the American doctor Clarence Douglas Ussher (1870–1955) and his wife, Elizabeth Barrows Ussher (1873–1915). Their mission's buildings at Van, in eastern Turkey, became a place of refuge for anyone in need—Armenians, Turks, and Russian soldiers—during the resistance some Armenians put up against the Turks. Eventually, both Clarence and Elizabeth became ill with typhus, a contagious disease. Elizabeth died of it, while Clarence developed pneumonia and was in a coma for some time. Clarence wrote an account of the Armenian genocide dedicated "to the memory of my beloved wife and the other martyrs, American and Armenian, who have laid down their lives for the name of Christ in Turkey during the Great World War."

William Ambrose Shedd (1865–1918) was another missionary with a similar story. He served in Urmia, in today's Iran, where thousands of Assyrian Christians lived. Like the Usshers, he and the other missionaries with him were caught in a siege and had to feed thousands of refugees in spite of limited supplies. Later, they and a large group of Assyrians had to flee to escape an approaching army of Turks and Kurds. He died of a fever during the march, and his second wife, Mary Lewis Shedd (1873–death unknown), wrote his biography, which is also a detailed account of the Assyrian genocide. "Is this the end?" she wondered at the close of her book, looking at the destruction of hundreds of thousands of homes. She remembered the promise in Psalm 126:5, "Those who sow in tears shall reap in joy." "God has not left Himself without witness here," she thought.

A first account of the Armenian genocide was written by Aurora Mardiganian (1901–1994), who was only a teenager at that time. Because of her beauty, Aurora was taken from her family and promised good treatment as one of the wives of a local rich man on condition that she convert to Islam. To pressure her, the man forced her to watch the cruel murder of her mother and siblings. She was forced to march over fourteen hundred miles, was kidnapped, and was sold into a Turkish slave market. She finally managed to escape first to the European nation of Georgia and then to the United States. In all her sufferings, she remembered the words an Eastern Orthodox priest had told her: "Always trust in God and remain faithful to Him."

> *May God grant and may we who know so well the wrongs that have been borne, so labor that the cause of these wrongs be removed. That will be done when Christ rules in the hearts of those who profess His name and is acknowledged by all, not merely as a great prophet but as the Savior for Whose coming prophecy prepared the way, Who is the fulfillment of revelation, and in Whom human destiny will find its goal.*
>
> —WILLIAM SHEDD

More Persecution in the Middle East and Africa

Persecution and genocides didn't end after World War I. Christians in the Middle East and Africa continued to suffer, particularly when countries became ruled by dictators or controlled by terrorist Islamic organizations, such as ISIS and Boko Haram.

Today Christians are particularly persecuted in Middle Eastern countries such as Iran, Yemen, and Libya and African countries such as Eritrea, Somalia, Sudan, and parts of Nigeria. Even if a government doesn't directly persecute Christians, it often makes life difficult for them. For example, some Muslim governments are not concerned with protecting Christians from violence or providing them with assistance in times of famine or war.

The Ugandan dictator Idi Amin

LIBRARY OF CONGRESS, PRINTS & PHOTOGRAPHS DIVISION, PHOTOGRAPH BY BERNARD GOTFRYD

An African dictator who persecuted Christians was Idi Amin (1925–2003). Amin wanted to turn Uganda into a Muslim country. He allowed only three forms of Christianity (Roman Catholic, Orthodox, and Anglican) and kept them under his control. Under his rule, about four hundred thousand Christians died, disappeared, or fled the country.

The best known of his victims is Anglican archbishop Janani Luwum (1922–1977), who spoke out against Amin's abuses and was arrested and accused of treason, together with two other men. The next day, an announcement on the radio said that the three had died in a car crash. But Luwum's body was later found full of bullets. In spite of the government's threats, forty-five thousand Ugandans attended Luwum's funeral.

One of the Christians who left Uganda was the Anglican bishop Festo Kivengere (1919–1988). He later wrote a book, *I Love Idi Amin*, to remind Christians that Jesus said to love and forgive their enemies. Kivengere was a talented preacher. When he told a Bible story, people thought they were right in the scene. For this reason, he was known as the Billy Graham of Africa.

Festo Kivengere

BUSWELL LIBRARY ARCHIVES & SPECIAL COLLECTIONS

Another African martyr was the Ethiopian pastor Gudina Tumsa (1929–1979), who was kidnapped with his wife, Tsehay Tolessa (1931–2014), after leading a Bible study. No one knew what happened to Gudina until thirteen years later when his body was found. Initially set free, Tsehay was arrested again in 1980 and kept in an overcrowded prison for ten years, where she suffered terrible torture.

Gudina's kidnapping was sudden but not unexpected. He had spoken out for years about the abuses of both Emperor Haile Selassie I (1892–1975) and his Marxist successor, Mengistu Haile Mariam (b. 1937). Like other Communist leaders, Mengistu tried to control the church. Under his rule, which lasted until 1987, thousands of Ethiopians were imprisoned and executed without trial. Gudina had been arrested twice before his final kidnapping. He could have left the country but decided to stay with his congregation.

As well as fighting for the freedom of the church, Gudina taught some important lessons about caring for people's bodies and souls, like Jesus and the early church did.

Janani Luwum, archbishop of Uganda, portrayed in one of ten statues of modern martyrs above Westminster Abbey's Great West Door, London. Work by Tim Crawley, 1998.

COPYRIGHT DEAN AND CHAPTER OF WESTMINSTER

> *Having been captured by Calvary love, you and I have only one option—the same time that we are hating and protesting against the evil, we love those who oppress us until they are set free from the bondage of oppressing.*
> —FESTO KIVENGERE

THE DEAD SEA SCROLLS

In late 1946 or early 1947, a young Arab shepherd working near Qumran, Israel, on the northwest shore of the Dead Sea, threw a rock into a cave on the side of a cliff and heard the sound of something breaking. When he and his friends went inside, they found a collection of large clay jars. Seven of them had some scrolls of parchment inside. At first, he thought of using the parchment as sandal straps. Later, he took them to a seller of antiques in Bethlehem.

As it turned out, the scrolls included portions of the Bible written about two thousand years earlier. They were valued at hundreds of thousands of dollars. After word of the discovery got out, people began to search the area, finding more than forty thousand fragments of scrolls in the years between 1947 and 1956.

These documents date from about 250 BC to AD 70. Before then, the oldest-known Hebrew transcriptions of the Bible dated about one thousand years later. What's more, when scholars compared transcriptions from different centuries, they discovered that, apart from a few spelling mistakes, they were identical. This meant that the Bible was transcribed correctly. For Christians who had often heard people say that the Bible can't be trusted because it was written a long time ago and had been transcribed by different people, this was encouraging. Now they could say with confidence that God had preserved His word.

Dead Sea Scrolls, found in the Qumran Caves near the Dead Sea in Israel
ALEFBET, ISTOCK

Great Questions of the Church

IS THE GOSPEL THE SAME IN EVERY CULTURE?

Foreign missionaries had worked hard in Africa. Besides preaching the gospel to people who had never heard it, they built schools and churches, opened new routes, and trained Africans to take over their work. With their emphasis on translating the Bible into the local languages and creating grammar books so that these languages could be learned, some missionaries had strengthened African cultures and made a way for African independence.

At the same time, many foreign missionaries had imposed their way of dressing or acting on Africans, as if those practices were part of being a Christian. When in the middle of the twentieth century most African nations became independent from Europe, some Africans got rid of all Western customs.

This rejection reached a dangerous extreme when, in an effort to promote their culture, some Africans began to teach that African religions are similar enough to Christianity that people could be saved without the Bible and without Christ just by following their traditions and living a good life.

The Nigerian theologian Byang Henry Kato (1936–1975) issued a strong warning against this teaching. He agreed that God gives a general revelation of Himself "through nature, conscience, history, and miracles." The Bible teaches that people can recognize God's glory just by looking at the sky (Psalm 19:1) and that much of God's law is written on their conscience (Romans 1:19–20).

But only "he who has the Son has life" (1 John 5:12), and no one can know God's Son without the Bible, where He has chosen to reveal Himself. And the gospel, Kato said, "is not a part of any people's culture," nor could it ever be because it's about "a historic person, Jesus the Christ…. The Jews did not have it. The Germans, the Americans, the Africans, the Europeans needed to get it through a messenger."

Kato spoke by experience because he first heard the gospel in a missionary school. At age seventeen, he decided to become a missionary too. He spent much of his life studying, teaching, preaching, writing, and promoting greater education and training for African pastors and Christians in general.

He died young, drowning in the Indian Ocean during a family vacation when he was only thirty-nine years old. Still, he left an important mark on the African church by insisting that the churches be first biblical, and then African. He knew it was important to present the gospel in a way that all Africans in their different situations and cultures could understand. But the message had to be the gospel, not African or Western beliefs.

The Kato family. From left to right: Deborah Bosede, Jummai Rahila, Paul Sanom, Byang Henry Kato, and Jonathan Nzuno.
COURTESY OF PAUL KATO

The Evangelical School of Theology in Bangui, the capital of the Central African Republic, was one of Kato's projects in his efforts to provide a better education for pastors and teachers. It was the first school of this kind in French-speaking Africa.

COURTESY OF DAVID STRINGER

Think about It

- Give some examples of something we can learn about God from general revelation, from looking at the beauty of creation or by listening to our consciences.

- What do you think of Kato's warning that people cannot learn the gospel through general revelation? Can the creation, our conscience, or anything in this world tell us that God became man to take the punishment we deserve for our sins so that He could reconcile us to Himself? How can we learn this?

- While the gospel message is the same for every nation, it has to be communicated in different languages and in ways that people can understand. Even the people who translated your Bible have worked hard to express every word in a way that was both faithful to the original and clear to readers.

- Think also of some small differences in the way churches in your country and around the world present the gospel. Do you agree or disagree that these differences can be allowed without changing the message of the gospel? Explain your answer.

East African Revival convention in Kabale, Uganda, 1945
CAMBRIDGE CENTRE FOR CHRISTIANITY WORLDWIDE

The East African Revival

In the 1930s, a Christian revival began to spread first in Uganda, then in Kenya and Tanzania. Some people attribute its beginnings to a meeting between a British missionary, John Edward (Joe) Church (1899–1989), and the Ugandan Simeoni Nsibambi (1897–1978), who were discouraged by the laziness and corruption of many churches.

Church and Nsibambi connected with other people who felt the same way and tried to bring a change. Each person talked to others, prayer groups formed, and preachers began to stress the repentance of sins and Christ's work of salvation. The Luganda hymn "Tukutendereza Yesu" (We praise You, Jesus), with its emphasis on what Christ has done for sinners, became particularly popular.

William Nagenda (1912–1973), another leader of the East African Revival, and Joe Church
CAMBRIDGE CENTRE FOR CHRISTIANITY WORLDWIDE

The revival continued for as long as fifty years and brought many people to Christ. Because of its location, it became known as the East African Revival. It is also known as the Balokole Revival, from the Luganda word *baloloke* (the saved ones), which some people called those who kept talking about salvation in Christ.

Initially, the revival was influenced by the Keswick teaching of a second blessing that gives complete victory over sin (see p. 169), but most leaders became aware of the dangers of this idea, as it led to extremes and distracted from the greatest blessing of all, which is Christ. They also encouraged people to avoid the temptation of breaking away from their local churches, helping them to see themselves as part of the unified kingdom of Christ.

Like in other revivals, there were problems with some people who joined just for the excitement, some who looked down on other Christians, and some who thought that shouting, crying, and jumping up and down were marks of a true Christian.

Simeoni Nsibambi and his wife, Eva Bakaluba, with their family
CAMBRIDGE CENTRE FOR CHRISTIANITY WORLDWIDE

Festo Kivengere, who played an important part in the revival, explained that "the devil is not afraid of people singing and jumping for joy in times of revival. …All he says is 'jump a little higher, and the higher you jump the more 'spiritual' you are! …So you could find the brethren fighting over whether you should shake, shout, be silent, or act in a particular way. But when you try and copy some kind of reaction, you produce a fake."

In spite of these misunderstandings and the terrible wars and persecutions happening at the same time, the churches in East Africa continued to grow, as thousands of true believers in Jesus were added to them.

An Evil Separation

From 1948 to 1994, the White minority government of South Africa imposed a separation between races similar to the segregation that had happened in the southern states of America. This policy was called *apartheid*, an Afrikaans word meaning "separateness."

But Black South Africans were not kept separate only from the Whites. They were also separated from each other so they could not unite to defend their rights. From 1961 to 1994, more than 3.5 million Blacks were removed from their homes and sent to some regions called Bantustans with very few resources.

In 1976, when a large number of Black students were killed by heavily armed police during a demonstration, the protest turned to a violent uprising that spread to other parts of the country.

Most White Christians approved of apartheid, basing their reasoning on a mistaken interpretation of Bible verses (see p. 207) and on the belief that people would be more at ease worshiping with those who looked and thought like them.

For many White South Africans, there was also a strong fear of what would happen to them if the Black population were empowered. "Like most other whites," Anglican bishop Frank Retief (b. 1942) confessed later, "our white-led church believed we were in a struggle for Western values and freedoms and that the liberation groups were all pawns of the communist regimes. Be that as it may, the fact of the matter is that we allowed ourselves to be misled into accepting a social, economic and political system that was cruel and oppressive."

The evangelical preacher Michael Cassidy (b. 1936) recommended that these fearful Whites choose "charity in spite of dangers, unselfishness in spite of risks, faith in spite of fear."

At the same time, the Anglican archbishop Desmond Tutu (b. 1931) encouraged Black South Africans to forgive those who had wronged them. "Forgiveness does not mean condoning what has been done," he said. "It means taking what happened seriously and not minimizing it; drawing out the sting in the memory that threatens to poison our entire existence. It involves trying to understand the perpetrators and so have empathy, to try to stand in their shoes and appreciate the sort of pressures and influences that might have conditioned them."

For many years, most people in the rest of the world remained silent about apartheid, which, along with Blacks, affected other South African minorities. In 1982, however, the World Alliance of Reformed Churches called it a sin and declared that any justification the church had given for it was "a travesty [distortion] of the gospel and, in its persistent disobedience to the word of God, a theological heresy."

They quoted John Calvin, a Reformer most Christians in South Africa respected, as saying, "None of the brethren can be injured, despised, rejected, abused, or in any way offended by us, without at the same time injuring, despising, and abusing Christ by the wrongs we do."

In 1991 South Africa's president Frederik Willem de Klerk (1936–2021) and his government officially ended apartheid. The next president, Nelson Mandela (1918–2013), had spent twenty-seven

Michael Cassidy and F. W. De Klerk

COURTESY OF MICHAEL CASSIDY & FRIENDS LEGACY FOUNDATION

Archbishop Desmond Tutu

BERNARD GOTFRYD, LIBRARY OF CONGRESS

Nelson Mandela

MAUREEN KEATING, LIBRARY OF CONGRESS

years in prison where he had time to reflect on Jesus's words, "Love your enemies, bless those who curse you, do good to those who hate you, and pray for those who spitefully use you and persecute you" (Matthew 5:44). As president, he decided to apply this teaching to his life and policies. Once again, as it has since the times of the Roman Empire, the Christian message provided the clearest direction on how to live with other people created in God's image.

The road to reconciliation is often difficult, but those South African churches that repented and returned to preaching Christ's good news to people of all races and colors, opening their doors to all, are finding that the same message still works wonders in people's hearts.

The Stellenbosch University Choir, South Africa, at a 2018 event

STELLENBOSCH UNIVERSITY CHOIR, LLANGOLLEN EISTEDDFOD

More Men and Women of the Modern Church

OTHER CHRISTIANS OF THE TWENTIETH-CENTURY CHURCH IN AFRICA

HARRY KAMBWIRI MATECHETA (1870–1962) served as a missionary in Ngoniland, a region of Malawi where foreigners were never able to survive because of bad weather and a great number of mosquitoes carrying malaria, a disease that can be deadly. The Ngoni were suspicious of Europeans and thought that Matecheta worked for them. Some even attacked the mission, stealing many supplies. In spite of this, Matecheta brought the gospel to thousands of people. By 1950 his church had over three thousand members—Christians who had been taught the Bible and catechism and were committed to submitting their lives to Christ and His church. Matecheta and his wife also provided medical help where needed and promoted the opening of schools at a time when most parents needed their children to work in the fields. These efforts were not always welcome—once a child threw a spear at Matecheta—but he never gave up.

DAMARI VIGOWA SAGATWA (1875–1960) was one of many women who were trained to take the gospel to local villages. She was also the first African to teach at the Church Missionary Society school in her hometown of Mamboya, Tanzania. She and her husband, **NUHU SAGATWA** (d. 1927), served as missionaries to different Tanzanian tribes. As well as proclaiming the gospel, she taught adults and children reading and writing. She continued to serve her missionary organization after the death of her husband, venturing into remote Tanzanian regions.

The Ethiopian **SOLAN GIDADA** (1899–1977) became blind when he was five years old as a result of smallpox, a contagious and often deadly illness. For much of his early life, he was a beggar in the streets. In 1920 he heard the gospel and became a Christian. From then on, his life changed. He learned **Braille** so he could read the Bible and devoted his life to telling people about Jesus. During World War I, he was arrested and imprisoned by the Italians who had come to occupy Ethiopia. They thought he was a spy for the British. Later, he was imprisoned again by the leaders of the Ethiopian Orthodox Church (the official state church), who didn't want people to leave their churches. In spite of this, he continued his mission. Through his efforts, six new churches were planted in Ethiopia.

AKILA TODI (1905–1992) was the first bishop of the Lutheran Church of Christ in Nigeria. Under his leadership, the church grew so much that there were congregations in almost every city. The church was also able to send missionaries to the Koma people, an isolated group living in a remote mountain region. Forty congregations were planted through this missionary work. This growth required new pastors, so Akila Todi established six Bible schools, one Bible college, and a seminary. The seminary was named after the Danish Niels Bronnum (1882–1966), the first Lutheran missionary to Nigeria.

MANCHE MASEMOLA (1913–1928), a young girl from the Pedi people of the southeastern region of Africa, refused to give up her Christian faith in spite of her parents' opposition. Not understanding why she had to obey God first, her parents beat her, forced her to drink a potion that was supposed to change her mind, and hid her clothes to prevent her from going to church. Once she told the local Anglican priest, "I shall be baptized with my own blood." This prediction came true because she died just before her baptism. Her mother continued to hate Christianity for a long time. Forty years later, however, she became a Christian and was baptized and changed her name to Magdalene.

A statue of Manche Masemola, one of the ten statues of modern martyrs above the main entrance of Westminster Abbey, London. Work by Tim Crawley, 1998

COPYRIGHT DEAN AND CHAPTER OF WESTMINSTER

LAMIN SANNEH (1942–2019) was an important African author. Born to a Muslim family in Gambia, West Africa, he read the Bible when he was a teenager. As he did, he discovered that God doesn't just ask to be honored, as Islam teaches, but desires to be loved because He loved us first in Christ. His writings have helped Christians understand how to relate to Muslims and how to appreciate the history, teachings, and example of Christians in parts of the world where they are now more numerous (Africa, Asia, and Latin America). He also corrected the critics who taught that Christian missionaries didn't respect people's cultures. While that was true in some cases, Sanneh pointed out that it was these missionaries who studied the local languages, recorded them, created grammar books, and taught people to value them.

Lamin Sanneh
COURTESY OF YALE DIVINITY SCHOOL

The Nigerian **TOKUNBOH ADEYEMO** (1944–2010) was one of the most important African teachers and scholars of the twentieth century. Believing that Africa had too many unprepared, corrupt, and selfish pastors and church leaders, he devoted his life to provide them with better training. "We need leaders who do not focus on greed, but see themselves as servants of the people," he said. He also challenged Christians to be better examples to others, like the salt and light Jesus told them to be (Matthew 5:13–16), and to have more faith in Christ's power for today instead of looking for immediate help in idols or ancestors.

Tokunboh Adeyemo
COURTESY OF BUSWELL LIBRARY ARCHIVES & SPECIAL COLLECTIONS

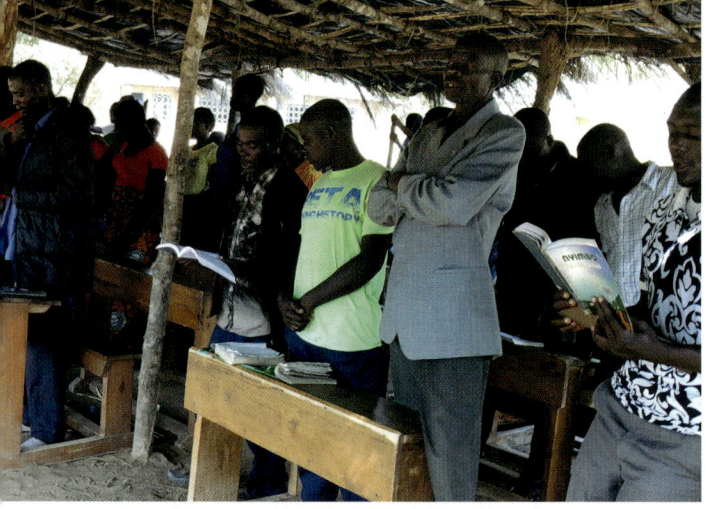

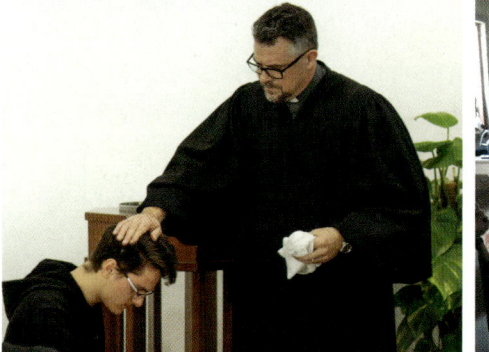
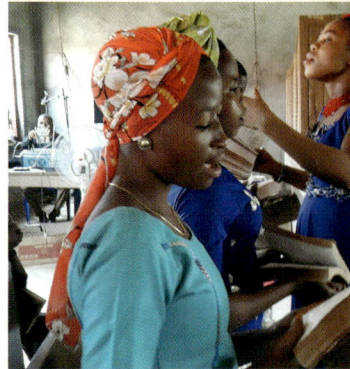

More Than Conquerors

When Jesus told His disciples that He would build His church and that the gates of hell would not prevail against it (Matthew 16:18) and when He sent them to make disciples of all nations (Matthew 28:19), they might not have imagined how large and long-lasting that church was going to be. They didn't even know that most of the nations of this world existed! But they obeyed, and Jesus has kept His word. He has built His church in spite of persecution, misunderstanding of His words, and the weakness of His people, and He has been with them always (Matthew 28:20). Two thousand years after Jesus's death, many people are still "added to the church daily" (Acts 2:47), and the good news of His life, death, and resurrection for the salvation of sinners is still being proclaimed.

In these two thousand years, the church has learned many lessons, sometimes the hard way. It has learned that Christ's kingdom is not of this world; that Christians will always be "strangers and pilgrims on the earth," looking for "a better, that is, a heavenly country" (Hebrews 11:13, 16); and that the gospel "is the power of God to salvation" (Romans 1:16), with no need of adding anything to it.

It has learned that "the word of God is living and powerful" (Hebrews 4:12) and will always accomplish what God wants,

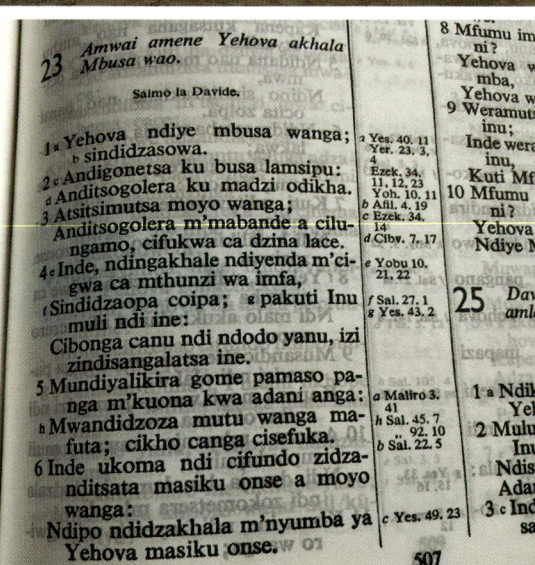
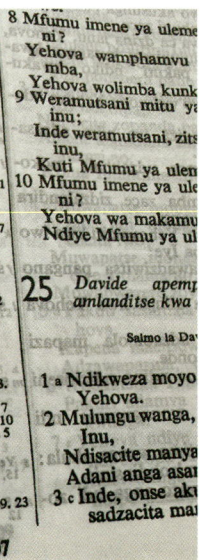

just like the rain causes grass and plants to grow, and no one is able to stop it (Isaiah 55:10–11).

Christians have also learned that in this world the church will always be persecuted and afflicted (John 15:18–21), but they can still "be of good cheer" because, Jesus said, "I have overcome the world" (John 16:33). In "tribulation, or distress, or persecution, or famine, or nakedness, or peril, or sword…we are more than conquerors through Him who loved us" (Romans 8:35–37). Christ is still building His church, and no enemy, earthly or spiritual, will ever prevail against it.

This book is not and could not be a full list of all the events that happened in the church during these two thousand years. I can only echo the author of the book of Hebrews, who wrote, "What more shall I say? For the time would fail me to tell" of many others (Hebrews 11:32) who have been kept by Christ as His precious possession through persecutions and troubles and in spite of their own missteps, falls, and fears. In fact, "out of weakness [they] were made strong" (Hebrews 11:34).

And I certainly could not include all those whose names never made the history books—Christians like you, your friends, your loved ones, and your pastor, who are no less important and no less loved.

  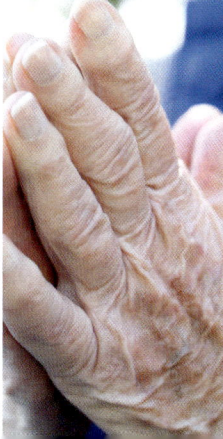

Glossary

abbess — A woman leading a convent of nuns.

abbey — A monastery or convent led by an abbot or abbess.

abbot — A man leading a monastery of monks or friars.

addiction — A strong, harmful need to have something.

altar — A raised place where a sacrifice is offered to God.

Anglican — From the Latin *anglicanus*, meaning "English." The Anglican Church consists of all the Protestant churches led by the archbishop of Canterbury.

annul — Cancel or make of no value.

apologist — From the Greek *apologia*, meaning "a defense." An apologist is a person who speaks in defense of a belief, cause, or religion.

apostle — From the Greek *apostolein*, meaning "to send." In the Bible, the word refers to one of the twelve people personally commissioned by Christ to spread the gospel in the world (the twelve disciples minus Judas, plus Paul). Today it is often used to indicate in a general sense someone who promotes an important message.

archbishop — Overseer of the bishops in one area.

arena — A building for sports or other entertainment with a large area surrounded by seats.

Arminian — Literally, a follower of the seventeenth-century teacher Jacob Arminius; in a broader sense, a person who emphasizes human choice in salvation.

atheism — The belief that there is no God.

Baptist — Christians who believe that baptism should be applied only when a person is old enough to believe in Christ.

basilica — For ancient Romans, a building for official meetings, court cases, and military drills. The church adopted the architecture of the basilica for its early buildings.

bishop — Initially, the word (*episkopos* in Greek) simply described an overseer of a church. Later, when cities began to have more than one church, it described an overseer over all the churches in one area.

brethren — A plural form of brother, sometimes used to indicate the members of a religious society or denomination.

Braille — A system of writing for the blind that uses characters made up of raised dots. It derives its name from its inventor, Louis Braille.

Buddhism	A religion that started in India between the sixth and fourth centuries BC. It can be more properly considered a philosophy because it doesn't include a belief in a god, only rules to live well based on the teachings of Siddhārtha Gautama (the Buddha).
Byzantine	Related to the Eastern Roman Empire.
caliph	Chief ruler in the Islamic government. He supervised both government and religion.
cannibal	A person who eats human flesh.
canon	From a Greek word meaning a "rule" or "standard." Something accepted as a rule or by rule, such as the list of books accepted as parts of the Bible.
cardinal	The highest authority in the Roman Catholic Church after the pope. The word comes from the Latin *cardinalis*, meaning "hinge" (hinges are an essential part of a door that make it turn). Since cardinals wore red, the name was later used for a red bird (crested finch).
catacomb	Underground cemetery used by Christians, who didn't cremate the bodies of their dead.
catechism	A summary of biblical teachings, usually in the form of questions and answers.
catholic	From a Greek word meaning "universal."
chant	A text that is spoken or sung to one tone with a set rhythm.
chaplain	A minister in charge of a chapel.
church order	A book of rules for a church.
civil war	A war between people of the same country.
clergy	Religious officials, such as priests, bishops, and ministers, who are authorized to lead religious services.
colporteur	A man or woman sent to distribute Bibles or other Christian literature.
commentary	A set of explanatory notes and comments on a text.
Communism	A system in which goods are held in common and private property is discouraged.
concentration camp	A place where large numbers of people, such as political prisoners or members of minorities, are forced to live in terrible conditions.
confession of faith	A document that summarizes and explains the beliefs of a religious group.
Confucianism	A religion that started in ancient China. It can be more properly considered a philosophy because it doesn't include a belief in a god, only rules to live well based on the teachings of the Chinese philosopher Confucius (551–479 BC).
congregation	The people attending a church.
Congregational	A church in which the congregation makes decisions by voting.
conscience	A sense of what is right and wrong.

convent	A place where nuns live together.
conversion	The act of changing, often used for a change from one religion to another.
council	A formal meeting, usually of people in authority.
covenant	A sacred agreement.
cowl	A hood or hooded cloak.
creed	A confession of faith, from the Latin *credo*, "I believe." The most famous Christian creeds are the Apostles' Creed and the Nicene Creed.
crusade	From the Latin *crux*, meaning "cross." A war that is considered holy.
crusader	A person fighting in a crusade.
cult	In Christianity, a religious group or teaching that is not in line with the main teachings of the Bible.
czar	Title for the emperor of Russia.
deacon	An officer of the church who usually cares for the material needs of the congregation.
deist	Someone who believes that God is indifferent to the world He created, leaving it to be governed by the laws He established
deity	The quality or state of being God.
denomination	A religious organization whose members share the same beliefs and practices. Some Protestant denominations are Anglican, Baptist, Lutheran, Presbyterian, and Reformed.
depose	To forcefully remove from office.
dictator	A ruler that imposes his or her will on others.
diet	Official meeting of the emperor and his princes.
disruption	The act of disrupting or interrupting the way things normally function.
divine	An adjective referring to God (as in "Jesus is divine") or to something related to God (as in "divine nature").
divinity	The quality or state of being divine. In earlier centuries, this word was also used to mean the formal study of religion, like in the book title *Marrow of Modern Divinity*.
doctrine	From the Latin *doctrina*, meaning "teaching."
ecumenical	Of a council, a meeting including representatives of the whole church, both in the East and the West.
ejection	The act of forcing or pushing out.
elder	An officer in the church, usually overseeing the preaching and the spiritual well-being of the congregation, making sure the church's teachings are according to the Bible.

elector	One of seven German princes, including three archbishops, who were eligible to vote to elect the Holy Roman Emperor (a title first used in the Middle Ages to indicate the ruler of the German regions).
elenctic	Meant to show that something is false.
Enlightenment	A movement that stressed the human power of learning and understanding the world through reason and experimentation.
Episcopalian	A type of church led by bishops, used especially of the Anglican Church.
equality	The condition of being considered on the same level as other people.
Eucharist	An ancient and more technical word used for the sacrament of the Lord's Supper coming from the Greek *eucharistô*, meaning "thanksgiving."
evangelization	The act of evangelizing, or bringing the gospel to others (from the Greek *euangelos*, meaning "good news.")
excommunicate	A form of church discipline, in which a person is cut off from church membership until he or she repents.
flog	To beat with a rod or whip.
friar	A male member of a Roman Catholic religious order, not restricted to a monastery.
fundamentalist	A follower of a movement in twentieth-century Protestantism (fundamentalism) emphasizing a literal interpretation of the Bible as fundamental (or essential) to the Christian faith.
galley	An ancient type of ship common in the Mediterranean sea moved by oars and sails.
genocide	From the Greek *genos* (race, kin) and the Latin *caedo* (kill). A purposeful extermination of a people or race.
Gnostic	A person who believes that true Christians must possess a special, secret knowledge.
gospel	The good news of the birth, death, and resurrection of Jesus to atone for the sins of believers.
habit	The clothes for a monk, priest, or nun that are typical of their order.
heresy	From a Greek word meaning "sect." The church used it to indicate a teaching that claims to be biblical but is not. Someone who promotes a heresy is called a *heretic*.
Hinduism	The main religion of India, which includes the worship of many gods, with a main spiritual power called Brahman and the belief that after death people return to life in different forms.
Holocaust	The massacre of Jews and other minorities by the Nazis during World War II.
Huguenots	French Protestants.
idol	An image of a person or thing that people worship.

idolatry	The practice of worshiping idols.
incarnate	Born in a human body and possessing a human soul and spirit.
indulgences	Formal promises by the Roman Catholic Church granting a shorter time in purgatory for those who meet certain requirements (for example, going on a pilgrimage, participating in a crusade, or buying a written document of indulgence). This reduction of time in purgatory could also be applied to other—for example, to relatives who had already died.
inquisition	A special court established by the Roman Catholic Church to examine people who seemed to have heretical ideas. It was also used to test the conversions to Christianity of some Muslims and Jews.
Islam	The religion of Muslims based on the teachings of Muhammad; also, the civilization built on the Muslim faith.
Islamic	Related to Islam.
Jehovah's Witnesses	A religious cult founded in the 1870s. Followers don't believe in the Trinity or in the divinity of Christ.
Jesuits	A religious order founded by Ignatius Loyola with the goal of spreading Christianity all over the world.
justification	From a Latin word that means "being made just," or "righteous." But the Greek word behind the Latin and English translations means "being declared righteous." This has been a major issue since the Reformation.
liberalism	In Christianity, the idea that Christians can modify biblical teachings in order to adapt to social and cultural changes.
martial art	A form of fight and self-defense, such as karate and judo.
martyr	A person who is put to death for his or her beliefs—in the case of Christians, for their faith in Christ.
Mass	Roman Catholic ceremony in which bread and wine are offered in a renewed sacrifice, with the understanding that they become the body and blood of Christ.
mediator	Someone who comes between two people to help them make peace or to ask one of them a favor on behalf of the other.
medieval	Related to the Middle Ages
Methodist	In today's language, a member of the denomination shaped by the teachings of John and Charles Wesley and some of their friends. Promoters of the Welsh Revival were also called Methodists but didn't share the Wesleys' Arminian views. For this reason, these Welsh believers are sometimes known as Calvinistic Methodists.
miniature	A very small portrait or painting.
modernism	A word Roman Catholics use to refer to what Protestants call liberalism.
monastery	A place for people, such as monks, who take a religious vow.
monasticism	The way of life followed by monks, nuns, or friars.

monk	A male member of a Roman Catholic religious order, usually restricted to a monastery.
Moravian	The Moravian church was started in Bohemia by a group of followers of Jan Hus. In the eighteenth century, it became an important part of Lutheran Pietism.
Mormon	A member of a religious group called the Church of Jesus Christ of the Latter-Day Saints. In spite of its name, it's not a Christian group because its members don't believe that Jesus and God are one and because it's based on what they believe is a new revelation.
mosque	Muslim place of worship.
Muslim	A follower of Islam.
mystic	A person who believes he or she can know God directly through experiences or intuitions.
nationalism	Exalting one nation over the others.
natural selection	In Darwin's teachings, the idea that random mutations in living beings lead to the survival of the strongest.
nun	A female member of a Roman Catholic religious order.
opium	An addictive drug made from poppies that can cause a soothing feeling.
ordain	To officially appoint a minister of God's word.
order	A community under a religious rule
ordination	The ceremony in which a minister was set apart for his work. In the Roman Catholic Church, ordination became a sacrament called holy orders. Roman Catholics believe that ordination gives priests a special mark on their souls so they can perform the Mass (changing bread and wine into the body and blood of Christ). Protestants ordain their ministers by laying hands on them, but they don't believe it's a sacrament.
orthodox	From a Greek word meaning both "right belief" and "right worship." When it's capitalized, it refers to the Eastern church, which officially divided from the Church of Rome in 1040.
pagan	From the Latin *paganus*, meaning "country-dweller." Christians used it to describe the worshipers of many gods.
parish	An area assigned to a priest or pastor.
Parliament	In some governments, a group of people that has the power to make laws or council the king.
patriarchate	In the Orthodox Church, a region overseen by a patriarch.
patriarch	In the Orthodox Church, an overseer of the churches in a particular region.
penance	Showing repentance for sin through confession and actions. For Roman Catholics, it is a sacrament that is also called confession, in which a person confesses sins to a priest and receives forgiveness by performing some prescribed actions or prayers.

persecute	To afflict or mistreat in a persistent manner, especially for religious reasons.
philosopher	A student of philosophy. See *philosophy* below.
philosophy	The study of ideas related to the meaning of life.
Pietism	A seventeenth- and eighteenth-century movement that encouraged Christians to show greater piety, usually through intense meditation and prayer in small groups, with an emphasis on practical rules and personal experiences.
piety	Devotion to God.
pilgrim	A person who goes on a journey, usually for religious reasons, with a specific goal.
pope	Initially, the word was used for any major bishop. Today, it is used for the head of the Roman Catholic Church.
prelate	Someone who holds superior rank in a church, such as an abbot or bishop.
Presbyterian	A type of church led by elders.
procession	A group of people moving in an orderly way, usually for a ceremony.
Protestant	Used to indicate the churches that broke with the Roman Catholic Church starting with the sixteenth-century Reformation.
pulpit	A raised platform used for preaching.
purgatory	According to Roman Catholic doctrine, a place where baptized sinners could be purified through fire until they could merit going to heaven.
Puritan	A name first given to Christians who wanted fewer formalities and better preaching in the Church of England under the reign of Elizabeth I. It was later used for Christians who wanted purity of worship and sincere devotion to God.
Quakers	A group of people who believed that God guides His people through an inner light.
reformation	A change for the better.
Reformed	Initially, a generic term to include all Protestants. Later, it was used specifically for a part of the Protestant Reformation that started in Switzerland and became prominent in the Netherlands, parts of Germany, and Hungary.
reformers	Men and women who promote a reformation.
relic	An object that is considered holy because of its connection with Christ or a saint.
Remonstrant	Member of a group of people who presented an official remonstrance, or protest, against the teachings of the Dutch church.
restoration	Bringing back to a condition that existed before.
revival	A return to attention or interest in culture or religion.
sack	An attack, usually on a city, taking it over by force.

sacrament	A religious act. Roman Catholics believe there are seven sacraments: baptism, Eucharist (Lord's Supper), penance, confirmation, matrimony (marriage), holy orders, and extreme unction (anointing the dying). They believe that Christians can use the sacraments to obtain more grace from God. Protestants keep only the two sacraments that were instituted by Christ (baptism and the Lord's Supper). They believe these sacraments are means of grace because they communicate the benefits of the same favor God has already given to believers.
scholar	A highly educated person or a specialist in a branch of study.
secession	The act of separating from a nation, church, or organization.
secular	Not religious.
seminary	A school for training ministers, such as priests or pastors.
successor	A person who holds a job or title after another.
sultan	The ruler of a Muslim state.
synod	A meeting of church leaders.
theologian	Someone who studies the nature and being of God.
theology	The study of the nature and being of God.
tiara	A type of crown.
tract	A paper printed for distribution.
transubstantiation	Roman Catholic doctrine teaching that during the Mass, the reality of bread and wine is changed into the reality of Christ's body and blood, even though the bread and wine look and taste the same.
Trinity	The unity of Father, Son, and Holy Spirit as one God in three persons.
tuberculosis	An infectious disease, mostly of the lungs. Before modern medicine, it was difficult to fight and could lead to death.
vestments	Special clothes worn by the clergy during a church service.
vow	A solemn promise.
Waldensians	A religious group begun by Peter Waldo that was eventually excommunicated by the Roman Catholic Church for preaching without a license. It eventually joined the Protestant Reformation and continued to be persecuted in Roman Catholic Italy.
witness	A person who gives evidence of a fact.

Index

A
abbess, 7, 249
abbeys, 35, 48, 249
abbot, 34, 249
Act of Secession, 152
addiction, 232, 249
Adeyemo, Tokunboh, 245
ad fontes, 73
Africa, 191–97, 235, 238, 240–45
Aksum, 28, 29
Al-Azhar University (Cairo), 67
Albigensians, 63
Alcuin of York, 47
Alexander, Archibald, 169
Alexander I, Czar, 161
Alexander II, Czar, 161
Alexander V, Pope, 72
Alexander VI, Pope, 69, 70
Alexandria, Egypt, 9
Alexius I Comnenus, Emperor, 56
Alexius IV, Byzantine prince, 57
Alexius V, Byzantine prince, 57
Alfred the Great, 50
Allen, Horace, 192–93
Alliance of Confessing Evangelicals, 221
al-Mahdi, Caliph, 43
Al-Malik al-Kāmil, Sultan, 55, 57
al-Mutawakkil, Caliph, 43
Alopen, 37, 38
altars, 66, 249
Ambrose of Milan, 25, 31
American Board of Commissioners for Foreign Missions, 162, 165, 166
American Civil Liberties Union, 219
American Revolutionary War, 137, 139
Ames, William, 103
Amin, Idi, 235, 238
Amphithéâtre des Trois-Gaules (Lyon), 4
Anabaptists, 98–99
Anderson, Rufus, 181
Anglican Church Missionary Society, 192, 193
Anglicans, 96, 105, 192, 249
Angulus Temple, 214
anno Domini (AD), 34
annul, 86, 249
Anselm of Canterbury, 60–61, 67
Anskar, 51
Anthony of Padua, 62
Antim of Iberia, 135
Antony, 20
apartheid, 235, 243–44
apologists, 9–10, 249
apostle, 1, 249
Arabia, 36, 38
archbishops, 12, 249
arena, 8, 249
Aristotle, 21
Arius, 16–17, 31
ark of the covenant, 194
Armenia, 3, 7, 236
Arminians, 103, 128, 249
Arnaud, Henri, 110
Arndt, Johann, 115
Asbury, Francis, 164
Asia, 36–39, 182–85, 227–33
    missions to, 186–87
Assumption of Mary, 206
Athanasius, 13, 15, 17, 24, 28
atheism, 169, 249
Auchterarder, Scotland, 130
Augsburg Confession, 97
Augustine of Canterbury, 34
Augustine of Hippo, 15, 25, 26–27, 65, 79, 82, 114
Australia, 131, 188
Avignon, France, 71
Azusa Street Mission, 173

B
Babylonian Captivity (papacy), 71
Bach, Johann Sebastian, 115
Balokole Revival, 242
baptism, 75
Baptist Confession of 1689, 104
Baptist Missionary Society, 180
Baptists, 99, 249
Barmen Confession, 199, 202
Barth, Karl, 204
Bartholomew (apostle), 7
Bartolomé de Las Casas, 70
Basil II, Byzantine emperor, 53
basilica, 20
Basil of Caesarea, 18, 21, 24
Battle of Tours, 43
Bavinck, Herman, 153, 154
Beaton, David, 89
Bede, 34, 50
Beecher, Lyman, 165
Behari Lal Singh, 186
Belgic Confession, 97
Bellarmine, Robert, 114
Benedict XI, Pope, 71
Benedict XIV, Pope, 123, 147
Benedict XVI, Pope, 224
Benedict of Nursia, 49
Benedict of Poland, 70
Berlin Wall, 199, 201
Bernard of Clairvaux, 61, 65
Besson, Pablo, 176, 177
Bethlen, Kata, 135
Beza, Theodore, 84
Bible Societies, 147
Bible translations, 27, 53, 93, 194
bishops, 7, 12, 30
Black Friars, 63
Blair, William N., 183
Blandina, 8
Bod, Peter, 135
Boers, 195
Bogerman, Johannes, 103
Bogomils, 63
Bogoyavlensky, Vasily Nikiforovich, 201
Bogue, David, 180
Boice, James Montgomery, 221
Boko Haram, 238
Bokwe, John Knox, 197
Boleyn, Anne, 86
Bonar, Horatius, 157
Bonhoeffer, Dietrich, 204
Boniface, 51
Boniface VIII, Pope, 71
Book of Common Prayer, 86, 88
Book of Mormon, 162, 168
Boston, Thomas, 130
Bosworth, Fred Francis, 215
Boxer Rebellion, 179, 184
Bradford, William, 121

INDEX • 257

Bradstreet, Anne, 121
Bradwardine, Thomas, 79
Braille, 244, 249
Brainerd, David, 137, 139
Breckinridge, Margaret Elizabeth, 171, 172
brethren, 77, 249
Brethren of the Common Life, 77
Bridges, Thomas, 176
British and Foreign Bible Society, 143, 147
British Missionary Society, 179
Brother Andrew, 201
Brown, Catharine, 166
Bruno of Cologne, 62
Bryan, William Jennings, 219
Bucer, Martin, 83
Buck, Pearl S., 218
Buddhism, 38, 182, 250
Bugenhaven, John, 91
Bulla, Peter, 188
Bullinger, Heinrich, 84, 97
Bunyan, John, 107, 109
"burnt-over district," 167
Byzantine, 250
Byzantine church, 20
Byzantine Empire, end of, 57
Byzantine icons, 46

C

caliph, 43, 250
Calvary Chapel, 220
Calvin, John, 81, 84, 96, 97, 98, 114, 243
Camisards, 124
Candidius, George, 115
Cane Ridge (camp meeting), 162, 165
Cảnh Thịnh, Emperor, 185
cannibals, cannibalism, 4, 250
canon, 102, 250
Canons of Dort, 102–3
Cappadocian Fathers, 18, 24
cardinal, 250
Carey, William, 179, 180, 181
Carmichael, Amy, 187
Carolingian Empire, 41
Carolingian Renaissance, 47
Cartwright, Robert, 189
Casalis, Eugenè, 195
Cassidy, Michael, 243
catacombs, 11, 250
catechism, 97, 250
Cathars, 63
cathedral, 11

Catherine II, Empress (Catherine the Great), 123, 134
Catherine of Aragon, 86
Catherine of Siena, 71, 76
catholic, 33, 250
Cavell, Edith, 205
Chalmers, Thomas, 155
chant, 250
chaplain, 107, 250
Charlemagne, 45, 46–47
Charles, Thomas, 126
Charles I, King, 100, 101, 104
Charles II, King, 101, 106, 108
Charles V, Emperor, 81, 82, 83, 97
Charles Emmanuel II, Duke of Savoy, 110
Charles Martel, 41, 43
Cherokees, 166
Chiang Kai-shek, 232
China, 38–39, 70, 230–31
  missions to, 182, 187
Chinese Inland Mission, 187
Chŏn Sam-dŏk, 185
Christianity, spread of, 6–7
Christianity Today (magazine), 217
Christian Reformed Church (Netherlands), 143, 152
Christian Science, 168
Christine de Pizan, 79
Christmas, 202
Chrysostom, John, 19
Church, John Edward (Joe), 242
Church of England, 86, 86, 88, 104, 105, 106, 126–27, 196
Church of Jesus Christ of the Latter-Day Saints, 168
Church of the Desert, 112
Church of the East, 36–37, 38
Church Mission Society (CMS), 180, 181
church order, 152, 250
circuit riders, 164
civil war, 89, 250
Clapham Sect, 140, 141
Clare of Assisi, 62
Claudius, bishop of Turin, 45
Clement III, Pope, 58
Clement V, Pope, 69, 71
Clement VII, Pope, 72
Clement XIV, Pope, 123, 134
Clement of Alexandria, 9
clergy, 88, 250
Clorinda, Rasa, 131
Clotilde, 34
Clovis, King of the Franks, 33, 34

Coillard, François, 195
Cold War, 212, 220
colporteur, 147, 250
Columba, 34
Columbanus, 35
Columbia, 223
Columbus, Christopher, 69, 70
commentary, 107, 250
Communism, 145, 201, 230, 250
Comonfort, Ignacio, 177
Conceição, José Manouel da, 176
concentration camps, 204, 250
Concordia Seminary, St. Louis, 160
Confessing Church, 202, 203, 204
confession of faith, 89, 250
confessions, 97
Confucianism, 182, 250
Congo, 193
congregation, 11, 250
Congregationalists, 99, 105, 250
conquest, 70
conscience, 77, 250
Constantine I, Emperor, 14, 15, 19, 38, 46
Constantine VII, Emperor, 53
Constantinople, 22, 46, 55, 57, 69, 134
convent, 7, 48, 251
conversion, 19, 138, 251
Coptic, 192
Coquarangon, 39
Cotton, John, 121
council, 251
Council of Carthage (397), 13
Council of Carthage (418), 15, 26
Council of Chalcedon (451), 15, 23
Council of Constance (1414–1418), 69, 72, 75, 79
Council of Constantinople (381), 15, 22
Council of Florence (1438–1445), 69, 75
Council of Nicaea (325), 15, 16–17
Council of Orange (529), 33
Council of Pisa (1409), 69, 72
Council of Rome (382), 15
Council of Trent (1545–1563), 81, 94, 145, 208
councils, relation to popes, 72
Court, Antoine, 124
Covenant, 108
Covenanters, 108
cowl, 62, 251
Craig, William, 130
Cranmer, Thomas, 81, 86–87
creeds, 2, 158, 251

Cristero War, 223, 224
Crosby-Schøyen Codex, 13
Crowther, Samuel Ajayi, 191, 192
crucifixion, 5
crusader, 251
crusades, 55, 56–57, 61, 64, 251
cults, 168, 251
Cultural Revolution, 227, 230
culture, and gospel, 240
Cyprian, 8, 13
Cyril, Byzantine missionary, 41, 43, 52, 53
Cyrillic, 52
czar, 134, 251

D

Damasus, Bishop, 30
Darby, John Nelson, 158, 217
Dark Ages, 41
Darrow, Clarence Seward, 219
Darwin, Charles, 143, 148, 203
Darwinism, 169
D'Aubigné, Jean Henri Merle, 157
deacon, 211, 51
Dead Sea Scrolls, 239
Decius, Emperor, 3, 5, 8
Declaration of Guilt, 209
Declaration of Independence (USA), 137, 139, 140
de Cock, Hendrik, 152–53
deists, 132
deity, 18, 251
de Klerk, Frederik Willem, 243
Denmark, 41, 51, 91
denominations, 126, 251
depose, 58, 251
Descartes, René, 116
Despard, George Pakenham, 176
Dévai, Matthias Biro, 90, 93
devotio moderna, 77
Dhuoda, 50
Dickens, Charles, 149
dictator, 149, 251
Didache, 11
Didodati, John, 103
diet, 251
Diet of Worms, 82
Diggers, 109
Dimbo, Lidia, 194
Din Limei, 184
Diocletian, Emperor, 3, 5, 7
Diognetus, 12
Dionysius Exiguus, 34
dispensations, 158
disruption, 155, 251
divine, 18, 251
divinity, 22
Dman, Diet, 205
Dober, Johann Leonhard, 125
Docetism, 22
doctrine, 11, 251
Doleantie, 143, 153
Dominicans, 63, 64
Dominic of Osma, 63
Down-Grade Controversy, 143
Drozdov, Filaret, Metropolitan, 161
Duff, Alexander, 181, 186
Durand, Marie, 124
Durand, Pierre, 124
Dutch Missionary Society, 195
Dutch Reformed Church in South Africa, 195
Dutton, Anne, 129
Dwight, Timothy, 165, 166

E

early Christians
    daily life of, 12
    reading the Bible, 13
Early Middle Ages, 40–53
East African Revival, 235, 242
Eastern Europe, Reformation in, 90
Eastern Orthodox Church, 33, 45, 63, 192, 206
East India Company, 181
Eckhart, Meister, 76
ecumenical, 16, 251
Eddy, Mary Baker, 168
Edict of Milan (313), 14
Edict of Nantes (1598), 81, 85, 112
Edward VI, King, 86–87, 88
Edwards, Jonathan, 137, 138, 165
Edwin, King of Northumbria, 35
Egeria, 25
Eighty Years War, 81, 101
Eisenhower, Dwight D., 212, 220
ejection, 106, 251
elder, 12, 251
Elector, 97, 252
elenctic, 114, 252
Eliot, John, 119, 121
Elizabeth I, Queen, 81, 88, 89
Elliot, Elisabeth, 223
Elliot, James, 225
Emmelia, 21
English Civil Wars, 104
English Puritans, 107
English Reformation, 86–88
English revival, 127–29
Enlightenment, 116, 200, 252
Enrico Dandolo, 56
Ephrem of Syria, 25
Episcopalianism, 105, 252
Episcopius, Simon, 103
equality, 144, 252
Equiano, Olaudah, 129
Erasmus, Desiderius, 69, 73
Erskine, Ebenezer, 130
Erskine, Ralph, 130
Ethelbert, King of province of Kent, 34, 35
Ethelburga, 35
Ethiopian Orthodox Church, 193, 194
Etienne de Bourbon, 64
Eucharist, 11, 252
Eudoxia, Emperor, 19
Eugene IV, Pope, 72
eugenics, 149, 203
Eusebius of Caesarea, 7
Evangelical Church in Germany, 209
evangelization, 7, 252
evolution, 148, 219
excommunication, 50, 252
explorations, 70
external and internal, 83

F

faith, and politics, 220
faith and works, 83
Falkland Islands, 176
Faraday, Michael, 148, 149
Fascism, 206, 209
Father Divine, 215
Fathme, Johannes, 194
feelings, 167
Felicitas of Carthage, 8
Ferdinand II, King, 70, 92
Ferrer, Vincent, 65
Finney, Charles Grandison, 162, 167, 214
First Dutch Secession, 151–52
First Secession (Scotland), 123, 130
First Vatican Council (1869–1870), 143, 145
flogging, 50, 252
Fontanini, Benedetto, 92
Formosus, Pope, 30
Formula of Concord, 97
Forty-Two Articles, 87
Fourth Lateran Council (1215), 55, 63, 64, 65, 66

Fox, George, 109
France
   Reformation in, 85
   revivals in, 124
Francis I, King, 84
Franciscans, 64
Francis of Assisi, 57, 62
Franco, Francisco, 207
Frederick I, Emperor, 56
Frederick II, Emperor, 55, 57
Frederick III, Elector, 97
Frederick IV, King, 131
Frederick William III, Prince, 143, 160
Frederick William IV, Prince, 160
Free Church (Scotland), 143, 155
Freetown, Sierra Leone, 191, 192
Free University of Amsterdam, 153
French Revolution, 132, 143, 144–45
friar, 57, 65, 252
Fritzsche, Gotthard Daniel, 160
Frumentius, 28
Fuller Theological Seminary, 217
fundamentalists, 216, 217, 252

G

Galen, Clemens von, 203
galley, 89, 252
Gallic Confession, 97
Galton, Francis, 149
Ganno, Aster, 194
Gansfort, Wessel, 77
Gardiner, Allen Francis, 176
Geddes, Jenny, 108
Geneva, 84
Genghis Khan, 70
genocide, 200, 236–37, 252
George, David, 140
Gerhard, Johann, 114
German revival, 125
Gidada, Solan, 244
Giertz, Bo, 205
Glorious Return, 101, 110
Glorious Revolution, 101, 106, 108
Gnostics, 10, 252
Gojong, Emperor, 183
Gomarius, Francis, 103
Goodwin, Thomas, 105
Gorbachev, Mikhail, 201
gospel, 172, 252
   and culture, 240
Gottschalk of Orbais, 48, 49, 50
grace, 26
Graham, Billy, 214
Graham, Isabella, 162, 171, 172

Graham, Ruth Bell, 214
Grant, Charles, 181
Gray, Lady Jane, 87
Great Awakening, 137–38, 165
Great Depression, 212, 215
Great Disappointment, 168
Great Ejection, 106
Great Purge (1936–1938), 200
Great Western Schism, 72
Greek Orthodox Church, 30, 41
Green, Ashbel, 169
Gregory I, Pope (Gregory the Great), 33, 34, 65, 94
Gregory VII, Pope, 55, 58
Gregory IX, Pope, 64
Gregory XI, Pope, 69, 71
Gregory of Nazianzus, 18, 24
Gregory of Nyssa, 18, 21, 24, 140
Gregory the Illuminator, 7
Griffiths, Ann, 126
Grimké, Francis James, 171, 172
Grindall, Edmund, 88
Groote, Geert, 77
Guinefort Martyr, 64
Gustav Vasa, King, 91
Gutenberg, Johannes, 69, 73
Gützlaff, Karl, 182
Güyük, Grand Khan, 70

H

habit, 62, 252
Hadrian II, Pope, 52
Haile Salassie I, Emperor, 235, 238
Hail Mary, 74
Haldane, Robert, 157
Hall, Rosetta Sherwood, 185
Hammon, Briton, 140
Hammon, Jupiter, 140
Han, Kyun-Chik, 229
Handel, George Frideric, 129
Hannington, James, 193
Harris, Howell, 123, 126
Hastings, Selina, 129
Hawaii, missions to, 166
Haynes, Lemuel, 140, 141
Haystack Prayer Meeting (Williamstown, Mass.), 165
Heidelberg Catechism, 97
Henry, Carl F. H., 217
Henry, Matthew, 107
Henry II, King of England, 59
Henry IV, King of Germany, 58
Henry IV, Emperor, 55

Henry VIII, King of England, 59, 81, 86, 93, 96
Henry of Navarre (King Henry IV of France), 85
Henry the Navigator, Prince, 70
heresy, 10, 252
Hernandez, Julián, 93
Herrnhut, 125
"higher life" movement, 159, 215
High Middle Ages, 40, 55–67
Hilda of Whitby, 50
Hildegard of Bingen, 76
Himmler, Heinrich, 202
Hinduism, 115, 252
Hitler, Adolf, 149, 199, 202–3, 204, 206
Hodge, A. A., 162, 169
Hodge, Charles, 169
Hog, James, 130
Hoksbergen, Dirk, 153
Holiness Movement, 173, 215
Holl, Karl, 157
Holocaust, 202–3, 205, 209, 252
Holy Land, 31
Holy Roman Empire, 58, 83
Honorable Restoration, 111
Hooker, Richard, 88
Hooper, John, 88
hospital, 21
House Church Movement (China), 231
Hripsime (nun), 7
Huguenots, 85, 112, 120, 124, 252
Hungary, 90
Hunt, Bruce F., 229
Hunter, John, 131
Hus, Jan, 69, 78, 82
Hutchinson, Lucy, 107
hymns, 129, 221

I

icons, 46
idolatry, 44–45, 253
idols, 12, 252
Ignatius Loyola, 94
Ignatius of Antioch, 8
incarnate, 22, 253
Independent Board for Presbyterian Foreign Missions, 212, 218
Index of Forbidden Books, 77
India, 7, 39, 131, 187
Indian Removal Act (1830), 166
indulgences, 77, 253
Innocent III, Pope, 55, 56
Innocent IV, Pope, 64, 69

Innocent X, Pope, 114
Innocent XI, Pope, 70
Innocent Veniaminov, metropolitan, 161
Inquisition, 64, 92, 253
International Congress on World Evangelization, 211
International Council on Biblical Inerrancy, 221
Ireland, 29
Irenaeus, 10, 13
Irene, Empress, 44
Isabella, Queen, 70, 92
ISIS, 238
Islam, 40, 42, 135, 141, 238, 253
 in Spain, 92
 spread to Africa, 192
Italy, 206
Ivan IV, Czar (Ivan the Terrible), 134
ixthus (Christian symbol), 12

J

Jamaica, 177
James VI, King of Scotland, 89
Jamestown, Virginia, 119
Jansen, Otto, 114
Japan, martyrs of, 111
Jehovah's Witnesses, 16, 168, 253
Jerome, 15, 27, 53, 73, 94
Jerusalem, fall to the Arabs, 41
Jerusalem council, 3
Jesuits, 81, 90, 94, 253
Jesus Christ
 crucifixion of, 3
 deity of, 16–17
 humanity of, 22
 images of, 44–45
 as Messiah, 6
Jesus People Movement, 220
Jews, persecution of, 202–3, 205
Jingwen, Liu, 231
John II, Pope, 30
John III, Pope, 52
John XII, Pope, 41
John XXIII, Pope, 76, 208
John of Damascus, 43
John of Montecorvino, 70
John of Pian del Carpine, 70
John of Wesel, 77
John Paul II, Pope, 199, 203, 223
Johnson, Richard, 131
Jones, Griffith, 126
Jones, Mary, 126
Judson, Adoniram, 186

Judson, Ann Hasseltine, 186
Judson, Emily Chubbuck, 186
Judson, Sarah Boardman, 186
Julian, Emperor, 15, 21
Julian of Norwich, 76
Junius, Robert, 115
justification, 157, 208, 253
Justin Martyr, 9

K

Ka'ba, 42
Kam, Joseph, 179, 186
Kant, Immanuel, 132, 167
Kassia, 50
Kato, Byang Henry, 240, 241
Kavel, Ludwig Christian, 160
Keble, John, 156
Kenya, 193
Kenyon, William (E. W.), 215
Kepler, Johannes, 148
Keswick Theology, 159
Khama III, King, 196
Khosrovidukht, 7
Ki-Choi, Chu, 229
Kim, Esther Ahn, 229
Kim, Joon Gon, 229
King James Version, 101
Kingsbury, Cyrus, 166
Kivengere, Festo, 238
Knox, John, 89
Korea, 182–83, 187, 228–29
Krapf, Johann Ludwig, 194
Kreyssig, Lothar, 203
Kryuchkov, Gennadi, 201
Kuyper, Abraham, 143, 153, 154

L

L'Abri, 210
Las Casa, Bartholomew de, 140
Laski, John, 90
late antiquity, 14–15
Lateran Treaty (1929), 199, 206
Latin, 74
Latin America, 223–25
Lausanne Convention, 199, 211
law and gospel, 83
Leaman, Charles, 232
Leeti, Esaia, 195
Lenin, Vladimir, 200
Leo I, Pope, 30
Leo III, Byzantine emperor, 44
Leo III, Pope, 41, 46
Leo V, Byzantine emperor, 44
Leo X, Pope, 81, 82

Leo XII, Pope, 147
Leoba, 51
Leopold II, King, 193
Letter to Diognetus, 12
Lewis, C. S., 209, 210
Li, Jeanette, 232
Liang Fa, 186
libellus, 5
liberalism, 167, 169, 216, 217, 253
liberation theology, 223, 224
Liberia, 192
Liddell, Eric, 233
Liele, George, 177
Ligonier Ministries, 221
Livingstone, David, 191, 196
Lloyd-Jones, Martyn, 209
Llull, Raymond, 57
Lohmeyer, Ernst, 204
Lollards, 78
London Missionary Society, 157, 180, 189, 196
Lord's Supper, 11, 66, 75, 78, 160
Louis XIII, King, 100
Louis XIV, King, 101, 114, 124
Louis XV, King, 124
Louise of Mecklenburg-Strelitz, 160
Luther, Martin, 81, 82–83, 98, 157, 160
 Catechisms of, 97
Lutheran Church-Missouri Synod, 160
Lutherans, Lutheranism, 91, 96, 98, 114, 157, 160, 208
Luwum, Janani, 235, 238
Luxeuil, France, 35
Lyon, France, 4, 5

M

Mabille, Adolphe, 195
Macaulay, Zachary, 140
Machen, J. Gresham, 212, 216–17, 218
MacIntyre, John, 182
Mackay, George Leslie, 187
MacKenzie, John, 197
Macrina, 21
Madagascar, 195
Madiai, Rosa, 146
Mandela, Nelson, 243
Mao Tse-tung, 227, 230, 231
Marcion, 10
Marguerite of Valois, 85
marriage, of priests, 66
Marrow Men, 123, 130
Marsden, Samuel, 188
Marshman, Joshua, 180

Marsilius of Padua, 69, 72
martial arts, 184, 253
Martin V, Pope, 72
Martin of Tours, 28
martyrs, 5, 8, 19, 253
    of Japan, 111
    of Vietnam, 185
Marx, Karl, 151, 200, 224
Mary (mother of Jesus), 31
Mary I, Queen, 81, 86, 87
Mary II of England, 101, 110
Mary of Guise, 89
Mary Stuart, 89
Masemola, Manche, 245
Mass, 66, 253
Massachusetts Bay Colony, 120
Mastricht, Petrus van, 116, 117
Matecheta, Harry Kambwiri, 244
Matilda of Canossa, Countess, 58, 60
Mayflower, 119
Mayflower Compact, 121
McCully, Ed, 223
McPherson, Aimee Semple, 214
Mecca, 42
mediator, 59, 95, 253
medieval, 48, 253
Mehmed II, sultan, 69
Meiji, Emperor, 111
Melanchthon, Philipp, 91, 97
Mendouça, Lourenço da Silva, 70
Mengistu Haile Mariam, 235, 238
Menelik I, King, 194
Methodists, 126, 127, 164, 253
Methodius, Byzantine missionary, 41, 52, 53
Mexican Revolt, 177
Mexican Revolution, 224
Michael III, Byzantine emperor, 43
Middle Ages, 40
Miller, Hugh, 148, 149
Miller, Lydia Falconer, 148, 149
Miller, Samuel, 169
Miller, William, 168
Milne, William, 186
Mincaye, 223
Mingdao, Wang, 230–31
miniature, 59, 253
Min Yong-ik, Prince, 183
Mirian III, King, 15, 29
missionary societies, 180
missions, missionaries
    to Asia, 70, 186–87
    to China, 182
    to eastern Europe, 52
    to the Hawaiians, 166
    to India, 131
    to Korea, 182–83
    in late antiquity, 28–29
    to Native Americans, 121, 139, 166
    to northern Europe, 51
    to Russia, 161
    to the Waorani, 225
modernism, 169, 253
Moffat, Robert, 196
Moffett, Samuel A., 233
monasteries, 20, 21, 48, 253
Mongols, 70
"Monkey Trial," 219
monks, 19, 20, 254
Moody, Dwight L., 165
Moon, Charlotte Digges "Lottie," 187
Moravian Church, 79, 125, 131, 254
More, Hannah, 140
Mormon, 254
Mormons, 16, 168, 254
Morrison, Robert, 179, 182
Morrison, William, 193
Mortara, Edgardo, 146
Moshoeshoe I, King, 195
mosque, 42, 254
Muggleton, Lodowicke, 109
Muggletonians, 109
Muhammad, 41, 42, 141
Münster, 81, 98
Muslims, 42–43, 254
    in Spain, 92
    took back Jerusalem, 55, 57
Mussolini, Benito, 199, 206
mystics, 76, 254
Myung-Sung, Empress, 183

N

Nadu, Tamil, 131
Nagasaki, 111
Nagenda, William, 242
Napoleon Bonaparte, 143, 144–45
National Association for the Advancement of Colored People (NAACP), 171
National Covenant, 108
nationalism, 202, 203, 254
Native Americans, 121
    missions to, 139, 166
natural selection, 148, 254
Nazism, 202–3, 209
Nee, Watchman, 233
Nero, Emperor, 3, 4
Nesib, Onesimos, 194
Netherlands, Reformation in, 85

Nettleton, Asahel, 167
Neumeister, Erdmann, 115
Nevin, John Williamson, 167
Nevius, Helen Coan, 181
Nevius, John Livingston, 181, 230
New Amsterdam, 119
Newman, John Henry, 156
new religious movements, 168
New South Wales, 123, 131
New Testament, 13, 15
Newton, John, 129
Nicene Creed, 22
Nicholas II, Czar, 200
Niemöller, Martin, 204
Nietzsche, Friedrich, 150, 200
Ninety-Five Theses (Luther), 82
Nino, 29
Nitschmann, David, 125
North Korea, 227, 228
nuns, 7, 254

O

Occom, Samson, 139
Odoacer, 15
Old Testament, 13, 15
Olevianus, Kaspar, 97
Olga, Queen of Russia, 53
opium of the people, 151, 254
Opukahaia, 162, 166
Orange Free State, 195
ordain, 28, 254
orders, religious, 62, 254
ordination of priests, 75, 254
Origen, 9
Oromo Bible, 194
orthodox, 33, 254
Orthodox Missionary Society, 161
Orthodox Presbyterian Church, 217
ostracon, 24, 27
Otto I, Emperor, 41
Ottoman Empire, 33, 90, 135, 235, 236–37
Our Father (prayer), 74
Owen, John, 107, 114, 117
Oxford Movement, 156–57

P

Pacific Islands, missions to, 188–89
Packer, James I., 211
pagan, 7, 254
Pal, Krishna, 180
Palmer, Phoebe, 159
Papal States, 145
parish, 127, 254

Parliament, 86, 254
Parr, Katherine, 87
patriarch, 30, 254
patriarchate, 46, 254
patriarchs, 33, 38
Patrick of Ireland, 29, 140
Patteson, John Coleridge, 189
Peace of Westphalia, 101
Paul
   conversion of, 3
   letters of, 13
Paul III, Pope, 70
Paulinus, Bishop, 35
Peale, Norman Vincent, 215
Pelagius, 26, 79, 114
penance, 35, 73, 254
penitentials, 35
Penn, William, 119, 120
Pentecostals, 173
   in Italy, 206
   in Latin America, 177
perfectionism, 128
Perkins, William, 88
Perpetua of Carthage, 8
persecution, 2–5, 7, 36, 255
   in Africa, 238
   in China, 230–31
   in Italy, 146
   of Jews, 202–3, 205
   in Korea, 228
   of Protestants, 85
Peter (apostle), 30
Peter I, Czar (Peter the Great), 123, 134, 161
Peter Abelard, 61
Peter Lombard, 67
Petri, Laurentius, 91
Petri, Olaus, 91
Philip II, King, 85, 87, 120
Philip II Augustus, King, 56
Philip IV, King, 71
Phillip, Arthur, 131
philosopher, philosophy, 9, 255
Pietists, 115, 125, 255
piety, 115, 255
pilgrims, 35, 255
Pilgrims (Massachusetts), 119, 120
Pillai, Satyanathan, 131, 181
Pineda, Juan Pérez de, 93
Pippin, 47
Pius VI, Pope, 144
Pius VII, Pope, 143, 144, 147
Pius IX, Pope, 143, 145, 147
Pius XI, Pope, 203, 206
Pius XII, Pope, 203, 206

Plancius, Peter, 115
Plütschae, Heinrich, 131
Plymouth, Massachusetts, 119, 120, 121
Poland, 90
Polycarp, 8
Pomare II, Chief, 189
pope, 27, 30, 33, 58, 94, 146, 255
positive thinking, 215
poverty, 155, 171
prayer books, 49, 74
preaching
   in language of the people, 74
   as a science, 167
prelate, 255
Presbyterians, 97, 105, 255
priest, marriage of, 66
Princeton Theological Seminary, 169, 217
printing press, 13, 69, 73
processions, 65, 255
Protestant churches, 45, 255
Protestant colleges, 114
Protestantism, on images, 45
Protestants, as "separated brethren," 208
Protten, Rebecca, 125
Prudentius of Spain, 25
Prussia, 160
psalms, 96, 129, 221
pulpit, 96, 255
Puritans, 88, 104, 107, 255

Q

quadriivium, 47
Quakers, 109, 120, 140, 255
Qur'an, 42, 43, 57

R

Rabaut, Paul, 124
Raberaba, Conrad, 188
racism, 203
Ranavalona, Queen, 195
Ranters, 109
Ratramnus of Corbie, 66
Rauschenbusch, Walter, 172
reason, 121
reason and revelation, 116
Reformation, 65, 78, 80–97, 255
   recovering of, 221, 224
   teachings of, 95
Reformed, 98, 160, 255
   on images, 45

Reformed Churches in the Netherlands, 143, 153
Reformed confessions, 97, 128
Reformers, 76, 255
Reign of Terror, 132, 143
relics, 64, 65, 255
religious experiences, 167
religious freedom, 120, 150, 218
Remonstrants, 103, 255
repentance, 35
Restoration, 111, 255
"Re-Thinking Missions," 218
Retief, Frank, 243
revivals, 47, 123–29, 255
Rhodes, Cecil John, 197
Richard I, King, 56
Ridley, William, 189
righteous and sinful, 83
Rockefeller, John D., Jr., 218
Rogerius, Abraham, 115
Roman Catholic Church, 33, 156, 208
   on images of Jesus and saints, 45
   in Latin America, 177
   on number of sacraments, 75
   and Protestant challenges, 176
   after Vatican II, 208
Roman Empire, 33
Romania, 90
Rosary, 74, 75
Ross, John, 182
Rousseau, Jean-Jacques, 132–33
Rowland, Daniel, 123, 126
Rufo, Paulus Ludwig, 194
Rumi, Abu, 194
Rush, Benjamin, 140
Russell, Charles Taze, 168
Russia
   Christianity in, 53
   missions to, 161
Russian church, 134
Russian Orthodox Church, 161
Russian Revolution, 199, 200, 209
Rutherford, Samuel, 105
Ryle, J. C., 156

S

sack of Rome, 15, 25, 255
sacraments, 11, 75, 256
Sagatwa, Damari Vigowa, 244
Sagatwa, Nuhu, 244
St. Augustine, Florida, 120
St. Bartholomew's Day Massacre, 85
Saint, Nate, 223
Saint, Rachel, 223

Saint, Steve, 223
Saladin, 55, 56, 57
Sanneh, Lamin, 245
Sastri, Vedanayagam, 131
Savonarola, Girolamo, 79
Scandinavia, 51
   Reformation in, 91
Schaeffer, Edith, 199, 210
Schaeffer, Francis, 199, 210, 211
Schleiermacher, Friedrich, 167
scholar, 14, 256
Schuller, Robert, 215
Schwartz, Christian Frederick, 131
Schweitzer, Albert, 150
Scofield, C. I., 158, 217
Scopes, John T., 219
Scots Confession, 97
Scottish Disruption, 155
Scottish Reformation, 89
Scottish Secession, 123, 130
secession, 130, 256
Second Commandment, 44, 46
Second Council of Lyon (1274), 69
Second Dutch Secession, 152
Second Great Awakening, 164–65
Second Helvetic Confession, 97
Second Lateran Council (1139), 55, 66
Second Vatican Council (1962–1965), 199, 208
secular, 48, 256
secular canons/canonesses, 48
Seekers, 109
seminary, 160, 256
Sendler, Irena Stanisława, 205
Seo Sang-ryun, 179, 182
Serfoji II, Prince, 131
Seventh Day Adventism, 168
Sharp, Granville, 140
Shedd, Mary Lewis, 237
Shedd, William Ambrose, 237
Sheppard, William Henry, 191, 193
Sietsma, Hein, 205
Sigismund, Emperor, 79
Sigismund of Hungary, 82
Silk Road, 36, 39
Simeon, Charles, 140
Simonton, Ashbel Green, 176
singing, 96, 129
slavery, 21, 70, 91, 140–41
   abolition of, 165, 195
      Christian support for, 197
Slessor, Mary, 197
Slovakia, 90
Smith, Chuck, 220
Smith, John, 168

Smith, Joseph, 162, 168
Society for the Propagation of the
   Gospel in Foreign Parts, 123
Society of Jesus. *See* Jesuits
Socinians, 99
Socinus, Faustus, 99
Socinus, Laelius, 99
Soga, Tiyo, 196
Sohn Yang-Won, 229
sola Deo gloria, 95
sola fide, 95
sola gratia, 95
sola Scriptura, 95, 173
solus Christus, 95
Solzhenitzyn, Aleksandr, 200–201, 209
Sontonga, Enoch Mankayi, 197
South Africa, 195, 197, 235, 243–44
South Korea, 227, 228
Soviet Union, 200–201, 220
Spain, Reformation in, 92
Spanish Civil War, 199, 207
Spanish Inquisition, 69, 92
Spinoza, Baruch, 116
Sproul, R. C., 220, 221
Spurgeon, Charles Haddon, 14, 157
Sri Lanka, 39
Stalin, Joseph, 200
Stephan, Martin, 160
Stephen I, Bishop, 30
Steward, Lyman, 216
Steward, Milton, 216
Stöckel, Leonhard, 90
Stott, John, 211
Stowe, Harriet Beecher, 165
Strauss, David Friedrich, 150, 151
Strehlow, Carl Friedrich Theodor, 189
successor, 19, 256
Suharto, Haji Mohammad, 232
sultan, 55, 56, 256
Sundaranandam, David, 181
Switzerland, Reformation in, 84
synod, 85, 256
Synod of Dort (1618–1619), 101, 103, 152–53

T

Taiwan, missions to, 187
Taizong, Emperor of China, 37, 38
Ta'unga, 188, 189
Taylor, Hudson, 187
Ten Boom, Corrie, 205
Tennent, Gilbert, 138
Tertullian, 10

Thaddeus (apostle), 7
Theodora, empress, 44
Theodosius I, Emperor, 15, 18
Theodulf of Orleans, 45, 51
theologian, 26, 256
theology, 67, 117, 256
Thirty-Nine Articles, 87, 156
Thirty Year's War, 100, 101, 148, 160
Thomas (apostle), 7
Thomas, John, 180
Thomas à Kempis, 77
Thomas Aquinas, 67
Thomas Becket, 59
Thomas of Kana, 39
Thomson, John, 138
Three-Self Patriotic Movement, 230
tiara, 71, 256
Tikhon of Zadonsk, Bishop, 161
Timkat, 194
Timothy I, Patriarch, 38, 39, 43
Ting, K. H., 230–31
Tiridates III, King, 3, 7
Tjalkabota, Moses, 189
Todi, Akila, 245
Tolessa, Tsehay, 238
Tolkien, J. R. R., 209
Toplady, Augustus, 128
Townsend, William Cameron (Cam), 212, 218
tracts, 121, 256
transubstantiation, 66, 78, 256
Transvaal, 195
Transylvania, 90, 135
Trinity, 18, 43, 256
trivium, 47
Trocmé, André, 205
Trocmé, Magda, 205
Trubar, Primož, 93
Tsai, Christiana, 232
tuberculosis, 139, 256
Tumsa, Gudina, 235, 238
Turkey, 237
Turretin, Francis, 114, 117
Tutu, Desmond, 243
Twisse, William, 105
Tyndale, William, 93

U

Uganda, 193, 238
Uhorskai, Pavel, 201
Underwood, Horace Grant, 187
Unitarians, 99
United States, 220
universities, 67

Urban II, Pope, 55, 56
Urban VI, Pope, 72
Ursinus, Bishop, 30
Ursinus, Zacharias, 97
Uruguay, 223
Ussher, Clarence Douglas, 237
Ussher, Elizabeth Barrows, 237

V

Vajda, Jaroslav, 221
Valdes of Lyon, 63
Valentinian II, Emperor, 31
Valla, Lorenza, 46, 170
van der Kemp, Johannes Theodore, 191, 195
Vatican State, 206
Venn, Henry, 181
Vermigli, Peter Martyr, 92, 98
vestments, 12, 256
Victoria Falls, 196
Vietnam, 185
Vietnam War, 220
Visigoths, 15, 25
Vladimir of Kyiv, 41
Vladimir the Great, 53
Voetius, Gisbertus, 114, 116, 117
Voltaire, 132–33
vow, 48

W

Waldensians, 63, 101, 110, 143, 256
Walther, Carl Ferdinand Wilhelm, 160
Wang Laiquan, 187
Waorani, 225
Ward, William, 180
Warfield, B. B., 162, 169, 170
Watts, Isaac, 129
Welsh revival, 123, 126
Wesley, Charles, 127, 128, 129
Wesley, John, 127, 128, 159, 164
Westminster Confession of Faith, 104
Westminster Larger Catechism, 104
Westminster Shorter Catechism, 104
Westminster Standards, 102, 104
Westminster Theological Seminary, 217
Wheatly, Phillis, 137, 140
White, Ellen, 168
Whitefield, George, 127, 128, 137
Wilberforce, William, 140, 141
Wilhelmina, Princess, 154
William I, Prince of Orange, 85
William III of Orange, 101, 106, 110
Williams, John, 179, 189
Williams, Roger, 119, 120
Williams, William (1717–1791), 126
Williams, William (1800–1878), 189
Winthrop, John, 119, 120
Wishart, George, 89
witnesses, 5, 256
World Alliance of Reformed Churches, 243
World Lutheran Federation, 208
World War I, 200, 202
World War II, 228
worship, 96
Wu Zetian, Buddhist Empress, 38
Wuzong, Emperor of China, 37, 38
Wycliffe, John, 69, 78
Wycliffe Bible Translators, 212, 218

X

Xiangchen, Allen Yuan, 233

Y

Yi, Gi Pung, 233
Youderian, Roger, 223
Yunbo, Bian, 231

Z

Zanchi, Jerome, 92
Ziegenbalg, Bartholomäus, 131
Zinzendorf, Nikolaus Ludwig von, 123, 125, 128
Zoroastrian religion, 38
Zurich, 84
Zwemer, Amy Elizabeth Wilkes, 192
Zwemer, Samuel Marinus, 192
Zwingli, Ulrich, 84, 98

Acknowledgments

This lengthy project has required the help of many people, starting with Dr. Michael Haykin, chair and professor of church history and director of the Andrew Fuller Center for Baptist Studies at the Southern Baptist Theological Seminary, Louisville, Kentucky, who has devoted many hours and exhibited infinite patience in reading my manuscript and kindly answering countless questions. I am also grateful to Rev. Michael Brown, URCNA missionary and pastor at Chiesa Riformata Filadelfia, Milan, Italy; and Dan Saxton, who have carefully read the whole manuscript and have supported me with valuable comments and words of encouragement. Dan has also checked the maps in this book, which have been patiently produced by the talented Tom Carroll, who often put up with last-minute changes.

I was deeply touched by the generosity of scholars who donated much of their time to give me advice on portions of my book, such as Dr. Paul Crawford, professor of ancient and medieval history, of the California University of Pennsylvania; Dr. Alfred J. Andrea, professor emeritus of medieval world history at the University of Vermont; Dr. S. Donald Fortson, professor of church history and pastoral theology at Reformed Theological Seminary, Charlotte, North Carolina; Dr. Travis Baker, medieval history scholar; Rev. Lee Gatiss, director of church society and lecturer in church history at Union School of Theology (UK); Dr. David Noe, department chair of philosophy and professor of classics at Calvin University, Grand Rapids, Michigan; Dr. Richard Bishop, early church history scholar; Dr. Phillip Cary, scholar-in-residence at Templeton Honors College, Eastern University, St. Davids, Pennsylvania; Professor Helen Vreugdenhil, adjunct lecturer in history at Redeemer University, Ancaster, Ontario, Canada; Dr. Baiyu Andrew Song, research associate and teaching fellow at Andrew Fuller Center of Baptist Studies, Louisville, Kentucky; and Rev. Chiu Luk, engaged in doctoral studies at the Southern Baptist Theological Seminary in Louisville, Kentucky.

I am also thankful for the advice of Sid Garland, international director-at-large of Africa Christian Textbooks; Marieke Ude, counselor at John Calvin Secondary School, Oswanka, Nigeria; and others who have chosen to remain anonymous.

I am equally grateful to my dear and faithful friend Kris Moberly and my former Sunday school students Lucy and Lucas Plotner, who have each read portions of the manuscript and have advised me on particular subjects.

Time and space would fail me to mention all the others who have answered my seemingly unending questions and have provided photos, but I remember you all with deep gratitude. As usual, I thank the wonderful RHB team that has been supporting me all along and has patiently agreed to my frequent requests to postpone the deadline.

Finally, a big thanks to my husband, Tom, and my children, who have listened to my discoveries, helped me to explore answers to my questions, and encouraged me when this project seemed to have no end in sight.